LIVING LANGUAGE®

PORTUGUESE
COURSEBOOK

REVISED & UPDATED

D0950287

PORTUGUESE
COURSEBOOK

REVISED & UPDATED

REVISED BY

JURA D. OLIVEIRA, PH.D.

CORNELL UNIVERSITY

Based on the original

by Oscar Fernández

Director Portuguese Program

New York University

◆

Based on the Method Devised

by Ralph Weiman, Former Chief of the

Language Section, U.S. War Department

LIVING LANGUAGE®
A Random House Company

This work was previously published under the titles *Conversation Manual Portuguese, Living Language™ Conversational Portuguese,* and *Living Language™ Conversational Portuguese, Revised and Updated* by Oscar Fernández.

Published by Living Language®, A Random House Company, New York, New York.

Living Language is a member of the Random House Information Group.

Random House, Inc., New York, Toronto, London, Sydney, Auckland

www.livinglanguage.com

If you are traveling, we recommend **Fodor's guides**

Living Language® publications are available at special discounts for bulk purchases for sales promotions or premiums, as well as for fund-raising or educational use. Special editions can be created in large quantities for special needs. For more information, write to Special Sales Manager, Living Language, 1745 Broadway, New York, NY 10019.

Printed in the United States of America

ISBN 1-4000-2024-7

10 9 8 7 6

CONTENTS

xi

INTRODUCTION

Living Language® Portuguese makes it easy to learn how to speak, read, and write Portuguese. This course is a thoroughly revised and updated version of *Living Portuguese: The Complete Living Language Course®*. The same highly effective method of language instruction is still used, but the content has been updated to reflect modern usage and the format has been clarified. In this course, the basic elements of the language have been carefully selected and condensed into forty short lessons. If you can study about thirty minutes a day, you can master this course and learn to speak Portuguese in a few weeks.

You'll learn Portuguese the way you learned English, starting with simple words and progressing to more complex phrases. Just listen and repeat after the native instructors on the recordings. To help you immerse yourself in the language, you'll hear only Portuguese spoken. Hear it, say it, absorb it through use and repetition.

This *Living Language® Portuguese Coursebook* provides English translations and brief explanations for each lesson. The first lessons cover pronunciation, laying the foundation for learning the vocabulary, phrases, and grammar that are explained in the later chapters. If you already know a little

Portuguese, you can use the book as a phrase book and reference. In addition to the forty lessons, there is a Summary of Portuguese Grammar, plus verb conjugations and a section on writing letters.

Also included in the course package is the *Living Language® Portuguese Dictionary*. It contains more than 18,000 entries, with many of the definitions illustrated by phrases and idiomatic expressions. More than 1,000 of the most essential words are highlighted to make them easy to find. You can increase your vocabulary and range of expression just by browsing through the dictionary.

Practice your Portuguese as much as possible. Even if you can't manage a trip abroad, watching Portuguese movies, reading Portuguese magazines, eating at Portuguese restaurants, and talking with Portuguese-speaking friends are enjoyable ways to help reinforce what you have learned with *Living Language® Portuguese*. Now, let's begin.

SOUTH AMERICAN (BRAZILIAN) vs. CONTINENTAL PORTUGUESE

Although the language spoken in Portugal and Brazil is essentially the same, there are certain differences, just as there are differences between British and American English. The structure of the language is much the same, but there are significant variations in word order, in pronunciation, and in intonation.

The manual and the dictionary follow the Brazilian version, while indicating significant Continental Portuguese variations.

SPELLING

1. Following Brazilian usage, the text will have many accent marks that are not used in Portugal. The first time such a form appears in the text, the variation used

in Portugal will be given in parentheses or in a footnote, and will be marked Ⓟ.

2. Differences in pronunciation that require different spellings, and variants of the same word, although pronounced the same way in both countries, will also be indicated.

BRAZIL	PORTUGAL	MEANING
ação	*acção*	action
Antônio	*António*	Anthony
diretor	*director*	director
otimista	*optimista*	optimist

These variants will also be given in parentheses, or in a footnote, and will be marked Ⓟ.

3. Other differences (vocabulary and word order) will be indicated in the same manner: *abacaxi (ananás Ⓟ)* pineapple; *Eu me diverti (Eu diverti-me Ⓟ)* I had a good time. At times Ⓑ will be used to indicate a particularly Brazilian form: *marrom* Ⓑ brown; *suetér* Ⓑ sweater.

4. In some cases the use of certain words or forms is optional; subject pronouns, the definite article (especially with possessives), etc. These optional forms will be given in parentheses.

5. The *Living Language® Portuguese Dictionary* gives the Continental Portuguese variation in parentheses. The designators Ⓟ and Ⓑ will be used only when they seem necessary for clarity.

COURSE MATERIAL

1. Two 90-minute cassettes or three 60-minute compact discs.

2. *Living Language® Portuguese Coursebook.* This book is designed for use with the recorded lessons, but it may also be used alone as a reference. It contains the following sections:

    Basic Portuguese in 40 Lessons
    Summary of Portuguese Grammar
    Verb Conjugations
    Letter Writing

3. *Living Language® Portuguese Dictionary.* The Portuguese/English–English/Portuguese dictionary contains more than 18,000 entries. Phrases and idiomatic expressions illustrate many of the definitions. More than 1,000 of the most essential words are highlighted.

INSTRUCTIONS

1. Look at page 1. The words in **boldface** type are the ones you will hear on the recording.

2. Now read Lesson 1 all the way through. Note the points to listen for when you play the recording. The first word you will hear is **Alberto**.

3. Start the recording, listen carefully, and say the words aloud in the pauses provided. Go through the lesson once and don't worry if you can't pronounce everything correctly the first time around. Try it again and keep repeating the lesson until you are comfortable with it. The more often you listen and repeat, the longer you will remember the material.

4. Now go on to the next lesson. If you take a break between lessons, it's always good to review the previous lesson before starting on a new one.

5. In the manual, there are two kinds of quizzes. With matching quizzes, you must select the English translation of the Portuguese sentence. The other type requires you to fill in the blanks with the correct Portuguese word chosen from the three given directly below the sentence. If you make any mistakes, reread the section.

6. Even after you have finished the forty lessons and achieved a perfect score on the Final Quiz, keep practicing your Portuguese by listening to the recordings and speaking with Portuguese-speaking friends.

LIVING LANGUAGE®

PORTUGUESE
COURSEBOOK

REVISED & UPDATED

LESSON 1

A. THE LETTERS AND SOUNDS

Some Portuguese sounds are fairly similar to English sounds. Listen to and repeat the following Portuguese names and notice which sounds are fairly similar and which are different:

Alberto	Albert	**Júlio**	Julius
Alfredo	Alfred	**Lúcia**	Lucy
Ana	Anna, Ann(e)	**Luís**	Louis
Antônio[1]	Anthony	**Manuel**	Manuel
Carlos	Charles	**Maria**	Mary
Cecília	Cecilia	**Mário**	Mario
Eduardo	Edward	**Maurício**	Maurice
Fernando	Ferdinand	**Miguel**	Michael
Francisco	Francis	**Paulo**	Paul
Glória	Gloria	**Pedro**	Peter
Guilherme	William	**Raimundo**	Raymond
Henrique	Henry	**Ricardo**	Richard
Isabel	Elizabeth	**Roberto**	Robert
João	John	**Rosa**	Rose
Jorge	George	**Tomás**	Thomas

NOTES

1. Each vowel is pronounced clearly and crisply.
2. A single consonant is pronounced with the following vowel.

---

[1] *António* ℗.

3. The accent mark (´ or ^) indicates the syllable that is stressed: *Tomás*.
   a. The acute accent mark (´) over *a, e, o* indicates an open pronunciation (in forming the sound there is a large opening between the roof of the mouth and the tongue): *Glória*.
   b. The circumflex accent mark (^) over *a, e, o* indicates a closed pronunciation (a smaller opening between the roof of the mouth and the tongue): *ângulo, cômodo, lê*.
4. The tilde *(til)* (~) over a vowel indicates a nasal sound: *irmã, alemão, botões*. It also indicates stress unless there is another written accent mark: *órfão (OR-fão); bênção (BEN-ção)*.

Now listen to the names of some cities:

Barcelona	Nova Iorque
Belém	Paris
Belo Horizonte	Porto
Brasília	Porto Alegre
Coimbra	Rio de Janeiro
Lisboa	Roma
Londres	Santos
Madrid	São Paulo

Now the names of some countries:

Alemanha (Germany)	Colômbia
Angola	Cuba
Argentina	Espanha (Spain)
Brasil	Estados Unidos (U.S.)
China	França
Inglaterra (England)	Moçambique
Itália	Portugal
México	Uruguai

B. VOWEL AND CONSONANT SOUNDS

Notice the following points (more detailed distinctions will be made later in the course):

VOWELS

a	approximates *a* in *ah, father.*
e	open, as explained above: *eh, best;* closed, approximates modified *a* as in *case;* compare *fez.*
i	as in *machine.*
o	open, as in *off;* closed, as in *rose.*
u	approximates *u* in *rule.*

CONSONANTS AND CONSONANT GROUPS

ch	as *ch* in *machine.*
h	is silent in initial position. See its pronunciation as part of the digraphs *ch, lh,* and *nh.*
lh	as *lli* in *million.*
m and n	at the beginning of a syllable, as in English: *fama, nabo, calma.* At the end of a syllable, *m* and *n* are not pronounced as consonants; they indicate the nasalization of the preceding vowel: *santo, canto, campo, amplo.*
nh	between vowels, similar to *ny* in canyon or like nasalized *y.* Important: the preceding vowel is also nasalized: *tenho, amanhã, ponho.*
s	between vowels as *z,* or as *s* in *rose;* initial *s,* or *ss,* as *ss* in lesson.

STRESS

1. Words ending in *a, e,* or *o* (or in one of these vowels and *s, m,* or *ns*) are stressed on the syllable before last:

casa	house
passaporte	passport
americano	American
programas	programs
homem	man
homens	men

2. Words ending in any other letter, including nasal vowels and diphthongs (two vowels pronounced in union), are stressed on the last syllable:

aqui	here
peru	turkey
manhã	morning
internacional	international
falar	to speak
descansei	I rested

3. Words not following the above rules have a written accent mark that indicates the stressed syllable:

café	coffee
difícil	difficult
português	Portuguese
pássaro	bird
júri	jury
órfão	orphan
água	water

LESSON 2

A. COGNATES: WORDS SIMILAR IN ENGLISH AND PORTUGUESE

Now listen to and repeat the following words that are similar in English and Portuguese.[1] Notice how Portuguese spelling and pronunciation differ from English.

acompanhar	to accompany	raça	race
agente	agent	restaurante	restaurant
centro	center	silêncio	silence
cheque	check	surpresa	surprise
certo	certain	teatro	theater
celebrar	to celebrate	exemplo	example
diferente	different	garantir	to guarantee
difícil	difficult	geral	general
importante	important	telefone	telephone
interessante	interesting	possível	possible
necessário	necessary	qualidade	quality
atenção	attention	tipo	type
caso	case	visita	visit

B. SPECIAL CONSONANT SOUNDS

Notice the following points:

1. *c* before *a*, *o*, and *u*, and before any other consonant (except *h*) is like *c* in *cat*:

---

[1] These words are called "cognates" and are descended from the same root.

carta   letter
secreto   secret *(adj.)*

2. *c* before *e* and *i* is like *c* in *center:*

cena   scene
sincero   sincere

3. *ç* (used only before *a, o,* or *u*) is like *c* in *face:*

moço   young man
nação   nation

4. *g* before *e* and *i* is like *s* in *measure:*

gente   people
gíria   slang

5. Otherwise *g* is like *g* in *go:*

gato   cat

6. *j* is similar to *j* before *e* and *i:*

jantar   to dine

7. *l* in Portuguese is formed with the tongue forward, the tip near the upper teeth:

livro   book
paletó   jacket (man's)

8. Final *l* is quite soft, almost like *w* in *cow:*

Brasil	Brazil
papel	paper
capital	capital

9. *qu* before *a* or *o* is like *qu* in *quota:*

quadro	picture

10. *qu* before *e* or *i* is usually like *k:*

Que?	What?
barquinha	small boat

11. *x* has the following sounds:

like *z:*

exame	examination
êxito	success

like *sh:*

caixa	box
mexer	to mix
xícara	cup

like *s* in *see:*

máximo	maximum
próximo	next

like *x* in *wax:*

táxi	taxi
sexo	sex

C. THE PORTUGUESE ALPHABET

LETTER	NAME	LETTER	NAME	LETTER	NAME
a	*a*	j	*i*	s	*esse*
b	*bê*	k	*ka*	t	*tê*
c	*cê*	l	*ele*	u	*u*
d	*dê*	m	*eme*	v	*vê*
e	*é*	n	*ene*	w	*dobliu*
f	*efe*	o	*ó*	x	*xis*
g	*gê*	p	*pê*	y	*ipsilão*
h	*agá*	q	*quê*	z	*zê*
i	*i*	r	*erre*		

LESSON 3

A. REGIONAL DIFFERENCES IN PRONUNCIATION

A language will vary somewhat in different countries where it is spoken, indeed, even in different parts of the same country. This is true of Portuguese.

Brazil, the fifth largest country in the world, has been attaining increased importance. It comprises about one-half of the continent of South America and accounts for about one-half of its total population. Its language is Portuguese, but with certain features that distinguish it from the language as spoken in Portugal. There are also some minor regional differences in Brazil itself. The *carioca* pattern of Rio de Janeiro (whose inhabitants are called *cariocas*) is quite distinctive. Farther south, as in São Paulo, and in the northern part of the country, one notices further minor differences, but the language is basically the same in all these cases.

The Portuguese language as spoken in Portugal is fundamentally the same language as is spoken in Brazil, but there are minor differences in syntax and significantly marked variations in pronunciation, intonation, and rhythm. Syllables are cut shorter and at times slurred over, with final vowels clipped sharply or practically dropped.

B. Pronunciation Practice

The following groups of words will give you an idea of some of the regional differences in pronunciation and will also provide additional practice in Portuguese pronunciation and spelling. The first pronunciation is as in São Paulo, the second as in Rio de Janeiro, and the third as in Portugal.

CONSONANTS

1. *d* is pronounced more forcefully in Rio de Janeiro and with some speakers approximates the *j* in *just;* this is especially true with *d* before *e* or *i:*

SÃO PAULO	RIO	PORTUGAL	
cidade	**cidade**	**cidade**	city
Bom dia.	*Bom dia.*	*Bom dia.*	Good morning.

2. *r* is pronounced with the tongue forward, along the top of the mouth with the tip near the base of the upper teeth (as in Spanish), with initial *r* and *rr* being more forceful, with the tongue vibrating in this position. This pronunciation can be heard in São Paulo and in Portugal. The *carioca r* is pronounced back in the

mouth, the upper back part of the tongue against the roof of the mouth (similar to a French back *r* and somewhat like *ch* in German).

SÃO PAULO	RIO	PORTUGAL	
carro	**carro**	**carro**	car, cart
caro	*caro*	*caro*	expensive
Rio	*Rio*	*Rio*	Rio

3. *s* between vowels is as *z* in *zeal*, or as *s* in *rose:*

fase	**fase**	**fase**	phase

s before a voiced consonant (produced with a vibration of the vocal cords, as *b, d, ge, gi, j, l, m, n, r, v, z*) tends to be as *z* in *azure*, as Portuguese *j:*

mesmo	**mesmo**	**mesmo**	same
Lisboa	*Lisboa*	*Lisboa*	Lisbon

Final *s* and *s* (and *x*) before a voiceless consonant (produced without a vibration of the vocal cords, as hard *c* and hard *g, f, p, qu, t*) are pronounced as *s* in *see* in São Paulo and by some *cariocas*, and as *sh* in *shine* in Portugal and by some *cariocas:*

costas	**costas**	**costas**	coasts
prosperidade	*prosperidade*	*prosperidade*	prosperity
moscas	*moscas*	*moscas*	flies

4. Initial *s, s* after a consonant, and *ss* are pronounced as *s* in *see* and *ss* in *passage:*

sempre	**sempre**	**sempre**	always
falso	*falso*	*falso*	false
passar	*passar*	*passar*	to pass

5. *t* before *e* or *i* is pronounced very forcefully by some *cariocas,* approximating the *ch* in *church:*

tinteiro	**tinteiro**	**tinteiro**	inkwell

VOWELS

1. *a* in a stressed position is "open" like the *a* in *father;* in unstressed positions and with the article *a* ("the") it tends to be more "closed" like the final *a* in *America;* this is particularly true in Portugal and in general with unstressed final *a:*

matar	**matar**	**matar**	to kill
a data	*a data*	*a data*	the date

2. *e,* in addition to the pronunciation indicated in Lesson 1, in a final unstressed position varies between the *i* in *did* and the *i* in *machine* in Brazil; it is clipped sharply in Portugal, being like a mute *e,* or is dropped:

breve	**breve**	**breve**	brief
verdade	*verdade*	*verdade*	truth

Stressed *e* before *j, ch, lh, nh* in Portugal can have the sound of final *a* in *America,* or of closed *e:*

cereja	**cereja**	**cereja**	cherry
igreja	*igreja*	*igreja*	church
fecha	*fecha*	*fecha*	he closes
venho	*venho*	*venho*	I come

e in an unstressed position is sometimes pronounced as *e* in *be* in parts of Brazil, as mute *e* in Portugal, or as *i* in *did* in both:

exercício	exercício	exercício	exercise
devagar	*devagar*	*devagar*	slowly
pedir	*pedir*	*pedir*	to ask
respeito	*respeito*	*respeito*	respect

3. *o,* in addition to the pronunciation already indicated in Lesson 1 ("open" as *o* in *off,* and "closed" as *o* in *oh*), is also pronounced like *oo* in *boot* in an unstressed position, quite regularly in Portugal, and less consistently in Brazil (for example, less so in São Paulo than in Rio de Janeiro); this applies also to the pronunciation of the definite article *o* ("the"), and to *o* in a final unstressed position:

todos	todos	todos	all
o movimento	*o movimento*	*o movimento*	the movement
os portu-	*os portu-*	*os portu-*	the Portuguese
gueses	*gueses*	*gueses*	

NASAL SOUNDS

1. *m, n,* and *nh,* nasal sounds, tend to nasalize the vowel preceding them; this nasal quality is especially strong in Brazil; in Continental Portuguese it may be slight or even absent:

campo	field	**nome**	name
tentar	to try	**menos**	less
cama	bed	**vinho**	wine
linha	line	**senhorita**	miss, young lady

m, n followed by a consonant, or in the final position, are not pronounced (do not close your lips in pronouncing the final *m;* merely nasalize the preceding vowel):

cantar	to sing	**falam**	they speak
também	also	**tem**	he has
sempre	always	**bom**	good
bomba	bomb	**um**	a, one

2. *ã* is nasalized:

lã	wool	**manhã**	morning

3. Nasal vowel combinations:

mãe	mother	**lições**	lessons
mão	hand	**põe**	he puts

4. A special case:

muito	much

•

SOME OTHER VOWEL COMBINATIONS

ai:	**pai**	father	**vai**	he goes
au:	**aula**	class	**causa**	cause
ei:	**falei**	I spoke	**sei**	I know
éi:	**hotéis**	hotels	**papéis**	papers
eu:	**meu**	my, mine	**seu**	your
	escreveu	he wrote	**museu**	museum
éu:	**céu**	sky	**chapéu**	hat
ia:	**diálogo**	dialogue		
ie:	**série**	series	**vienense**	Viennese
ié:	**dieta**	diet	**viela**	alley, lane
io:	**próprio**	proper, (one's) own		
iu:	**partiu**	he left		
oi:	**noite**	night	**coisa**	thing
ói:	**herói**	hero		

	lençóis	bed sheets		
ou:	**outro**	another, other		
	comprou	he bought		
ua:	**água**	water	**quando**	when
ué:	*suéter* Ⓑ	sweater		
ui:	**cuidar**	to take care (of)		
uo:	**quota**	quota		

WORD GROUPS

Keep in mind that the information given about pronunciation applies to word groups as well as to individual words:

1. *s* between vowels is like *z* in *zeal:*

todososamigos   all the friends
(todos os amigos)

2. Voiced *s* before a voiced consonant is like *z* in *azure:*

osdemais   the rest
(os demais)

RHYTHM AND INTONATION

To speak Portuguese well, you should not only pronounce individual words and word groups correctly, but you should try to use the proper rhythm and intonation. Pay attention to these and try to imitate them in the following examples.

1. In a declarative statement the tone level is normal, with a slight drop at the end:

A escola está aberta.   The school is open.
A escola está aberta.

2. In a question there is a slight rise at the end:

A escola está aberta?   Is the school open?
A escola está aberta?

3. Compare:

Ele está aqui?	**Ele está aqui.**
Is he here?	He is here.
Ele está aqui?	**Ele está aqui.**

4. Exclamations and phrases said with emotion will affect inflection and may show a rise at the end:

Ele está ferido!	He is wounded (hurt)!
Ele está ferido!	
Não me diga!	You don't say!
Não me diga!	

LESSON 4

A. MORE ENGLISH-PORTUGUESE COGNATES

Building up a Portuguese vocabulary is facilitated by the great number of words that are similar in English and Portuguese. These words are descended from the same root and are called cognates. Some of these words are spelled exactly the same (although they may differ considerably in pronunciation):

PORTUGUESE	ENGLISH	PORTUGUESE	ENGLISH
animal	animal	hospital	hospital
capital	capital	hotel	hotel
central	central	motor	motor
chocolate	chocolate	original	original
envelope	envelope	regular	regular
favor	favor	total	total

There are many Portuguese words you will have no difficulty in recognizing despite minor differences. Some of these differences are:

1. The Portuguese word has an accent mark:

área	area	*júnior*	junior
cônsul	consul	*rádio*	radio

2. The Portuguese word has a single consonant:

antena	antenna	*comercial*	commercial
anual	annual	*oficial*	official

3. The Portuguese word adds *-a*, *-e*, or *-o:*

lista	list	*problema*	problem
mapa	map	*restaurante*	restaurant
parte	part	*revolta*	revolt

4. The Portuguese word ends in *a* or *o*, the English word in *e:*

causa	cause	*nota*	note
figura	figure	*rosa*	rose
medicina	medicine	*tubo*	tube
minuto	minute	*uso*	use

5. The Portuguese word is slightly different in other respects:

automóvel	automobile	*origem*	origin
especial	special	*questão*	question

B. General Spelling Equivalents

1. Portuguese *c (qu)* = English *k (ck):*

franco	frank	*ataque*	attack
parque	park	*saco*	sack

2. Portuguese *f* = English *ph:*

filosofia	philosophy	*frase*	phrase, sentence
físico	physical	*telefone*	telephone

3. Portuguese *t* = English *th:*

autor	author	*simpatia*	sympathy
autoridade	authority	*teatro*	theater

4. Portuguese *ç* = English *ce:*

força	force	*raça*	race

5. Portuguese *i* = English *y:*

estilo	style	*ritmo*	rhythm
mistério	mystery	*sistema*	system

6. Portuguese *o* and *u* = English *ou:*

corte	court	*sopa*	soup
hora	hour	*anunciar*	to announce
montanha	mountain	*curso*	course
som	sound	*fundar*	to found

7. Portuguese *-ia* and *-io* = English *-y:*

companhia	company	*secretária*	secretary
família	family	*dicionário*	dictionary
história	history	*território*	territory
		necessário	necessary

8. Portuguese *-ia, -a,* and *-o* = English *-e:*

ausência	absence	*diferença*	difference
distância	distance	*justiça*	justice
experiência	experience	*comércio*	commerce
notícia	notice, news	*silêncio*	silence
polícia	police	*serviço*	service

9. Portuguese *-ção* = English *-tion:*

atenção	attention	*imitação*	imitation
cooperação	cooperation	*informação*	information
descrição	description	*satisfação*	satisfaction
estação	station	*tradução*	translation

10. Portuguese *-o* = English *-al:*

eterno	eternal	*político*	political

11. Portuguese *-oso* = English *-ous:*

delicioso	delicious	*famoso*	famous
numeroso	numerous	*religioso*	religious

12. Portuguese *-dade* = English *-ty:*

cidade	city	*possibilidade*	possibility
oportunidade	opportunity	*qualidade*	quality

LESSON 5

A. DAYS AND MONTHS

segunda-feira or **segunda**	Monday
terça-feira or **terça**	Tuesday
quarta-feira or **quarta**	Wednesday
quinta-feira or **quinta**	Thursday
sexta-feira or **sexta**	Friday
sábado	Saturday
domingo	Sunday

janeiro[1]	January
fevereiro	February
março	March
abril	April
maio	May
junho	June
julho	July
agosto	August
setembro	September
outubro	October
novembro	November
dezembro	December

B. Numbers 1–10

um *(masc.)*, **uma** *(fem.)*	one
dois *(masc.)*, **duas** *(fem.)*	two
três	three
quatro	four
cinco	five
seis	six
sete	seven
oito	eight
nove	nine
dez	ten
Um mais um: dois.[2]	One and one are two.
Um mais dois: três.	One and two are three.
Dois mais dois: quatro.	Two and two are four.
Dois mais três: cinco.	Two and three are five.

---

[1] With initial capital letters in Portugal: *Janeiro*, etc.
[2] This form is good for oral use. Another form: *Um mais um igual a dois*, etc.

Três mais três: seis.	Three and three are six.
Três mais quatro: sete.	Three and four are seven.
Quatro mais quatro: oito.	Four and four are eight.
Quatro mais cinco: nove.	Four and five are nine.
Cinco mais cinco: dez.	Five and five are ten.

C. Colors

vermelho	red
azul	blue
verde	green
preto, negro	black
branco	white
amarelo	yellow
marrom Ⓑ, **castanho** Ⓟ	brown
gris Ⓑ, **cinzento** Ⓟ	gray

D. Seasons

a primavera[3]	spring
o verão	summer
o outono	autumn
o inverno	winter

E. North, South, East, West

o norte	north
o sul	south
o leste, este	east
o oeste	west

[3] With initial capital letters in Portugal: *Primavera*, etc.

F. Morning, Noon, and Night

manhã	morning
meio-dia	noon
tarde	afternoon
noite	evening, night

G. Yesterday, Today, Tomorrow

ontem	yesterday
hoje	today
amanhã	tomorrow
Ontem foi quinta-feira.	Yesterday was Thursday.
Hoje é sexta-feira.	Today is Friday.
Amanhã é sábado.	Tomorrow is Saturday.

QUIZ 1

Try matching these two columns:

1.	*sexta-feira*	a.	January
2.	*outono*	b.	summer
3.	*quinta-feira*	c.	June
4.	*primavera*	d.	winter
5.	*oito*	e.	October
6.	*janeiro*	f.	white
7.	*inverno*	g.	autumn
8.	*verde*	h.	Sunday
9.	*junho*	i.	eight
10.	*verão*	j.	spring
11.	*segunda-feira*	k.	west
12.	*quatro*	l.	Thursday
13.	*outubro*	m.	four
14.	*domingo*	n.	ten
15.	*oeste*	o.	red
16.	*vermelho*	p.	black
17.	*preto*	q.	green
18.	*dez*	r.	Friday

19. *branco*   s. gray
20. *cinzento*   t. Monday

ANSWERS

1—r; 2—g; 3—1; 4—j; 5—i; 6—a; 7—d; 8—q; 9—c;
10—b; 11—t; 12—m; 13—e; 14—h; 15—k; 16—o; 17—
p; 18—n; 19—f; 20—s.

LESSON 6

A. GREETINGS

DE MANHÃ	IN THE MORNING
bom dia	good day
Bom dia.	Good morning.
senhor	Mr.
Campos	Campos
Bom dia, senhor (Sr.) Campos.	Good morning, Mr. Campos.
como	how
vai *(está)*	are (you) getting along
o senhor[1]	you
Como vai *(está)* **o senhor?**	How are you?
muito	very
bem	well
Muito bem.	Very well.
obrigado	thank you
Muito bem, obrigado.	Very well, thank you.
e	and
o senhor	you

[1] "You" is translated by *o senhor (masc.)* and *a senhora (fem.)* and by their
plural forms *os senhores* and *as senhoras*.

E o (a) senhor(a)?	And you?
bem	well
Bem, obrigado(a).	Fine, thank you.

DE TARDE   IN THE AFTERNOON

boa	good
tarde	afternoon
Boa tarde.	Good afternoon.
Boa tarde, Dona Maria.	Good afternoon, Dona Maria.
Como vai *(está)* a senhora?	How are you?
Muito bem, obrigada.[2]	Very well, thank you.
E o senhor?	And you?
Muito bem, obrigado.	Very well, thank you.

DE NOITE   IN THE EVENING

boa	good
noite	evening, night
Boa noite, Cecília.	Good evening, Cecilia.
Boa noite, Pedro.	Good evening, Peter.
Boa noite, Dona Maria.	Good evening, Dona Maria.
Boa noite, Pedro.	Good evening, Peter.

B. How's the Weather?

Que tempo faz?	How's the weather?
Hoje está frio.	It's cold today.
Está quente.	It's hot.
Está ventando.	It's windy.

---

[2] A man answers *obrigado*, a lady *obrigada*, for "thank you." Mr. and Mrs. Campos, *o senhor Campos* e *a senhora Campos;* however, it is more common to address a married woman by *Dona* and her first name: *Dona Maria,* etc. *Seu* is the colloquial form for *senhor* (mister). It is used in everyday speech before a man's first name: *Seu Paulo, como vai o senhor?* These forms of address correspond somewhat to those used in the southern U.S.: Miss Josie, Mr. Ralph, etc.

Está ensolarado.	It's sunny.
Faz sol.	It's sunny.
Está bom tempo.	It's nice weather.
Está chuvoso.	It's rainy.
Está chovendo.	It's raining.
Está nevando.	It's snowing.
Que tempo horrível!	What terrible weather!
Que dia lindo!	What a nice day!
Que tempo lindo!	What nice weather.

C. WORD STUDY

classe	class
considerável	considerable
diferença	difference
elemento	element
glória	glory
mãe	mother
operação	operation
pai	father

QUIZ 2

1. manhã
2. senhora
3. Como vai (está) o senhor?
4. Muito bem.
5. Bom dia.
6. Boa noite.
7. de manhã
8. tarde
9. Obrigado.
10. Pedro
11. Qué tempo faz?
12. Boa tarde.
13. Como?

a. Good afternoon.
b. in the morning
c. How's the weather?
d. morning
e. Thank you.
f. Mrs.
g. Peter
h. Sir or Mr.
i. How?
j. Good morning.
k. It's raining.
l. How are you?
m. Very well. (Fine.)

| 14. *senhor* | n. afternoon |
| 15. *Está chovendo.* | o. Good evening. Good night. |

ANSWERS

1—d; 2—f; 3—l; 4—m; 5—j; 6—o; 7—b; 8—n; 9—e; 10—g; 11—c; 12—a; 13—i; 14—h; 15—k.

LESSON 7

A. WHERE IS . . . ?

onde	where
há	is there (there is)
Onde há . . . ?	Where is there . . . ?
um	a
hotel	hotel
Onde há um hotel?	Where is there a hotel?
bom	good
restaurante	restaurant
Onde há um bom restaurante?	Where is there a good restaurant?
onde	where
é	is
Onde é?	Where is it?
Onde é a delegacia de policía?	Where is the police station?
Onde é o aeroporto?	Where is the airport?
Onde é a farmácia?	Where is the drugstore?
Onde é o restaurante?	Where is the restaurant?

Onde é a estação?	Where is the station?
Onde é o correio?	Where is the post office?
Onde é o banheiro?	Where is the restroom?

Note: There is a tendency to use *ficar* with fixed location: *Onde fica o restaurante? Onde fica a estação?*

B. CAN YOU . . . ?

o senhor pode dizer-me	can you tell me
O senhor pode dizer-me . . . ?	Can you tell me . . . ?
O senhor pode dizer-me onde há um hotel?	Can you tell me where there is a hotel?
O senhor pode dizer-me onde há um bom restaurante?	Can you tell me where there is a good restaurant?
O senhor pode dizer-me onde fica a estação do metrô?Ⓑ	Can you tell me where the subway station is?
O senhor pode dizer-me onde fica a estação rodoviária?	Can you tell me where the bus station is?
O senhor pode dizer-me onde fica o correio?	Can you tell me where the post office is?

QUIZ 3

1. *Onde há um hotel?*	a. Where is the subway station?
2. *Onde é a estação do metrô?*	b. Can you tell me where the bus station is?
3. *O senhor pode dizer-me . . . ?*	c. Can you tell me . . . ?

4. *O senhor pode dizer-*   d. the post office
   me onde fica a
   estação rodoviária?
5. *o correio*   e. Where is there a hotel?

ANSWERS
1—e; 2—a; 3—c; 4—b; 5—d.

C. DO YOU HAVE . . . ?

O senhor tem . . . ?	Do you have . . . ?
dinheiro	(any) money
cigarros	(any) cigarettes
fósforos	(any) matches
fogo *(lume* ℗)	a light
Preciso de . . .	I need . . .
papel	(some) paper
tinta	ink
um selo	a (postage) stamp
sabonete	soap
pasta de dente (dentes)	toothpaste
uma toalha	a towel

Onde posso comprar . . . ?	Where can I buy . . . ?
um dicionário	a dictionary
um dicionário inglês-português	an English-Portuguese dictionary
alguns livros em inglês	some English books ("some books in English")
algumas roupas	(some) clothes

D. In a Restaurant

o café da manhã	breakfast
(o pequeno-almoço Ⓟ)	
o lanche	snack[1]
o almoço	lunch
o jantar	dinner
a sobremesa	dessert

O que é que o senhor deseja?	What will you have? ("What do you wish?")
Pois não?	Can I help you?
Eu queria o menu (a ementa Ⓟ), por favor.	I would like the menu, please.
Sim, senhor.	Yes, sir.
Eu queria um sanduíche de queijo, por favor.	I would like a cheese sandwich, please.
Eu queria um hambúrguer, por favor.	I would like a hamburger, please.
Pois não.	Sure/Certainly.

Temos ...	We have ...
pão	bread
pão e manteiga	bread and butter
sopa	soup
carne	meat
carne de vaca	beef

[1] *Lanche* is the Portuguese word for *lunch*, but observe that its meaning is *snack*.

bife/filé	steak (beefsteak)
bisteca	pork chop
carne de porco	pork
presunto	ham
peixe	fish
bacalhau	cod
camarão, camarões	shrimp *(sing. and pl.)*
lagosta	lobster
frango, galinha	chicken
arroz	rice
ovos	eggs
ovos fritos	fried eggs
ovos mexidos	scrambled eggs
verduras *(legumes* Ⓟ*)*	vegetables
batatas	potatoes
fritas	French fries
batatinha frita	potato chip
feijão	black beans
salada	salad
salada de alface	lettuce salad
tomate	tomato
água	water
vinho	wine
cerveja	beer
torrada	toast
rabanada	French toast
geléia	jelly
café com leite	coffee with milk
açúcar	sugar
sal	salt
pimenta	pepper
fruta	fruit
abacaxi *(ananás* Ⓟ*)*	pineapple
banana	banana
laranja	orange
maçã	apple

O senhor quer um cafezinho?	Would you like a cup of coffee (demitasse)?[2]
Sim, eu quero dois cafés.	Yes, I want two cups.
Sim, por favor.	Yes, please.
Eu quero uma xícara de chá, por favor.	I want a cup of tea, please.
Eu queria uma garrafa de água.	I would like a bottle of water.
Pois não. Olhe aqui.	Sure. Here.
Obrigado.	Thank you.
De nada, às ordens.	You are welcome./Don't mention it.
Por favor, eu queria . . .	Please, I would like . . .
um guardanapo	a napkin
uma colher	a spoon
uma colher de chá	a teaspoon
uma faca	a knife
um prato	a plate
um copo	a glass
uma garrafa de vinho	a bottle of wine
uma garrafa de cerveja	a bottle of beer
um chope *(uma caneca* Ⓟ*)*	draft beer
mais uma garrafa	another bottle
um pouco mais disso	a little more of that
mais pão	more bread
Quanto é?	How much?
A conta, por favor.	The check, please.

[2] In Brazil coffee is normally served only in small cups.

QUIZ 4

1. *carne*	a. fish
2. *batata*	b. water
3. *água*	c. vegetables
4. *O que é que o senhor deseja?*	d. I need soap.
5. *ovos*	e. The check, please.
6. *frango*	f. breakfast
7. *peixe*	g. a spoon
8. *uma garrafa de vinho*	h. coffee with milk
9. *Preciso de sabonete.*	i. What will you have?
10. *Eu queria pão.*	j. dessert
11. *café com leite*	k. meat
12. *açúcar*	l. a knife
13. *verduras (legumes)*	m. eggs
14. *uma xícara de chá*	n. Can/could I have some bread?
15. *um pouco mais de pão*	o. chicken
16. *uma faca*	p. a cup of tea
17. *sobremesa*	q. some more bread
18. *o café da manhã (o pequeno-almoço)*	r. sugar
19. *uma colher*	s. a bottle of wine
20. *A conta, por favor.*	t. potato

ANSWERS
1—k; 2—t; 3—b; 4—i; 5—m; 6—o; 7—a; 8—s; 9—d;
10—n; 11—h; 12—r; 13—c; 14—p; 15—q; 16—l; 17—j;
18—f; 19—g; 20—e.

LESSON 8

This lesson and several that follow are longer than the others. They contain information about grammar you need to know from the start. Try to understand each point, and, as the course continues, observe examples of the points mentioned. Refer back to the sections on grammar as often as necessary. Try to develop an understanding and feeling for the basic features of Portuguese grammar rather than a mere memorization of rules.

A. To Speak: *Falar*

SINGULAR

eu falo	I speak
(tu falas)	you speak *(familiar)*
ele fala	he speaks
ela fala	she speaks
o senhor fala	you speak *(masc.)*
a senhora fala	you speak *(fem.)*
você fala	you speak

PLURAL

nós falamos	we speak
(vós falais)	(you speak)
eles falam	they speak *(masc.)*
elas falam	they speak *(fem.)*
os senhores falam	you speak *(masc.)*
as senhoras falam	you speak *(fem.)*
vocês falam	you speak

The forms in parentheses are generally to be avoided.

NOTES

1. These forms, which make up the present tense, translate English "I speak," "I am speaking," "I do speak."
2. In Portugal *tu* (you) is used in very familiar speech, as between members of a family and very close friends. It is rarely used in Brazil. Brazilians use *você* and *vocês*, which are the more informal way of "you," when talking to friends, fellow students, and younger people. In both countries, the form *o senhor/a senhora*, is the less "familiar" or "polite" way of expressing "you," mostly with anyone who is older. When in doubt, it is best to use these polite forms. The plural *vós* is considered fairly archaic and is never used in Brazil today; *vocês* generally takes its place in Portugal and Brazil. *Os senhores* and *as senhoras* are the "polite" or less "familiar" plural forms of "you."
3. Notice that there are six endings:

SINGULAR

—*o*   indicates the speaker (I).
(—*as*)   indicates the person spoken to (you). This is
                the familiar form.
—*a*   indicates someone or something spoken about
                (he, she, it), or spoken to (you).

PLURAL

—*amos*   indicates two or more people including the
                speaker (we).
(—*ais*)   indicates the persons spoken to (you). *This
                form is rarely used.*
—*am*   indicates those spoken about (they),
                or spoken to (you, plural).

These are the endings for verbs with infinitives ending in -*ar*, like *falar*. (Other verbs also have six endings.)

ele fala	he speaks
ela fala	she speaks
eles falam	they speak *(masc.)*
elas falam	they speak *(fem.)*

4. Notice that the verb form used with *ele, ela, o senhor, a senhora,* and *você* is the same: *fala.* The plurals of these have the same form: *falam.*
5. Notice that several forms of the subject pronouns differ depending on whether men or women are speaking or are being spoken about.[1]

Later on you will learn the other regular verb forms, for verbs with infinitives ending in *-er* and in *-ir.* Some other common *-ar* verbs that are conjugated like *falar* are:

chamar	to call
trabalhar	to work
visitar	to visit

B. *THE* AND *A* (DEFINITE AND INDEFINITE ARTICLES: GENDER AND NUMBER OF NOUNS)

THE

	SINGULAR		PLURAL	
M.	**o menino**	the boy	**os meninos**	the boys
F.	**a menina**	the girl	**as meninas**	the girls

A (AN)/SOME

	SINGULAR		PLURAL	
M.	**um menino**	a boy	**uns meninos**	some/a few boys
F.	**uma menina**	a girl	**umas meninas**	some/a few girls

---

[1] This is also true when the pronouns refer to masculine or feminine nouns (see Section 13 of the Portuguese Grammar Summary).

Portuguese nouns have number (singular or plural) and gender (masculine or feminine). The gender and number are classifications that require agreement of articles, adjectives, and pronouns. Usually the *-o* ending indicates a masculine noun; the *-a* ending indicates a feminine noun. You should learn the gender of the noun, that is, whether it is masculine or feminine.

The *-s* ending of the plural is pronounced like the double *ss* of *miss*. When the word that follows the articles starts with a vowel or a voiced consonant *(b, d, g, j, l, m, n, v, z)*, it is pronounced like the English *z:*

os homens /z/	the men
as avenidas /z/	the avenues
as casas /s/	the houses

QUIZ 5

1. *eu*   a. they speak *(masc.)*
2. *nós*   b. she speaks
3. *o senhor fala*   c. she
4. *ele*   d. you speak (to friends, *pl.*)

5. *eles falam*   e. I
6. *vocês falam*   f. you speak *(masc. sing.* "polite")

7. *as senhoras falam*   g. he
8. *ela*   h. we speak
9. *nós falamos*   i. you speak (*fem. pl.* "polite")

10. *ela fala*   j. we

ANSWERS
1—e; 2—j; 3—f; 4—g; 5—a; 6—d; 7—i; 8—c; 9—h; 10—b.

C. CONTRACTIONS

These prepositions MUST form contractions with the definite articles *(a, o, as, os)*:

de + o = do	*de + os = dos*	of/from[2]
de + a = da	*de + as = das*	
a + o = ao	*a + os = aos*	to/for/at (when it denotes hour)
a + a = à	*a + as = às*	
em + o = no	*em + os = nos*	in/on/at (in reference to place)
em + a = na	*em + as = nas*	

do menino	of the boy
da menina	of the girl
dos meninos	of the boys
das meninas	of the girls
ao menino	to the boy
à menina	to the girl
aos meninos	to the boys
às meninas	to the girls
no bolso	in the pocket
nos bolsos	in the pockets
na praia	on the beach
nas praias	on the beaches

Contractions of *de* and *em* with the indefinite article (*um* and its other forms) are optional, with both contracted and noncontracted forms being used:

de um menino or *dum menino*	of a boy
de uma escola or *duma escola*	of a school
em umas cidades or *numas cidades*	in some cities

[2] It also expresses the possessive case in English: *O livro do menino* (The boy's book).

D. PLURALS

1. Nouns in Portuguese have plural forms with which all other words (articles/adjectives) must agree. Most words ending in a single vowel, oral or nasal, or in an oral diphthong, form the plural by adding -s:

a mesa grande	**as mesas grandes**	the big table(s)
o elefante	**os elefantes**	the elephant(s)
a maçã fresca	*as maçãs frescas*	the fresh apple(s)
a mãe	*as mães*	the mother(s)
a lei	*as leis*	the law(s)
o véu verde	*os véus verdes*	the green veil(s)

2. Words ending in -ão form the plural by changing to -ões:

a lição	**as lições**	the lesson(s)
o avião	**os aviões**	the airplane(s)

However, there are a few words that do not follow this rule. They are exceptions and must be memorized separately:

by changing the -ão into -ães:

pão	bread	**pães**	breads
alemão	German	**alemães**	Germans
capitão	captain	*capitães*	captains

by just adding -s:

irmão	brother	**irmãos**	brothers
mão	hand	**mãos**	hands
cidadão	citizen	*cidadãos*	citizens
cristão	Christian	*cristãos*	Christians
órfão	orphan	*órfãos*	orphans

3. Words ending in *m* change the *m* to *n* before adding *-s* (this has no effect on pronunciation):

o homem	the man	**os homens**	the men
o jardim	the garden	**os jardins**	the gardens

4. Words ending in *-r, -s* and *-z* add *es:*

a flor	the flower	**as flores**	the flowers
o país	the country	**os países**	the countries
a voz	the voice	*as vozes*	the voices

Exceptions:

o lápis/os lápis	the pencil(s)
o ônibus/os ônibus	the bus(es)
o campus/os campus	the campus(es)
simples	simple, plain (adj.)

5. Words ending in *-al, -el, -ol,* or *-ul* drop the *l* and add *is:*

o jornal	the newspaper	**os jornais**	the newspapers
o papel	the paper	**os papéis**[3]	the paper
o espanhol	the Spaniard	*os espanhóis*	the Spaniards
o fuzil	the rifle	*os fuzis*	the rifles

Exceptions: Words ending in an unstressed *-il* change to *eis:*

difícil	**difíceis**	difficult
fácil	**fáceis**	easy
útil	*úteis*	useful

E. ADJECTIVES

o aluno alto	the tall student *(masc.)*
a aluna alta	the tall student *(fem.)*

---

[3] Note that words ending *-el* and *-il* receive a written accent in the plural: *-éis* and *-óis*.

os alunos altos	the tall students *(masc.)*
as alunas altas	the tall students *(fem.)*

Notice that a descriptive adjective tends to follow the noun it modifies and agrees with it in gender and number, that is, the adjective is masculine if the noun is masculine, plural if the noun is plural, etc.

The adjective, when used without the noun, indicates through its form whether the noun referred to is masculine or feminine, singular or plural:

(ele) **É espanhol.**	He's Spanish.
(ela) **É espanhola.**	She's Spanish.
(eles) **São espanhóis.**	They're Spanish. *(masc.)*
(elas) **São espanholas.**	They're Spanish. *(fem.)*

F. POSSESSION

English -*'s* or -*s'* is translated by *de* (of):

a caneta do João	John's pen ("the pen of John")
os cadernos	the professors' notebooks
dos professores	("the notebooks of the professors")

G. ASKING A QUESTION

To ask a question, use the same word order as when making a statement. In spoken Portuguese, it is only the intonation that indicates the difference between a statement and a question.

Ele fala português.	He speaks Portuguese.
Ele fala português?	Does he speak Portuguese?

Repeat the verb of the question in answering the question. Usually no subject or object pronouns are used in the answer.

There are three short possible answers:

Ele fala português?	Fala.	Yes, he does.
	Sim, fala.	
	Fala, sim.	

If the question presents more than one verb, just use the auxiliary in the answer:

Ele está estudando português?	Is he studying Portuguese?
Está.	Yes, he is.
Ele vai estudar português?	Is he going to study Portuguese?
Vai.	Yes, he is.

H. NEGATION

The word for both "no" and "not" is *não*. A statement is made negative by placing *não* before the verb. There are three short possible ways to answer in the negative:

Ele fala português?	Does he speak Portuguese?
Não fala.	No, he doesn't.
Não, não fala.	
Não fala não.	

REVIEW QUIZ 1

1. *Boa* _____ (afternoon), *senhor Coelho.*
   a. *manhã*
   b. *tarde*
   c. *obrigada*

2. *Pode dizer-me* _____ (where) *é o correio?*
   a. *onde*
   b. *bom*
   c. *quando*

3. *Quero café* _____ (with) *leite.* •
   a. *de*
   b. *mais*
   c. *com*

4. *Café com* _____ (milk).
   a. *açúcar*
   b. *vinho*
   c. *leite*

5. *Um pouco* _____ (more) *de carne.*
   a. *mais*
   b. *copo*
   c. *outro*

6. *No dia sete de* _____ (January).
   a. *março (Março* Ⓟ*)*
   b. *janeiro (Janeiro* Ⓟ*)*
   c. *outubro (Outubro* Ⓟ*)*

7. _____ (Wednesday), *cinco de setembro.*
   a. *sexta-feira*
   b. *sábado*
   c. *quarta-feira*

8. _____ (how) *vai (está) o senhor?*
   a. *amável*
   b. *como*
   c. *cedo*

9. *Boa* _____ (evening), *Dona Maria.*
   a. *com*
   b. *noite*
   c. *eu*

10. *Por favor, eu queria uma garrafa de* _____ (wine).
    a. *chá*
    b. *vinho*
    c. *água*

ANSWERS
1—b; 2—a; 3—c; 4—c; 5—a; 6—b; 7—c; 8—b; 9—b;
10—b.

LESSON 9

A. INTRODUCTIONS

Você and its plural form *vocês* are used in addressing members of the family, children, and close friends. In all other cases *o senhor, a senhora, os senhores,* and *as senhoras* are used to express "you." When in doubt, it is safer to use the *o/a senhor/a* forms. These words can also mean "Mr." or "Mrs." when they precede a proper name: *Sr.* Smith, *Sra.* Smith. Notice that in Portuguese people are usually addressed by their given name: *Sr. Paulo.* However, the word *senhor* in this position is customarily pronounced *seu* in conversation in Brazil: *Seu Paulo.* Likewise, it is better to use *dona* preceding an older or married woman's given name.

Bom dia, seu Joaquim. Como vai o senhor?	Good morning, *seu* Joaquim (Mr. Joaquim). How are you, sir?
Bom dia. Vou bem, obrigado. E a senhora?	Good morning. Fine, thank you. And you?
Bem, obrigada.	Fine, thanks.
Oi, João. Quero apresentar a dona Teresa para você.	Hi João. I want to introduce dona Teresa (Mrs. Teresa) to you.
Muito prazer em conhecer a senhora. João Silva.	I'm glad to meet you, ma'am. João Silva.

O prazer é todo meu.	The pleasure is all mine.
Oi, Paulo. Tudo bem?	Hi, Paulo. Is everything O.K.?
Tudo bem, obrigado.[1] E você?	Fine, thanks. And you?
Tudo legal.[2]	Everything's cool (right/correct).
Ruim.	Not so good.
Mais ou menos.	So-so.
Paulo, esta é a minha amiga Glória.	Paulo, this is my friend Glória.
Muito prazer.	Nice to meet you. (Much pleasure.)
Igualmente.	Likewise.
Bom dia, Paulo. Quero apresentar a minha esposa[3] para você.	Good morning, Paulo. I want to introduce my wife to you.
Muito prazer. Como a senhora tem passado?	Nice to meet you. How have you been?
Muito bem, obrigada.	Very well, thank you.
O senhor é estrangeiro?	Are you a foreigner?
Sim. Sou.	Yes. I am.
O senhor é americano?	Are you an American?
Sim. Sou. E você? Você é brasileira?	Yes. I am. And you? Are you Brazilian?
Sim, senhor. Sou brasileira.	Yes, sir. I am Brazilian.
A senhora fala português?	Do you speak Portuguese?

---

[1] A woman replies: *obrigada*.
[2] Very informal and colloquial form of greeting in Brazil.
[3] Also: *mulher*.

Um pouco.	A little.
Um pouquinho *(um bocadinho* Ⓟ*).*	Just a little.
Mais ou menos.	More or less./So-so.
Qual é o seu nome?	What's your name? *(informal)*
O meu nome é Pedro.	My name is Pedro.
Qual é o nome do senhor?	What's your name? *(formal)*
O meu nome é Pedro. E o seu?	My name is Pedro. And yours?
Como você se chama?	What's your name ("how do you call yourself")? *(informal)*
Eu me chamo Pedro.	My name is Peter.
Como a senhora se chama?	What's your name? *(formal)*
Eu me chamo Maria.	My name is Mary.
Qual é o nome dele?	What's his name?
O nome dele é Carlos.	His name is Charles.
Qual é o nome dela?	What is her name?
O nome dela é Ana.	Her name is Ana.
Qual é o seu sobrenome?	What's your family name?
Smith.	Smith.
Qual é o sobrenome dele?	What's his family name?
Silva.	Silva.
Boa noite, doutor (Dr.) Sérgio.	Good evening, Dr. Sergio.
Como está a sua senhora?[4]	How is your wife?
Ela está bem, obrigado.	She's fine. Thank you.

[4] More formal phrase for wife.

B. I Had a Good Time!

eu	I
me diverti *(diverti-me* Ⓟ*)*	had a good time ("amused myself")
muito	very much
Eu me diverti *(diverti-me* Ⓟ*)* **muito.**	I had a good time.
eu também	I also
gostei muito	I liked it very much
Eu também gostei muito.	I also enjoyed it very much.
Eu não me diverti.	I did not have a good time.
Que pena! Sinto muito.	That's too bad! I'm sorry.
Você está gostando *(está a gostar* Ⓟ*)* **da praia?**	Are you enjoying the beach?
Sim. Gosto muito *(gosto imenso* Ⓟ*).*	Yes. I am enjoying it very much.
Até logo.	Good-bye.
Até breve.	Good-bye.
até amanhã	until tomorrow
boa noite	good evening/good night
Até amanhã.	See you tomorrow.
Boa noite.	Good night.
Até já.	See you soon.
até	until
a volta	the return
Até a volta.	See you when you get back.
passe	get along
bem	well
Passe bem.	Good-bye. Good luck. Take it easy.

C. What's New?

Como vai, Manuel?	How's it going, Manuel?
Bem, e você, João?	Well, and how are you, John?
mais	more

ou	or
menos	less
Mais ou menos.	So-so.
Ruim.	Not so good.
o que	what
há	is there
de	of
novo	new
O que há de novo?	What's new?
nada	nothing
e	and
você	you
que	what
está	are you
fazendo *(a fazer* Ⓟ*)*	doing
agora	now
Nada. E você? Que está fazendo *(a fazer* Ⓟ*)* **agora?**	Nothing. And you? What are you doing now?
pouca	little
coisa	thing
nada	nothing
importante	important
Pouca coisa. Nada importante.	Not much. Nothing important.
Até logo.	So long./See you later.
Até amanhã.	See you tomorrow./Until tomorrow.
Até logo mais.	See you later./Until later.
Até à vista.	See you later (one of these days).
Até outro dia.	See you another day.
Adeus.	Good-bye.
Tchau Ⓑ.	Good-bye.

Obrigado(-a).   Thank you.
De nada.   You're welcome.

D. WORD STUDY

comédia	comedy
constante	constant
contrário	contrary
desejo	desire
longo	long
norte	north
órgão	organ
simples	simple
vendedor(-a)	vendor

QUIZ 6

1. *Como vai?*	a. Not much.
2. *Até logo.*	b. I would like to introduce my friend to you.
3. *Boa noite.*	c. See you tomorrow.
4. *Que há de novo?*	d. What's new?
5. *Pouca coisa.*	e. I'm very glad to meet you.
6. *Quero apresentar o meu amigo para você.*	f. How are you?
7. *Até amanhã.*	g. Good night.
8. *novo*	h. Good luck (Good-bye).
9. *Muito prazer em conhecer você.*	i. new
10. *Passe bem.*	j. So long.

ANSWERS
1—f; 2—j; 3—g; 4—d; 5—a; 6—b; 7—c; 8—i; 9—e; 10—h.

LESSON 10

A. To Be or Not to Be

Ser and *estar* both mean "to be" in Portuguese. *Ser* expresses a more permanent quality, feature, or condition, and a fixed location, origin, possession, and time. *Estar* describes a more temporary condition, quality, feature, or state that has changed or is changeable, and is used to discuss the weather. It is also used to denote health and emotions. Observe examples for particular uses of each verb.

1. Ser:

eu sou	I am
(tu és)	you are *(fam.)*
ele *(ela, o senhor,* etc.) **é**	he (she, you) is, are
nós somos	we are
(vós sois)	(you are)
eles *(elas, os senhores,* etc.) **são**	they, you, etc., are

Study the following phrases with *ser* and note its usage.

Ele é médico.	He is a doctor.
Ele é brasileiro.	He is Brazilian.
Ela é jovem.	She is young.
Eles são inteligentes.	They are intelligent.
É ele.	It is he.
Nós somos estudantes.	We are students.
O homem é alto.	The man is tall.
A sala é pequena.	The room is small.

A mesa é de madeira.	The table is made of wood.
Coimbra é em Portugal.	Coimbra is (located) in Portugal.
De onde (*donde*) você é?	Where are you from?
Sou dos Estados Unidos.	I'm from the U.S.
Onde é o correio?	Where is the post office?
De quem é isto?	Whose is this?
Isto é dele.	This is his.
Quanto é?	How much is it?
É cedo/tarde.	It is early/late.
É uma hora.	It is one o'clock.
São duas.	It is two o'clock.
É preciso.	It's necessary.
É importante.	It's important.

2. Estar:

eu estou	I am
tu estás	you are (*fam.*)
ele (*ela, o senhor,* etc.) está	he (she, you, etc.) is, are
nós estamos	we are
(vós estais)	(you are)
eles (*elas, os senhores,* etc.) estão	they (they, you, etc.) are

Now study these phrases with *estar,* noting the usage of this verb.

Onde está (o) meu irmão?	Where is my brother?
Ele está em casa.	He is home.
Estou cansado.	I'm tired.
Estamos prontos.	We are ready.
O café está frio.	The coffee is cold.
As janelas estão abertas.	The windows are open.
Hoje está quente.	Today it is hot.

O Paulo está doente?[1]　Is Paul sick?
Eles estão tristes.　They are unhappy.
Você está feliz aqui?　Are you happy here?
Ele não está aqui.　He is not here.

QUIZ 7

1. *Ele é inteligente.*	a. Whose is it?
2. *É preciso.*	b. Where are you from?
3. *Ele é médico.*	c. They are Brazilians.
4. *Sou aluno.*	d. He is a doctor.
5. *É uma hora.*	e. It's early.
6. *Nós somos médicos.*	f. It is two o'clock.
7. *É de madeira.*	g. He is intelligent.
8. *Donde é o senhor?*	h. It is necessary.
9. *Eles estão em casa.*	i. I am a student.
10. *É cedo.*	j. It is one o'clock.
11. *Estou cansado.*	k. It's made of wood.
12. *Eles são brasileiros.*	l. We are doctors.
13. *De quem é?*	m. They are home.
14. *É tarde.*	n. I'm tired.
15. *São duas.*	o. It's late.

ANSWERS

1—g; 2—h; 3—d; 4—i; 5—j; 6—l; 7—k; 8—b; 9—m;
10—e; 11—n; 12—c; 13—a; 14—o; 15—f.

B. IT IS ...

É ...　It is ...
É verdade.　It's true.
Não é verdade.　It's not true.
É meu (*seu, dele, dela,* etc.)　It's mine (yours, his, hers, etc.)
É muito mau.　It's very bad.
É grande/pequeno.　It's big/small.

---

[1] It means that he's sick today or for a while, but if he's a sickly person: *Ele é doente.*

Está caro/barato.	It's expensive/cheap.
É perto.	It's near.
É longe.	It's far.
É difícil.	It's difficult.
É fácil.	It's easy.
É pouco.	It's little. It's not much.
É muito pouco.	It's very little.
É muito.	It's a lot.
É bastante.	It's enough.
Não é bastante.	It's not enough.
Está[2] ...	It is ...
Está certo!	Fine!/Yes!/O.K.
Está bem.	All right.
Está chato Ⓑ.	It's boring.
Está agradável.	It's nice.
Está aqui (ali).	It's here (there).
Não está frio.	It's not cold.
Está chovendo.	It's raining.
É para o senhor.	It's for you.

C. WORD STUDY

cadeia	chain
carta	letter
completo	complete
creme	cream
eterno	eternal
fonte	fountain
oficial	officer
sistema	system

[2] For the difference between *é* and *está* see parts 1 and 2 of this section and also section 38 of the grammar summary.

QUIZ 8

1. *É muito.*	a. It's enough.
2. *É fácil.*	b. It's not true.
3. *É perto.*	c. It's very bad.
4. *É bastante.*	d. It's near.
5. *Não é verdade.*	e. It's mine.
6. *É muito mau.*	f. It's true.
7. *É pequeno.*	g. It's here.
8. *É verdade.*	h. It's small.
9. *É meu.*	i. It's easy.
10. *Está aqui.*	j. It's a lot.

ANSWERS
1—j; 2—i; 3—d; 4—a; 5—b; 6—c; 7—h; 8—f; 9—e;
10—g.

LESSON 11

A. TO HAVE AND HAVE NOT: *TER*

1. To have:

eu tenho	I have
(tu tens)	you have (*fam.*)
ele tem	he has
nós temos	we have
(vós tendes)	(you have)
eles têm	they have

2. Not to have:

eu não tenho	I don't have
(tu não tens)	you don't have (*fam.*)

ele não tem	he doesn't have
nós não temos	we don't have
(vós não tendes)	(you don't have)
eles não têm	they don't have

3. Study expressions with *ter:*

Tenho tempo.	I have time.
Não tenho tempo.	I don't have time.
Tenho fome. *(Estou com fome.)*[1]	I am hungry. ("I have hunger.")
Tem alguém em casa?	Is there anyone at home?
Quantos anos você tem?	How old are you?
Ele tem 20 anos.	He is 20 years old.
Eles têm que ir ao correio agora.[2]	They have to go to the post office now.
Nós temos que fazer tudo isto?	Do we have to do all this?
Temos sede. *(Estamos com sede.)*	We are thirsty. ("We have thirst," etc.)
Ele tem frio. *(Ele está com frio.)*	He is cold.
Eles têm calor. *(Eles estão com calor).*	They are warm.
O senhor tem razão.	You are right.

---

[1] The first form, *Tenho fome*, etc., is more common in Portugal; the second form given, *Estou com fome*, etc., is more common in Brazil.
[2] *Ter que* means to have to.

B. I KNOW ONLY A LITTLE PORTUGUESE

O senhor fala português?	Do you speak Portuguese?
Falo.[3]	I speak (it).
Não falo.	I don't speak (it).
Muito bem.	Very well.
Não falo muito bem.	I don't speak (it) very well.
Um pouco *(bocadinho* Ⓟ*).*	A little.
Muito pouco.	Very little.
Só um pouco.	Just a little./Only a little.
Mais ou menos.	So-so./More or less.
Ainda não.	Not yet.
Mal.	Poorly.
Só sei umas poucas palavras.	I know only a few words.
Não posso dizer muita coisa em português.	I can't say much in Portuguese.
O seu amigo fala português?	Does your friend speak Portuguese?
Não, o meu amigo não fala português.	No, my friend doesn't speak Portuguese.
O senhor compreende português?	Do you understand Portuguese?
Compreendo.	I understand (it).
Compreendo tudo mas não falo.	I understand everything but I don't speak (it).
Não, não compreendo português.	No, I don't understand Portuguese.
O senhor me compreende *(compreende-me* Ⓟ*)?*	Do you understand me?
Não compreendo muito bem.	I don't understand very well.
Você já sabe falar português?	Do you already know how to speak Portuguese?

[3] In colloquial Brazilian speech, usually the object pronoun is omitted whenever it is clear from the context what is being referred to.

Ainda não sei nada.	I don't know anything yet.
Nós sabemos um pouco *(bocadinho* Ⓟ*).*	We know a little.
O senhor sabe ler português?	Can you read Portuguese?
Leio mas não falo.	I read (it) but I don't speak(it).
Não, não sei.	No, I can't.
Estou aprendendo.	I'm learning (it).
Eu preciso praticar mais.	I need to practice (it) more.
Eu quero aprender.	I want to learn (it).
O que o senhor disse?	What did you say?
Eu não entendi o que você disse.	I didn't understand what you said.
O senhor fala muito depressa.	You speak too fast. You're speaking too fast.
Fale mais devagar.	Speak slower.
Você podia Ⓟ *falar mais devagar, por favor?*[4]	Could you speak slower, please?
Dá para você Ⓑ **falar mais devagar?**[5]	Could you speak slower?
Dá para você repetir?	Can you repeat it?
Outra vez, por favor.	Again, please.
Claro.	Sure.
Pois não.	Of course./Sure.
Desculpe, mas não compreendi nada.	Excuse (me), but I didn't understand anything.
Compreende agora?	Do you understand now?
Sim, compreendo.	Yes, I understand.
Que quer dizer isso em português?	What does that mean in Portuguese?

[4] *Faz favor* Ⓟ.
[5] *Dá para você:* Idiomatic expression very common in Brazilian colloquial speech with the meaning of: Can/could you; it's/would it be possible for you.

Como se diz "Thanks" em português?	How do you say "Thanks" in Portuguese?
Como se escreve essa palavra?	How do you spell ("write") that word?
Você podia escrever o seu endereço, por favor?	Could you write your address, please?
Você podia escrever, por favor?	Could you write it, please?

C. Do You Speak Portuguese?

Bom dia, senhor.	Good morning, sir.
Bom dia.	Good morning.
O senhor fala português?	Do you speak Portuguese?
Sim, falo.	Yes, I do. ("I speak")
Não falo inglês.	I don't speak English.
O senhor é português?	Are you Portuguese?
Não senhor, sou brasileiro. Mas tenho um amigo que é português.	No sir, I'm Brazilian. But I have a friend who is Portuguese.
Há quanto tempo o senhor está nos Estados Unidos?	How long have you been in the United States?
Três meses.	Three months.
O senhor vai aprender inglês em pouco tempo. Não e muito difícil.	You'll soon learn English. It's not very difficult.
Eu acho que é mais difícil do que o senhor diz.	I think it's more difficult than you say.
Eu acho que é mais fácil aprender a falar do que a escrever.	I think it's easier to learn to speak than to write.
Talvez. Porém, a pronúncia inglesa é muito difícil. O senhor não acha?	Perhaps. However, English pronunciation is very difficult. Don't you agree?

Sim, acho que o senhor tem razão.	Yes, I think that you're right.
Não sei, talvez.	I'm not sure, perhaps.
O senhor fala muito bem português.	You speak Portuguese very well.
Morei vários anos no Brasil.	I lived in Brazil for several years.
O senhor tem uma boa pronúncia.	You have good pronunciation.
Muito obrigado. Mas preciso praticar.	Thank you. But I need to practice.
Com licença, o avião vai sair.	If you'll excuse me, the plane is about to leave.
Boa sorte e boa viagem.	Good luck and have a pleasant trip.
Adeus.	Good-bye.
Adeus.	Good-bye.

QUIZ 9

1. *Compreendo mas não falo.*	a. Do you speak Portuguese?
2. *Compreende agora?*	b. I need to practice.
3. *Não falo muito bem.*	c. a little
4. *O senhor fala muito depressa.*	d. What did you say?
5. *Como se escreve essa palavra?*	e. Could you repeat (it), please?
6. *O senhor fala português?*	f. not very well
7. *Preciso praticar.*	g. I didn't understand (it) very well.
8. *um pouco*	h. I understand (it) but I don't speak (it).
9. *Você pode repetir, por favor?*	i. Speak slower.

10. *não muito bem*	j. I don't speak (it) very well.
11. *Fale mais devagar.*	k. How do you say "Thanks" in Portuguese?
12. *Falo (-o) mal.*	l. You speak too fast.
13. *Que disse o senhor?*	m. Do you understand now?
14. *Como se diz "Thanks" em português?*	n. How do you spell that word?
15. *Não compreendi muito bem.*	o. I speak (it) poorly.

ANSWERS

1—h; 2—m; 3—j; 4—l; 5—n; 6—a; 7—b; 8—c; 9—e; 10—f; 11—i; 12—o; 13—d; 14—k; 15—g.

D. EXCUSE ME AND THANK YOU

Desculpe.	Excuse me (asking pardon for something done).
Com licença. *(Dá licença. ℗)*	Excuse me (asking permission to do something, as to leave, etc.).
Com licença? *(Dá licença? ℗)*	May I?
Faça o favor de repetir.	Please repeat (it). ("Do the favor to repeat (it).")
Com muito prazer.	Gladly. ("With much pleasure.")
Às suas ordens.	At your service. ("At your orders.")
Em que posso servi-lo?	What can I do for you? ("In what can I serve you?")
Pois não?	Can I help you?
Pois não.	Sure./Of course.
Obrigado *(masc. form).*	Thank you.

Obrigada *(fem. form).*	Thank you.
Muito obrigado(-a).	Thank you very much.
O senhor é muito amável.	You are very kind. That's very kind of you.
Obrigado.	Thank you.
Muito obrigado.	Many thanks.
Muitíssimo obrigado.	Many, many thanks.
De nada.	Don't mention it.
Não há de quê.	Don't mention it.
Não é nada.	It's nothing.
Não foi nada.	Don't mention it. ("It wasn't anything.")
Por favor, fique à vontade!	Please make yourself comfortable.
Foi um prazer!	It was a pleasure!

E. WORD STUDY

banda	band
chofer	chauffeur
composição	composition
comun	common
consciência	conscience
decoração	decoration
descrição	description
missão	mission
numeral	numeral
região	region

LESSON 12

A. *THIS* AND *THAT* (DEMONSTRATIVE PRONOUNS AND ADJECTIVES)

The demonstrative pronouns *este* (this) and *esse* and *aquele* (that) agree in gender and number with the nouns they modify. Note that their forms vary according to distance:

This/these: *este, -a; -es, -as* (near speaker)
That/those: *esse, -a; -es, -as* (near the person being spoken to)
               aquele, -a; -es, -as (far from both)[1]

Before something not mentioned or uncertain, use the neuter forms, which are invariable: *isto* (this, these) and *isso* and *aquilo* (that, those).

The prepositions *de* (of/from, and possessive) and *em* (in/on/at) make contractions:[2]

de + este, estas, isto, etc.:   *deste, destas, disto*, etc. (of/from this, these)
de + esse, aquele, isso, etc.:   *desse, daquele, disso*, etc. (of/from, that, those)
em + esse, aquelas, aquilo, etc.:   *nesse, naquelas, naquilo*, etc. (in/on, that, those)

---

[1] The words *aqui* (here), *aí* (there) and *lá* or *ali* (over there) are helpful in determining the proper demonstrative pronoun.

[2] The preposition *a* (to) makes contractions with only the *aquele* form: *àquele, -s; àquela, -s;* and *àquilo*.

O que é isto aqui?	What is this here?
O que é isso aí?	What is that there?
O que é aquilo lá?	What is that over there?
Quem é este menino aqui?	Who is this boy here?
Quem é essa menina aí?	Who is that girl there?
Quem são aquelas meninas lá?	Who are those girls over there?
Este carro é seu?	Is this your car?
Não, o meu é aquele.	No, mine is that one.
Por favor, o senhor podia me dar aquela lá?	Please, could you give me that one *(fem.)*?
Eu fico com este aqui.	I'll take this one *(something masc.)*.
Esta cidade é bonita.	This town is pretty.
Por que você não quer aquilo?	Why don't you want that?
Quando aconteceu isto?	When did this happen?
Não entendo esta palavra.	I don't understand this word.
Não posso entender isto.	I can't understand this.
Não sei nada disto.	I don't know anything about/of this.
Dentro deste hotel.	Inside this hotel.
Perto daquela casa.	Near that house.
Ele mora neste apartamento.	He lives in this apartment.
Não pensei nisto.	I didn't think about this.
Você gosta disto?	Do you like this?
Neste momento . . .	At this moment . . .

QUIZ 10

1. *Fico com este.*   a. that one
2. *O que é aquilo?*   b. That lady.
3. *Aquele livro é dele.*   c. I don't like this.
4. *essa*   d. It is this one here.

5. *Não entendo isto.*   e. This one.
6. *perto desta cidade*   f. I'll take this one.
7. *É esta aqui.*   g. I don't understand this.
8. *Este.*   h. What is that?
9. *Essa senhora.*   i. That book is his.
10. *Não gosto disto.*   j. near this city

ANSWERS
1—f; 2—h; 3—i; 4—a; 5—g; 6—j; 7—d; 8—e; 9—b;
10—c.

B. MORE OR LESS THAN

1. More *(mais):*

mais devagar	slower
mais difícil	more difficult
mais fácil	easier
mais longe	farther
mais perto	nearer
mais que isso	more than that
mais dum ano	more than a year

2. Less *(menos):*

menos devagar	less slowly
menos difícil	less difficult
menos fácil	less easy
menos longe	less far, not as far
menos perto	not as near
menos que isso	less than that
menos dum ano	less than a year

The English "than" translates into *do que.*

REVIEW QUIZ 2

1. _____ (this) *menino*.
   a. *esta*
   b. *este*
   c. *essa*

2. *Quero* _____ (those, fem.)
   a. *essas*
   b. *estes*
   c. *aquele*

3. *Tenho* _____ (here) *os livros*.
   a. *isso*
   b. *aqui*
   c. *como*

4. *O senhor fala muito* _____ (fast).
   a. *devagar*
   b. *bem*
   c. *depressa*

5. *Amanhã vou* _____ (there).
   a. *lá*
   b. *aqui*
   c. *esse*

6. _____ (where) *está?*
   a. *aqui*
   b. *onde*
   c. *como*

7. *É* _____ (far) *daqui*.
   a. *longe*
   b. *perto*
   c. *ali*

8. *Hoje é* _____ (Friday).
   a. *quinta-feira*
   b. *sexta-feira*
   c. *fevereiro*

9. *É muito* _____ (expensive).
   a. *caro*
   b. *barato*
   c. *pouco*
10. *As janelas estão* _____ (open).
    a. *fechadas*
    b. *abertas*
    c. *ali*

ANSWERS
1—b; 2—a; 3—b; 4—c; 5—a; 6—b; 7—a; 8—b; 9—a;
10—b.

C. AND, OR, BUT

1. And *(e):*

O Roberto e o João são irmãos.	Robert and John are brothers.

2. Or *(ou):*

Cinco ou seis dólares.	Five or six dollars.
Vou com o meu irmão ou com a minha irmã.	I'm going with my brother or with my sister.

3. But *(mas):*

Quero ir mas não sei quando.	I want to go, but I don't know when.
Desejo estudar mas não posso.	I want to study, but I can't.

4. Nor, not even *(nem):*

Nem o meu cunhado me visitou.	Not even my brother-in-law visited me.
nem . . . nem	neither . . . nor
Nem o soldado nem o marinheiro veio.	Neither the soldier nor the sailor came.
Ela nem riu nem chorou.	She neither laughed nor cried.

D. WORD STUDY

desenvolvimento	development
diversão	diversion
líquido	liquid
obrigação	obligation
ocupação	occupation
pálido	pale
popular	popular
sólido	solid
teatro	theater
viagem	voyage

QUIZ 11

1. *inglês*	a. five or six days
2. *e*	b. He is not French but English.
3. *mas*	c. seven or eight hours
4. *cunhado*	d. English
5. *irmão*	e. but
6. *cinco ou seis dias*	f. tomorrow
7. *quando*	g. brother-in-law
8. *Ele não é francês mas inglês.*	h. and
9. *amanhã*	i. when
10. *sete ou oito horas*	j. brother

ANSWERS
1—d; 2—h; 3—e; 4—g; 5—j; 6—a; 7—i; 8—b; 9—f;
10—c.

LESSON 13

A. WHERE?

The verbs *ser* (to be) or *ficar* (to be, to stay) are inter-
changeable when they imply a permanent location of somebody or something. On the other hand, if the location of
something/somebody can be moved or is temporary, the
verb *estar* must be used instead.

1. Where?

Onde?	Where?
Aqui.	Here (near the speaker).
Aí.	There (near the person spoken to).
Ali.	There/Over there (far from both).
Lá dentro.	In there.
Lá fora.	Out there.
Em cima *(de).*	On top (of)
Embaixo *(de).*	Under.
Daqui. Daí. Dali.[1]	From here. From there. From over there.
À direita. À esquerda.	To the right. To the left.
Na[2] **esquina.**	On the corner.

---

[1] Contractions of *de* + *aqui, aí* or *ali.*
[2] The word *em (on/in/at)* contracts with the articles: em + *a, -s = na, -s; em*
+ *o, -s = no, -s.*

No parque.	At the park.
Onde fica isso?	Where is that?
É aqui mesmo.	It's right here.
A que distância fica?	How far is it from here?
É mais adiante.	It's farther on.
Fica longe?	Is it far?
É perto daqui?	Is it near (from) here?

Names of countries and continents are either masculine or feminine and require an article.[3] Remember that in Portuguese some prepositions make contractions with articles. However, names of cities do not require an article.[4]

2. To where?

Para onde?	To where?
Para onde eles vão?	(To) Where are they going?
Eles vão para o cinema.	They're going to the movies.
Eles vão para Lisboa.	They are going to Lisbon.
** E você?**	And you?
Eu vou para o Rio.	I'm going to Rio.

3. From where?

De onde?	From where?
De onde você vem?	Where are you from? Where do you come from?
Eu venho de Portugal e ele vem do Brasil.	I come from Portugal, and he comes from Brazil.
De onde as (os) senhoras (-eŝ) são?	Where are you *(pl.)* from?

•

[3] Main exceptions: *Portugal, Angola, Moçambique, Israel, Cuba,* and *Porto Rico.*
[4] Main exceptions: *o Rio de Janeiro; o Porto.*

Eu sou dos Estados Unidos e ela é da Itália.	I'm from the U.S., and she's from Italy.
Por⁵onde?	Which way (through where/by where)?
Por onde o ônibus vai?	Where does the bus go (through)?
Por aqui.	This way/by here.
Por ali.	That way/by there.
Pela praça.	By the square.
Pelo parque.	By the park.

4. Other examples:

Onde você mora?	Where do you live?
Eu moro em Londres.	I live in London.
Eu moro nos Estados Unidos.	I live in the United States.
Onde eles estão?	Where are they?
Eles estão no hotel.	They are at the hotel.
Eu estou aqui.	Here I am.
Ele está em casa.	He's at home.
Onde estão os bilhetes?	Where are the tickets?
Estão aqui.	They are here.
Estão aqui mesmo.	They are right here.
Estão ali.	They are over there (away from us).
Estão aí.	They are there (near you).
Eles estão por aí.	They're over there somewhere.
Você pode pôr aí.	You can put it there (near you).
Onde está o táxi?	Where's the taxi?
Como eles vêm?	How are they coming?
Eles vêm de ônibus.	They are coming by bus.
Ele vem de avião.	He's coming by plane.

---

⁵ The word *por (by/through)* contracts with the articles: *por + o, -s = pelo, -s; por + a, -s = pela, -s.*

B. ASKING DIRECTIONS

Por favor, onde fica o correio?	Please, where is the post office?
Não é muito longe.	It's not very far (from here).
Fica no centro.	It is downtown.
É perto daqui?[6]	Is it near here?
O correio fica na esquina da Rua Liberdade com a Avenida América.	It's on the corner of Liberdade Street and America Avenue.
Dá para ir andando?	Can I walk there?/Is it within walking distance?
Claro. Primeiro, você vai em frente até à rua Liberdade, lá você vira à esquerda.	Sure. First, go straight ahead as far as Liberdade Street, where you turn left.
O correio fica à direita do Banco do Brasil.	The post office is to the right of the Bank of Brazil.
É aqui que se troca dólar?	Is this where one can exchange dollars?
Não. A loja fica do outro lado da rua.	No. The shop is on the other side of the street.
Eu tenho que atravessar a rua?	Do I have to cross the street?
Sim, você tem.	Yes, you have to.
Onde ele mora?	Where does he live?
Ele mora em São Paulo, mas agora está na França.	He lives in São Paulo, but he's in France now.
Onde você vai agora?	Where are you going now?
Eu vou até à esquina.	I'm going as far as the corner.

---

[6] *daqui:* contraction of *de + aqui*

C. HERE AND THERE

O João mora aqui?	Does John live here?
Não, não mora aqui.	No he doesn't live here.
Mora ali.	He lives there.
Ela está aqui.	She is here.
Como se vai lá?	How do you get there?
Vira à esquerda/à direita.	Turn to your left/right.
Você segue em frente.	Go straight ahead.
(Você vai em frente.)	
Lá na Africa.	Over there in Africa.
Aqui na América.	Here in America.
Ele já vem.	He's coming right away.
Vem cá!	Come here!

D. NEAR AND FAR

Perto daqui.	Near here.
Muito perto.	Very near.
Perto da cidade.	Near the city.
Perto do parque.	Near the park.
Ao lado da igreja.	Next to the church.
É longe?	Is it far?
É longe daqui?	Is it far from here?
É muito longe.	It is very far.
Não é tão longe.	It's not very far.
Fica a duas quadras Ⓑ (dois quarteirões) daqui.	It's two blocks from here.
Fica a uma milha daqui.	It's a mile from here.
Fica a mil quilômetros daqui.[7]	It's a thousand kilometers from here.

---

[7] *quilómetros* Ⓟ.

QUIZ 12

1. *De onde?*	a. Where are they?
2. *Vem cá.*	b. in there
3. *aqui*	c. to the left
4. *à direita*	d. It's far.
5. *ali*	e. here
6. *É aqui mesmo.*	f. Come here.
7. *Onde eles estão?*	g. Near here?
8. *à esquerda*	h. to the right
9. *É longe.*	i. there
10. *lá dentro*	j. out there
11. *Ele está por aí.*	k. as far as
12. *Fica perto?*	l. It's right here.
13. *lá fora*	m. Where from?
14. *até*	n. He's somewhere around here.
15. *Perto daqui?*	o. Is it near?

ANSWERS

1—m; 2—f; 3—e; 4—h; 5—i; 6—l; 7—a; 8—c; 9—d; 10—b; 11—n; 12—o; 13—j; 14—k; 15—g.

LESSON 14

A. I, YOU, HE, ETC. (SUBJECT PRONOUNS)

eu	I
(tu)	(you)
você	you *(masc./fem.—informal)*
o senhor, a senhora	you *(masc. formal)*, you *(fem. formal)*

ele, ela	he, she
nós	we
(vós)	(you)
vocês	you *(masc./fem.—informal)*
os senhores, as senhoras	you *(masc. formal)*, you *(fem. formal)*
eles, elas	they

B. USING SUBJECT PRONOUNS: CONJUGATING IN THE PRESENT TENSE

Portuguese regular verbs fall into three categories according to the ending of the infinitive: *-ar, -er,* or *-ir.* For example, *falar* (to speak); *comer* (to eat); *abrir* (to open).

Verbs are conjugated in the various persons, numbers, and tenses by adding the inflectional ending to the stem, which is obtained by dropping the infinitive ending:

fal*ar;* com*er;* abr*ir.*

1. I:

The first person singular of the present tense of all three categories is formed by dropping the ending of the infinitive and adding *-o.*

eu falo	I speak
eu como	I eat
eu abro	I open

2. You, he, she, it, you, they:

Although at times the form *tu* is used,[1] its plural form *vós* is never employed. So, there is no need to memorize all the verbal forms, and they will not be given here. For more

---

[1] More frequently in Portugal than in Brazil.

detailed information on verbal conjugation see Section 39 of the grammar summary.

Usually *you* (*singular* and *plural*) is expressed by *você, vocês, o senhor, a senhora, os senhores,* or *as senhoras.* Note that the same endings put on the verb stem of the second person *you* are used for the third person *he, she,* and *it.* The same thing happens in the second and third person plural: The *-ar* verbs take the endings *-a* in the singular and *-am* in the plural. The *-er* and *-ir* verbs take the endings *-e* and *-em* in the singular and plural, respectively.

EXAMPLES

FALAR		TO SPEAK
você	*fala*	you speak
a senhor, a senhora	*fala*	you speak
ele, ela	*fala*	he, she speaks
vocês	*falam*	you speak (*plural*)
os senhores, as senhoras	*falam*	you speak (*plural*)
eles, elas	*falam*	they speak (*masc.*), they speak (*fem.*)

COMER		TO EAT
você	*come*	you eat
o senhor, a senhora	*come*	you eat
ele, ela	*come*	he, she eats
vocês	*comem*	you eat (*plural*)
os senhores, as senhoras	*comem*	you eat (*plural*)
eles, elas	*comem*	they eat (*masc.*), they eat (*fem.*)

ABRIR		TO OPEN
você	*abre*	you open
o senhor, a senhora	*abre*	you open
ele, ela	*abre*	he, she, it opens

vocês	abrem	you open (plural)
os senhores, as senhoras	abrem	you open (plural)
eles, elas	abrem	they open (masc.), they open (fem.)

3. We:

The first person plural *nós* is formed by adding to the stem of the verb the endings *-amos*, *-emos*, and *-imos* for *-ar, -er,* and *-ir* verbs, respectively.

nós falamos	we speak
nós comemos	we eat
nós abrimos	we open

There are a few verbs that do not follow the pattern mentioned above. These are called *irregular* verbs, and they have to be learned individually.

C. IT'S ME (I), YOU, HE, ETC. (DISJUNCTIVE PRONOUNS)

Sou eu.	It's me (I).
És tu.	It's you. (fam.)
É ele.	It's him (he).
É ela.	It's her (she).
É o senhor.	It's you (masc.).
É a senhora.	It's you (fem.).
É você.	It's you.
Somos nós.	It's us (we).
São eles.	It's them (they) (masc.).
São elas.	It's them (they) (fem.).

D. *IT* AND *THEM* (OBJECT PRONOUNS)

(See Lesson 15 for more on object pronouns.)

	SINGULAR	PLURAL
Masculine	*o* it	*os* them
Feminine	*a* it	*as* them

O senhor tem o dinheiro?	Do you have the money?
Tenho. (Sim, tenho-o.)	Yes, I have it.
O senhor tem a carta?	Do you have the letter?
Tenho. (Sim, tenho-a.)	Yes, I have it.
O senhor viu João e Pedro?	Did you see John and Peter?
Vi. (Sim, vi-os.)	Yes, I saw them.
O senhor viu Maria e Ana?	Did you see Mary and Anna?
Vi. (Sim, vi-as.)	Yes, I saw them.

Notice that the pronoun is masculine if the word to which it refers is masculine, plural if the word to which it refers is plural, etc. In conversation, a short answer is often given, just as the verb form shown above. If the object pronoun is used in the answer, it can follow the verb, as shown above in parentheses. If the verb is preceded by words such as an expressed subject, adverb, etc., the object pronoun can precede the verb: *Sim, eu os tenho; Sim, Paulo os tem; Não os tenho,* etc. Notice that *o, os, a, as* are also used to mean "you": *Não o vi.* I didn't see you *(masc. sing.).*

E. MY, YOUR, HIS, ETC. (POSSESSIVE ADJECTIVES)

1. The possessive adjectives agree with the word they refer to in gender *(masc.* or *fem.)* and number *(sing.* or *plural),* and not with the possessor as in English. For example: *meu carro (masc. sing.); minhas casas (fem. plural).*

	MASCULINE	FEMININE	
eu	*meu(s)*	*minha(s)*	my
você(s)	*seu(s)*	*sua(s)*	your
nós	*nosso(s)*	*nossa(s)*	our

2. Although grammatically the words *seu/sua* (either singular or plural) refer to the third person, such usage will be misunderstood since its meaning implies "your" in spoken language.[2] If the possessor is clearly indicated, the article alone may be sufficient.

Ele perdeu o passaporte.   He lost his passport.

3. Otherwise, the contracted forms *dele/-s, dela/-s*, should be used after the noun in order to express the meaning of "your."

Eu fui com o irmão dele.   I went with his brother.
Nós vamos ficar na casa   We are going to stay in their
deles.   house.
Sua irmã e a dela.   Your sister and her sister.

4. Often the possessives are not used before parts of the body, clothing, etc., unless the possessor is not clear (*Onde está o meu livro?* Where is my book?).

Ela colocou o dinheiro na   She put her money in her
bolsa.   purse.
Ele fechou os olhos.   He closed his eyes.
Eu lavei as mãos.   I washed my hands.

Study the following examples:

SINGULAR
meu amigo   my friend *(masc.)*
minha amiga   my friend *(fem.)*
(teu amigo)   (your friend) *(familiar)*
(tua amiga)   (your friend) *(familiar)*
seu amigo   your friend

[2] It is mostly in literature that *his her, their* are expressed by *seu*.

sua amiga	your friend
o amigo dele	his friend
a amiga dele	his friend
os amigos dele	his friends
o amigo dela	her friend
a amiga dela	her friend
as amigas dela	her friends
nosso amigo	our friend
nossa amiga	our friend
seu amigo	your friend (their friend)
sua amiga	your friend (their friend)

PLURAL

meus amigos	my friends *(masc.)*
minhas amigas	my friends *(fem.)*
(teus amigos)	(your friends) *(familiar)*
(tuas amigas)	(your friends) *(familiar)*
seus amigos	your (his, her) friends
suas amigas	your (his, her) friends
as amigas deles	their friends
a amiga deles	their friend
os amigos delas	their friends
as amigas delas	their friends
o amigo delas	their friend
nossos amigos	our friends
nossas amigas	our friends
seus amigos	your friends (their friends)
suas amigas	your friends (their friends)

SINGULAR

meu parente	my relative
minha sobrinha	my niece
seu sobrinho	your (his, her) nephew
sua prima	your (his, her) cousin *(fem.)*
nosso primo	our cousin *(masc.)*
nossa sogra	our mother-in-law

seu sogro	your (their) father-in-law
sua tia	your (their) aunt
o pai dela	her father
a mãe dele	his mother

PLURAL

meus parentes	my relatives
minhas sobrinhas	my nieces
seus sobrinhos	your (his, her) nephews
suas primas	your (his, her) cousins
nossos primos	our cousins
nossas sogras	our mothers-in-law
seus sogros	your (their) fathers-in-law
suas tias	your (their) aunts
os pais deles	their parents
os pais dele	his parents
os parentes dele	his relatives

Other examples:

Even though the use of the definite article with possessive adjectives is optional, there is a tendency to use it both in Brazil and Portugal. However, it is omitted in a direct address:

Meu Deus, onde estão meus óculos!	My God, where are my glasses!
Meus amigos, como estão?	My friends, how are you?

MASCULINE SINGULAR

Onde está o meu irmão?	Where is my brother?
Onde está o seu irmão?	Where is your (his, her) brother?
Onde está o nosso irmão?	Where is our brother?
Onde está o seu irmão?	Where is your (their) brother?
Onde está a prima dele?	Where is his (female) cousin?
Onde está o primo dele?	Where is his (male) cousin?

FEMININE SINGULAR

Onde está a minha irmã?	Where is my sister?
Onde está a sua irmã?	Where is your (his, her) sister?
Onde está a nossa irmã?	Where is our sister?
Onde está a sua irmã?	Where is your (their) sister?
Onde está a prima dela?	Where is her (female) cousin?
Onde está o primo dela?	Where is her (male) cousin?

Notice that, like possessive adjectives, possessive pronouns reflect the number and gender of the thing possessed.

MASCULINE PLURAL

Onde estão os meus chapéus?	Where are my hats?
Onde estão os seus chapéus?	Where are your (his, her) hats?
Onde estão os nossos chapéus?	Where are our hats?
Onde estão os seus chapéus?	Where are your (their) hats?
Onde estão os chapéus dele?	Where are his hats?

FEMININE PLURAL

Onde estão as minhas luvas?	Where are my gloves?
Onde estão as suas luvas?	Where are your (his, her) gloves?
Onde estão as nossas luvas?	Where are our gloves?
Onde estão as suas luvas?	Where are your (their) gloves?
Onde estão as luvas dela?	Where are her gloves?

F. IT'S MINE, YOURS, HIS, ETC. (POSSESSIVE PRONOUNS)

There are two forms of possessive pronouns, one without the definite article and stressing the possessor:

É meu (carro).	It's mine (my car; something *masc.*).
É sua.	It's yours (something *fem.*).
É nosso.	It's ours (something *masc.*).
São dele.	They are his.
É deles.	It's theirs.

and one with the definite article, indicating the possessor, but with some thought on the object possessed:

É o meu.	It's mine.
É o seu.	It's yours.
É o nosso.	It's ours.
É o seu.	It's yours.
É o dele.	It's his (something *masc.*).
É a dele.	It's his (something *fem.*).
É o deles.	It's theirs.
São os dele.	They are his.
São os dela.	They are hers.
São os deles.	They are theirs.

Other examples:

Meus amigos e os seus.	My friends and yours.
Seu livro é melhor que o nosso.	Your book is better than ours.
De quem é a luva?—É minha.	Whose glove is this?—It's mine.

LESSON 15

A. ME, YOU, HIM, ETC./TO ME, YOU, HIM, ETC. (DIRECT AND INDIRECT OBJECT PRONOUNS)

Object pronouns are always used in conjunction with a verb, and they take the place of the real objects.

1. The direct object pronouns in Portuguese are:

me	me
o, a	you
o, a	him, her, it
nos	us
os, as	you
os, as	them

2. The position of the pronouns (either direct or indirect) in relation to the verb varies. With a one-word verb, Brazilian usage favors placing pronouns before the verb, whereas Continental Portuguese favors them after the verb. Whenever the pronoun follows a verb, it must be connected by a hyphen.

Ele comprou o carro.	He bought the car.
Ele o comprou. Ⓑ	He bought it.
Ele comprou-o. Ⓟ	He bought it.

3. He saw me, you, her, etc.:

Você o viu.[1]	You saw him.
Você a viu.	You saw her.
Ele me viu.	He saw me.
Ele o viu.	He saw you/him. (you *masc.*)

---

[1] In Continental Portuguese:

Você viu-o.	*Ele viu-a.*
Você viu-a.	*Eles viram-nos.*
Ele viu-me.	*(Eles viram-vos.)*
(Ele viu-te.)	*Nós vimo-los.*
Ele viu-o.	*Nós vimo-las.*

Brazilian usage favors the object pronoun before the verb, Continental Portuguese favors it after the verb. For more information on the position of the object pronouns, see Section 19 of the grammar summary.

Ele a viu.	He saw you/her. (you *fem.*)
Ele nos viu.	He saw us.
Nós os vimos.	We saw you/them. (you *masc.*)
Eles as viram.	They saw you/them. (you *fem.*)

4. Indirect object pronouns:

The indirect object is the person (or thing) that ultimately receives the object. In Portuguese the second and third person indirect object pronouns (singular and plural) are exactly the same. In English, the indirect object is sometimes introduced by the preposition "to," sometimes not. Example: He gave *me* the book. He gave the book *to me*. The Portuguese indirect object pronouns are:

me	to me
lhe	to you
lhe	to him/to her
nos	to us
lhes	to you
lhes	to them
Você me deu o livro.[2]	You gave me the book. (You gave the book to me.)
Ele me deu o livro.	He gave me the book. (He gave the book to me.)
Ela nos deu o livro.	She gave us the book.
Eu lhe dei o livro.	I gave you/him/her the book.
Ela lhe deu o livro.	She gave you/him/her the book.
Eu lhes dei o livro.	I gave you/them the book.

---

[2] In Continental Portuguese: *Você deu-me o livro; Ele deu-me o livro; Ele deu nos o livro; Eu dei-lhe o livro; Ela deu-lhe o livro; Eu dei-lhes o livro.*

5. As mentioned above, object pronouns may precede or follow the verb. When the pronouns follow the verb, they must be attached with a hyphen: *Disse-me*. In Brazilian speech, however, it is common to start a statement with a pronoun: *Me disse*. Due to its frequency, this must be considered an acceptable colloquial pattern even though it is not considered the best form to begin a sentence or a clause with an object pronoun. Also, in Brazilian speech it has become quite common to use the subject pronoun instead of the object pronoun:

Eu vi ele. (for: *Eu o vi*)	I saw him.
Eu vi ela. (for: *Eu a vi*)	I saw her.
Eu vi você. (for: *Eu o vi*)	I saw you.

Remember that in Brazilian Portuguese there is a tendency not to use the pronoun whenever its reference is clear from the context:

Você comprou o livro?	Did you buy the book?
Sim. Eu (o) comprei.	Yes. I bought (it).

6. Generally, an object pronoun used with an infinitive may precede or follow the infinitive if a preposition comes before the infinitive (however, with the prepositions *a* and *em* the pronoun comes after the infinitive):

para me falar or	
para falar-me	to speak to me

In the above case, and when the infinitive follows another verb, Brazilian usage usually favors using the object pronoun before the infinitive:

Ele quer me falar.   He wants to speak to me.

When the direct pronouns *o, a, os,* and *as* follow an infinitive, the final *-r* of the infinitive is dropped, the preceding vowel receives an accent in the first and second conjugations (*-ar* and *-er*), and an *l* is added to the direct object pronoun:[3]

Você vai levá-las?   Are you going to take them?
Muito prazer em conhecê-lo.   I'm very pleased to meet you.
Preciso abri-lo.   I need to open it.

B. I'M SPEAKING TO YOU

Eu lhe digo. Digo-lhe.	I'm speaking to you.
Eu digo para você.	I'm speaking to you.
Ele lhe diz. Diz-lhe.	He's saying (it) to you.
Ele diz para você.	He's saying (it) to you.
Quem me escreveu uma carta?	Who has written me a letter?
Não sei quem lhe escreveu.	I don't know who has written to you.
Não sei quem escreveu para você.	I don't know who has written to you.

C. HE GAVE IT TO ME, YOU, HIM, ETC.

In Continental Portuguese, the direct object pronoun, if used with an indirect object, can be contracted with the noun, forming such new forms as *mo, lho, no-lo, mas, lhos,* etc.: *Ele mo deu.* (He gave it to me). These forms are somewhat awkward and are generally avoided, especially in conversation, and they are never used in Brazilian speech. Thus, the

---

[3] The *ir* verbs do not need an accent since the final *-i* automatically receives the stress.

direct object pronoun may be omitted: *Ele me deu* (He gave
it to me). Or, the direct object may be used and the indirect
object replaced by the prepositional form. Note that the subject pronouns (*você, o senhor, a senhora, ele, ela, nós*, etc.)
are used following a preposition except in the first person
when the form *mim* must be used.

Ele o deu para mim.	He gave it to me.
Ele o deu para você.	He gave it to you.
Eu o dei para ela.	I gave it to her.
Ele o deu para nós.	He gave it to us.
Ela o deu para os senhores.	She gave it to you.
Ela o deu para vocês.	She gave it to you.

D. I'M SPEAKING ABOUT YOU, HIM, HER, ETC.

Falo de você.	I'm speaking about you.
Você fala de mim.	You're speaking about me.
Ela fala dele.	She's speaking about him.
Ele fala dela.	He's speaking about her.
Falamos dos senhores.	We're speaking about you.
Eles falam de nós.	They're speaking about us.
Eles falam deles.	They're speaking about them.

E. MYSELF, YOURSELF, HIMSELF, ETC. (REFLEXIVE PRONOUNS)

A reflexive construction is formed by a verb and an object
pronoun that refers back to the subject. Note the forms for
"myself," "yourself," etc. in Portuguese:

me	myself
se	yourself
se	himself, herself, itself
nos	ourselves

se   yourselves
se   themselves

Here is the conjugation of a reflexive verb in the present:

Eu me lavo.   I wash myself.
Você se lava.   You wash yourself.
Ele/ela/o senhor se lava. He/she/it washes himself,
                              herself, itself.
Nós nos lavamos.   We wash ourselves.
Vocês se lavam.   You wash yourselves.
Eles/elas se lavam.   They wash themselves.

Other examples:

Como o senhor se chama? What's your name?
Nós nos vemos no espelho. We see ourselves in the
                               mirror.
Eu me conheço bem.   I know myself well.

The reflexive construction may have a reciprocal meaning (each other) as well:

Eles se gostam.   They like each other.
Eles se escrevem.   They write to each other.

There are verbs that are reflexive in Portuguese but not in English. For example:

Eu me divirto.   I'm having a good time.
Nós nos levantamos.   We get up.
Eu não me sinto bem.   I don't feel well.
Ele se senta.   He sits down.

Some of these reflexive verbs use a preposition before a following object:

Eles se despedem dos amigos deles.	They are taking leave of ("saying good-bye to") their friends.
Eu não me lembro disto.	I don't remember this.
Ela se ri de nós.	She is laughing at us.

F. IDIOMATIC USES OF *SE*

When there is an unidentified subject, the pronoun *se* is used in many expressions with the English meaning of "one," "they," "people," etc. Notice that the verb takes the third person singular form:

Como se vai para o centro?	How does one go downtown?
Diz-se que . . .	It's said that . . . They say that . . .
Onde se compra isto?	Where can one buy this?
Come-se bem aqui.	One eats well here ("The food is good here").

The *se* form is often used where the passive form would be used in English:

Fala-se português aqui.	Portuguese is spoken here.
As portas se abrem às oito.	The doors open at eight.

QUIZ 13

1. *Senta-se.*	a. We get up.
2. *Nós nos vemos.*	b. They are taking leave.
3. *Divirto-me.*	c. He gave it to them.
4. *Disse-me.*	d. She laughs.
5. *Nós nos levantamos.*	e. I wash myself.
6. *Eu me lavo.*	f. I'm having a good time.
7. *Ri-se.*	g. They write to each other.
8. *Escrevem-se.*	h. He told me.

9. *Deu-lhes.*   i. We see ourselves.
10. *Despedem-se.*   j. He sits down.

ANSWERS
1—j; 2—i; 3—f; 4—h; 5—a; 6—e; 7—d; 8—g; 9—c;
10—b.

REVIEW QUIZ 3

1. *É* _____ (she).
   a. *ele*
   b. *ela*
   c. *eu*
2. *Somos* _____ (us).
   a. *eles*
   b. *nos*
   c. *nós*
3. *Dou o livro a* _____ (him).
   a. *ele*
   b. *o senhor*
   c. *o*
4. *(her) vestido* _____.
   a. *dela*
   b. *delas*
   c. *de mim*
5. _____(our) *cartas.*
   a. *o nosso*
   b. *as nossas*
   c. *os nossos*
6. *Onde estão* _____ (my) *livros?*
   a. *mim*
   b. *os meus*
   c. *a nossa*
7. *Seu livro é melhor que o* _____ (ours).
   a. *nossos*
   b. *nosso*
   c. *seu*

8. *Falamos* _____ (about him).
   a. *do senhor*
   b. *deles*
   c. *dele*

9. *Ele* _____ (us) *deu.*
   a. *se*
   b. *nos*
   c. *nossos*

10. *Como se* _____ (call) *o senhor?*
    a. *lavo*
    b. *chama*
    c. *vemos*

11. *Nós nos* _____ (wash).
    a. *lava*
    b. *lavam*
    c. *lavamos*

12. _____ *-se* (They take leave).
    a. *despedem*
    b. *levantam*
    c. *sente*

13. _____ *-me* (sit down).
    a. *diz*
    b. *lavo*
    c. *sento*

14. *Falo-* _____ (to him).
    a. *a eles*
    b. *o senhor*
    c. *lhe*

15. *Não se* _____ (dare).
    a. *atreve*
    b. *lavam*
    c. *levantamos*

ANSWERS
1—b; 2—c; 3—a; 4—a; 5—b; 6—b; 7—b; 8—c; 9—b;
10—b; 11—c; 12—a; 13—c; 14—c; 15—a.

LESSON 16

A. A Few Action Phrases

Cuidado!	Watch out!
Tenha cuidado!	Be careful! Watch out!
Atenção!	Attention! Watch out!
Depressa!	Hurry up!
Mais depressa.	Faster.
Devagar.	Slowly.
Mais devagar.	Slower.
Já vou.	I'm coming.
Vamos embora.	Let's leave.
Vamos lá.	Let's go.
Vamos!	Come on!
Depressa!	Let's hurry!
Não há pressa.	There's no hurry.
Estou com pressa.	I'm in a hurry.
Não estou com pressa.	I'm not in a hurry.
Um momento!	Just a minute!
Venha já!	Come right away!
Imediatamente.	Immediately.
Agora mesmo!	Right now!
Aqui mesmo.	Right here.
Cedo.	Soon.
Mais cedo.	Sooner.
Mais tarde.	Later.
Muito bem.	Very well.
Está certo.	Alright.

QUIZ 14

1. *Cuidado!*   a. slower
2. *Estou com pressa.*   b. Right now!

3. *Um momento!*	c. Come right away!
4. *cedo*	d. I'm coming.
5. *imediatamente*	e. Watch out!
6. *mais tarde*	f. later
7. *mais devagar*	g. I'm in a hurry.
8. *Já vou.*	h. Just a minute!
9. *Venha já!*	i. immediately
10. *Agora mesmo!*	j. soon

ANSWERS

1—e; 2—g; 3—h; 4—j; 5—i; 6—f; 7—a; 8—d; 9—c;
10—b.

B. May I Ask?

Posso lhe fazer uma pergunta?	May I ask you a question?
Gostaria de lhe perguntar uma coisa.	I'd like to ask you something.
Pode me dizer *(dizer-me* ℗*)?*	Can you tell me?
Podia me dizer *(dizer-me* ℗*)?*	Could you tell me?
Queira me dizer *(dizer-me* ℗*).*	Please tell me.
Tenha a bondade de me dizer *(dizer-me* ℗*).*	Please tell me.
Faça o favor de me dizer *(dizer-me* ℗*).*	Please tell me.
Quer me dizer *(dizer-me* ℗*).*	Will you tell me?
Que quer dizer o senhor?	What do you mean?
Quero dizer que . . .	I mean that . . .
Que quer dizer isso?	What does that mean?
Quer dizer . . .	It means . . .

C. Word Study

barreira	barrier
caráter	character
curioso	curious
curiosidade	curiosity
dicionário	dictionary
exército	army
freqüentemente	frequently
grau	degree
oficial	official
pena	pity

LESSON 17

A. Numbers

Notice that in Portuguese the numbers one and two have feminine forms that agree with feminine words: *dois meninos e duas meninas,* etc. However, if the number is placed after the noun, there is no need for agreement since the word *número,* which is masculine, is understood: *a lição trinta e dois.*

um *(masc.)* **uma** *(fem.)*	one
dois *(masc.)* **duas** *(fem.)*	two
três	three
quatro	four
cinco	five
seis	six
sete	seven

oito	eight
nove	nine
dez	ten
onze	eleven
doze	twelve
treze	thirteen
catorze *(quatorze* Ⓟ*)*	fourteen
quinze	fifteen
dezesseis *(dezasseis* Ⓟ*)*	sixteen
dezessete *(dezassete* Ⓟ*)*	seventeen
dezoito	eighteen
dezenove *(dezanove* Ⓟ*)*	nineteen
vinte	twenty
vinte e um *(uma)*	twenty-one
vinte e dois *(duas)*	twenty-two
vinte e três	twenty-three
trinta	thirty
trinta e um *(uma)*	thirty-one
trinta e dois *(duas)*	thirty-two
trinta e três	thirty-three
quarenta	forty
quarenta e um *(uma)*	forty-one
quarenta e dois *(duas)*	forty-two
quarenta e três	forty-three
cinqüenta[1]	fifty
cinqüenta e um *(uma)*	fifty-one
cinqüenta e dois *(duas)*	fifty-two
cinqüenta e três	fifty-three

[1] *cinquenta* Ⓟ.

sessenta	sixty
sessenta e um *(uma)*	sixty-one
sessenta e dois *(duas)*	sixty-two
sessenta e três	sixty-three
setenta	seventy
setenta e um *(uma)*	seventy-one
setenta e dois *(duas)*	seventy-two
setenta e três	seventy-three
oitenta	eighty
oitenta e um *(uma)*	eighty-one
oitenta e dois *(duas)*	eighty-two
oitenta e três	eighty-three
noventa	ninety
noventa e um *(uma)*	ninety-one
noventa e dois *(duas)*	ninety-two
noventa e três	ninety-three
cem	one hundred
cento e um *(uma)*	a hundred and one
cento e dois *(duas)*	a hundred and two
cento e três	a hundred and three
mil	one thousand
mil e um *(uma)*	a thousand and one
mil e dois *(duas)*	a thousand and two
mil e três	a thousand and three

B. MORE NUMBERS

120 cento e vinte
122 cento e vinte e dois (duas)
130 cento e trinta
140 cento e quarenta

150 cento e cinqüenta
160 cento e sessenta
170 cento e setenta
178 cento e setenta e oito
200 duzentos, duzentas
300 trezentos, trezentas
400 quatrocentos, quatrocentas
500 quinhentos, quinhentas
600 seiscentos, seiscentas
700 setecentos, setecentas
800 oitocentos, oitocentas
900 novecentos, novecentas
1965 mil novecentos e sessenta e cinco
1,000,000 um milhão (de)

Notice that in addition to the numbers one and two, the plural hundred forms also have feminine forms: *duzentos, duzentas*, etc. *Milhão* uses *de* before a completing noun: *um milhão de dólares*.

FIRST, SECOND, THIRD
The following ordinal numbers each have four forms, masculine singular and plural and feminine singular and plural: *primeiro, primeiros, primeira, primeiras*, etc.

primeiro	first
segundo	second
terceiro	third
quarto	fourth
quinto	fifth
sexto (x = s)	sixth
sétimo	seventh
oitavo	eighth
nono	ninth
décimo	tenth

TWO AND TWO

Dois e dois: quatro.	Two and two are four.

(Also used: *Dois mais dois são quatro; Dois mais dois igual a quatro.*)

Quatro e dois: seis.	Four and two are six.
Dez menos dois: oito.	Ten minus two is eight.
Sete vezes três: vinte e um.	Seven times three is twenty-one.
Oito vezes oito: sessenta e quatro.	Eight times eight is sixty-four.
Vinte e um dividido por sete: três.	Twenty-one divided by seven is three.
A Primeira Dama está no terceiro andar.	The First Lady is on the third floor.
A segunda avenida.	(The) Second Avenue.
O quinto capítulo.	The fifth chapter.

QUIZ 15

1. *mil*	a. 1002
2. *onze*	b. 32
3. *cem*	c. 102
4. *terceiro*	d. 324
5. *trinta*	e. 11
6. *vinte*	f. 1000
7. *sessenta e sete*	g. 67
8. *trezentos e vinte e quatro*	h. 71
9. *trinta e dois*	i. 3rd
10. *cento e dois*	j. 875
11. *oitocentos e setenta e cinco*	k. 83
12. *setenta e um*	l. 555
13. *mil e dois*	m. 20

14. *quinhentos e cinqüenta e*   n. 30
    cinco
15. *oitenta e três*   o. 100

ANSWERS
1—f; 2—e; 3—o; 4—i; 5—n; 6—m; 7—g; 8—d; 9—b;
10—c; 11—j; 12—h; 13—a; 14—l; 15—k.

LESSON 18

A. How Much?

Quanto custa isto?	How much does this cost?
Custa quarenta centavos.	It costs forty cents.
Quanto é uma libra (*um quilo*) **de café?**	How much is a pound (a kilogram) of coffee?
Estamos vendendo a oitenta centavos a libra (*o quilo*).	It costs eighty cents a pound (a kilogram). ("We're selling at eighty cents," etc.)
Qual é o preço?	What is the price?
Quanto são as camisas?	How much are the shirts?
Quanto é o sorvete?	How much is the ice cream?

B. It Costs . . .

Custa . . .	It costs . . .
Este livro custa sessenta cruzeiros.	This book costs sixty cruzeiros.
Ele comprou um carro por dez mil dólares.	He bought a car for ten thousand dollars.
A viagem de navio é oitocentos dólares.	The trip by ship is eight hundred dollars.

É (muito) caro.	It's (very) expensive.
É barato.	It's cheap.
Onde é que eu pago?	Where do I pay?
Não dá para fazer por menos?	Can't you charge less?
Não dá para fazer um desconto?	Can't you make a discount?
Pode-se trocar depois?	Can it be exchanged later?
Vou ficar com este.	I'll take this.

C. My Address Is . . .

Eu moro na Rua do Passeio *(no) (número)*, duzentos e trinta.	I live at 230 Passeio Street.
Ele mora na Praça da Bandeira.	He lives on Bandeira Plaza.
A loja é na Avenida Rio Branco.	The store is on Rio Branco Avenue.

D. My Telephone Number Is . . .

O número de meu telefone é três, dois, oito, oito.	My telephone number is 3288.
O número de seu telefone é quatro, zero, oito, dois, zero.	Their telephone number is: 4-0820.
Não esqueça o número de meu telefone; é dois, um, zero, cinco.	Don't forget my telephone number: 2105.
Linha, por favor. Vou discar o número.	Line, please. I'm going to dial the number.
O número sete, um, dois, oito, não responde.	Number 7128 does not answer.

E. The Number Is . . .

O número é . . .	The number is . . .
Meu número é . . .	My number is . . .
Moro no quarto número trinta.	I live in room 30.
O número de meu apartamento é cento e vinte.	My apartment number is 120.
Moro na Quinta Avenida, trezentos e trinta e dois, quinto andar.	I live at 332 Fifth Avenue, fifth floor.

F. Word Study

absoluto	absolute
aspecto	aspect
barra	bar
câmbio	exchange (money)
certo	certain
combinação	combination
maneira	manner
perigo	danger

LESSON 19

A. What's Today?

O dia.	The day.
A semana.	The week.
O fim de semana.	The weekend.
O mês/os meses.	The month/the months.
Que dia da semana é hoje?	What day is today?
Hoje é segunda-feira.[1]	Today is Monday.
É sexta.	It's Friday.
Vou lá na terça.[2]	I'll go there on Tuesday.
Qual é a data?	What's the date?
Hoje é . . .	Today is . . .
Estamos a . . .	It's the . . .
um *(primero)* de maio.[3]	1st of May.
onze de abril.	11th of April.
quatro de julho.	4th of July.
quinze de setembro.	15th of September.
vinte e um de junho.	21st of June.
vinte e cinco de dezembro.	25th of December.
dezessete *(dezassete* Ⓟ*)* de novembro.	17th of November.
treze de fevereiro.	13th of February.
vinte e oito de agosto.	28th of August.

[1] Usually the word *feira* is omitted in conversation.
[2] The preposition *em*, which contracts with the article, is used with the days of the week. Remember that *sábado* and *domingo* are masculine: *na segunda, na quinta*, but *no sábado* and *no domingo*.
[3] In Portugal, *Maio*, etc.

B. SOME DATES

A América foi descoberta em mil quatrocentos e noventa e dois.	America was discovered in 1492.
Os portugueses descobriram o Brasil em mil e quinhentos.	The Portuguese discovered Brazil in 1500.
O presidente Roosevelt faleceu em mil novecentos e quarenta e cinco.	President Roosevelt died in 1945.
O pai dele faleceu em mil novecentos e oitenta e dois.	His father died in 1982.
Que aconteceu em mil novecentos e oitenta e nove?	What happened in 1989?
Estivemos lá em mil novecentos e noventa ou noventa e um.	We were there in 1990 or 1991.

C. WORD STUDY

cena	scene
conclusão	conclusion
condição	condition
consideração	consideration
decisão	decision
estação	season
pessoa	person
sinal	signal

QUIZ 16

1. *É segunda-feira.*   a. on the 25th of June
2. *Que dia do mês é hoje?*   b. on the 28th of February
3. *no dia primeiro de julho* c. on the 13th of August

4. *no dia vinte*   d. 1605
5. *no dia onze de abril*   e. It's Monday.
6. *no dia vinte e oito de*   f. What day of the month is
   fevereiro   it?
7. *no dia vinte e cinco de*   g. died
   junho
8. *mil seiscentos e cinco*   h. on the 1st of July
9. *no dia treze de agosto*   i. on the 11th of April
10. *faleceu*   j. on the 20th

ANSWERS
1—e; 2—f; 3—h; 4—j; 5—i; 6—b; 7—a; 8—d; 9—c;
10—g.

LESSON 20

A. WHAT TIME IS IT?

(a) hora (fem.)   hour
(o) minuto (masc.)   minute
(o) segundo (masc.)   second
a meia-noite   midnight
o meio-dia   noon

In order to tell the time in Portuguese, use *é* if the hour is
singular: *uma hora, meio-dia,* and *meia-noite.* Use *são* if the
hour is plural: *duas horas, três,* etc.

Por favor, diga-me que   Please tell me what time
   horas são?   it is?
Que horas são?   What time is it?
São . . .   It is . . .
É . . .   It is . . .
É uma hora.   It's 1:00.

É uma e cinco.	It's 1:05.
É uma e dez.	It's 1:10.
É uma e quinze.	It's 1:15.
É uma e um quarto.	It's 1:15.
É uma e meia.	It's 1:30.

To tell time past the half hour, *são* and *faltam* can be used interchangeably.

São dez para as duas.	It's 1:50. It's ten of two.
Faltam dez para as duas.	
São quinze para o meio-dia.	It's 11:45 A.M.
Faltam quinze . . .	
São vinte para a meia-noite.	It's 11:40 P.M.
Faltam vinte . . .	
São duas (horas).	It's 2:00.
São três.	It's 3:00.
São quatro.	It's 4:00.
São cinco.	It's 5:00.
São seis.	It's 6:00.
São sete.	It's 7:00.
São oito.	It's 8:00.
São nove e meia.	It's 9:30.
São dez horas.	It's 10:00.
São onze.	It's 11:00.
É meio-dia e meia.	It's 12:30 P.M.
É meia-noite e meia.	It's 12:30 A.M.
São quinze para as duas.	It's a quarter to two.

B.   AT WHAT TIME?

Notice that it is the article *a*, not the preposition *a*, that is used before the word *hora* in time expressions such as "At what time . . ." Remember that the preposition *a* contracts with the definite article:

A que horas?	(At) what time?
A que horas você chegou?	At what time did you arrive?
Cheguei às dez *(horas)*.	I arrived at ten.
À uma *(hora)*.	At 1:00.
Às duas *(horas)*.	At 2:00.
Às cinco e meia.	At 5:30.
À meia-noite.	At 12:00 midnight.
Ao meio-dia.	At 12:00 noon.

In conversation, since Portuguese does not have the expressions A.M. and P.M., use *da manhã, da tarde,* and *da noite*[1] when clarification is needed.

O avião sai às três e dez da tarde.	The plane leaves at 3:10 P.M.

Other examples:

Que horas o senhor tem?	What time do you have?
Que horas são pelo seu relógio?	What time is it by your watch?
Você podia me dizer que horas são?	Could you tell me the time?
A senhora sabe que horas são?	Do you know what time is it?
Ainda não são quatro.	It's not four yet.
A que horas sai o trem *(comboio* ℗*)*?	What time does the train leave?
Às nove em ponto.	At 9 o'clock sharp.
Quase às nove.	About 9 o'clock.
São dez horas de manhã.	It's 10 A.M.
Às oito e quarenta da noite.	At 8:40 P.M.
Às seis da tarde.	At 6 P.M.
Às dez da noite	At 10 P.M.

[1] Lit. "of the morning," "of the afternoon," and "of the evening."

Lá pelas sete da manhã   Around 7:00 A.M.

Notice that to indicate A.M. or P.M., *da manhã, da tarde*, or *da noite* is added.

C. IT'S TIME

Está na hora.	It's time.
Está na hora de fazê-lo.	It's time to do it.
Está na hora de partir.	It's time to leave.
Está na hora de irmos para casa.	It's time for us to go home.
Tenho muito tempo.	I have a lot of time.
Não tenho tempo.	I don't have any time.
Ele está perdendo *(a perder Ⓟ)* **o tempo.**	He's wasting his time.
Ela vem de vez em quando.	She comes from time to time.

D. WORD STUDY

avanço	advance
banco	bank
capítulo	chapter
contente	content
delicioso	delicious
fruta	fruit
inimigo	enemy
milhão	million
permanência	permanence
rico	rich

QUIZ 17

1. *Está na hora de fazê-lo.*   a. She comes from time to time.
2. *Que horas são?*   b. It's 9:00.
3. *É uma.*   c. At what time?

4. *São três.*	d. It's time to do it.
5. *São nove.*	e. It's 2:00.
6. *É meia-noite.*	f. It's 1:00.
7. *A que horas?*	g. I don't have any time.
8. *Não tenho tempo.*	h. It's 3:40 P.M.
9. *É uma e um quarto.*	i. It's noon.
10. *São quatro horas.*	j. It's 3:00.
11. *São duas.*	k. It's 1:05.
12. *Ela vem de vez em quando.*	l. It's 4:00.
13. *É meio-dia.*	m. What time is it?
14. *É uma e cinco.*	n. It's 1:15.
15. *São três e quarenta da tarde.*	o. It's midnight.

ANSWERS
1—d; 2—m; 3—f; 4—j; 5—b; 6—o; 7—c; 8—g; 9—n;
10—l; 11—e; 12—a; 13—i; 14—k; 15—h.

LESSON 21

A. Past, Present, and Future

PASSADO	PRESENTE	FUTURO
ontem	*hoje*	*amanhã*
yesterday	today	tomorrow
ontem de manhã	*esta manhã*	*amanhã de manhã*
yesterday morning	this morning	tomorrow morning
ontem à tarde	*hoje à tarde*	*amanhã à tarde*

yesterday afternoon	this afternoon	tomorrow afternoon
ontem à noite	*hoje à noite*	*amanhã à noite*
last night, last evening	this evening, tonight	tomorrow night, tomorrow evening

B. MORNING, NOON, AND NIGHT

Esta manhã.	This morning.
Ontem de manhã.	Yesterday morning.
Amanhã de manhã.	Tomorrow morning.
Hoje ao meio-dia.	Today at noon.
Ontem ao meio-dia.	Yesterday at noon.
Amanhã ao meio-dia.	Tomorrow at noon.
Hoje à tarde.	This afternoon.
Ontem à tarde.	Yesterday afternoon.
Amanhã à tarde.	Tomorrow afternoon.
Hoje à noite.	Tonight.
Ontem à noite.	Last night.
Amanhã à noite.	Tomorrow night.
Esta semana.	This week.
A semana passada.	Last week.
A semana que vem.	Next week.
A próxima semana.	Next week.
Dentro de duas semanas.	In two weeks.
Há duas semanas.	Two weeks ago.
Este mês.	This month.
O mês passado.	Last month.
O mês que vem.	Next month.
No próximo mês.	Next month.
Dentro de dois meses.	In two months.
Há dois meses.	Two months ago.
Este ano.	This year.
O *(no)* **ano passado.**	Last year.
O *(no)* **próximo ano.**	Next year.
Dentro de dois anos.	In two years.

Há dois anos.	Two years ago.
Há quanto tempo?	How long ago?
Há pouco tempo.	A short time ago.
Há muito tempo.	A long time ago.
Agora.	Now.
Agora mesmo.	Right now.
Por agora.	For the time being.
Neste instante.	At this moment.
Dentro em pouco.	In a little while.
Daqui a pouco.	In a little while.
Quantas vezes?	How many times?
Uma vez.	Once.
Duas vezes.	Twice.
Cada vez.	Each time.
Raras vezes.	Seldom.
Muitas vezes.	Often.
Algumas vezes.	Sometimes.
Às vezeş.	Sometimes.
De vez em quando.	From time to time.
Mais uma vez.	Again.
Pela primeira vez.	For the first time.
De manhã cedo.	Early in the morning.
De madrugada.	Very early in the morning.
Ao anoitecer.	In the evening ("at nightfall").
No dia seguinte.	On the following day.
De hoje a quinze dias.	In two weeks.
De hoje a oito dias.	A week from today.
Dentro de uma semana.	In a week.
Na quarta-feira da próxima semana.	Next Wednesday.
Na segunda-feira da semana passada.	Monday a week ago.
No dia cinco deste mês.	On the fifth of this month.
No dia cinco do mês passado.	On the fifth of last month.
Em princípios de março.	Early in March.

Em fins de maio.	Late in May.
Aconteceu há oito anos.	It happened eight years ago.

C. WORD STUDY

ambição	ambition
brilhante	brilliant
capital	capital
contato	contact
departamento	department
mamãe	mama
monumento	monument
obstáculo	obstacle
recente	recent

QUIZ 18

1. *ontem de manhã*	a. last year
2. *hoje à tarde*	b. last night
3. *amanhã à tarde*	c. today at noon
4. *ontem à noite*	d. now
5. *o próximo mês*	e. in two weeks
6. *agora*	f. in a little while
7. *a semana passada*	g. yesterday morning
8. *o ano passado*	h. right now
9. *hoje ao meio-dia*	i. It happened eight years ago.
10. *dentro em pouco*	j. this afternoon
11. *esta semana*	k. sometimes
12. *Aconteceu há oito anos.*	l. within a week
13. *em fins de maio*	m. tomorrow afternoon
14. *há dois meses*	n. next month
15. *de vez em quando*	o. last week
16. *dentro de uma semana*	p. each time
17. *agora mesmo*	q. from time to time
18. *às vezes*	r. toward the end of May

19. *dentro de duas semanas*   s. this week
20. *cada vez*   t. two months ago

ANSWERS

1—g; 2—j; 3—m; 4—b; 5—n; 6—d; 7—o; 8—a; 9—c;
10—f; 11—s; 12—i; 13—r; 14—t; 15—q; 16—l; 17—h;
18—k; 19—e; 20—p.

REVIEW QUIZ 4

1. *Ele comprou um carro por* _____ (two thousand)
   dólares.
   a. *três mil*
   b. *quatrocentos*
   c. *dois mil*
2. *O número de seu telefone é* _____ (4-0820).
   a. *dois, cinco, zero, sete, nove*
   b. *cinco, zero, oito, nove, zero*
   c. *quatro, zero, oito, dois, zero*
3. _____ (It's time) *de partir.*
   a. *a que horas*
   b. *há muito tempo*
   c. *está na hora*
4. *Que dia do mês é* _____ (today)?
   a. *agora*
   b. *hoje*
   c. *tempo*
5. *Dia* _____ (17) *de dezembro.*
   a. *dezessete (dezassete* Ⓟ)
   b. *vinte e sete*
   c. *quinze*
6. *É* _____ (1:10).
   a. *uma e cinco*
   b. *uma e dez*
   c. *onze*
7. *São* _____ (7:00).

    a. *sete*
    b. *nove*
    c. *seis*

8. *É* _____ (12:00 noon).
    a. *meia-noite*
    b. *meio-dia*
    c. *duas*

9. *Às* _____ (3:40).
    a. *falta um quarto para as três*
    b. *três e quarenta*
    c. *uma e meia*

10. _____ (yesterday) *de manhã.*
    a. *hoje*
    b. *ontem*
    c. *esta*

11. *A* _____ (week) *passada.*
    a. *semana*
    b. *noite*
    c. *amanhã*

12. *dentro de dois* _____ (months).
    a. *semana*
    b. *dias*
    c. *meses*

13. *Há dois* _____ (years).
    a. *meses*
    b. *anos*
    c. *dias*

14. *Na* _____ (Wednesday) *da próxima semana.*
    a. *segunda-feira*
    b. *sexta-feira*
    c. *quarta-feira*

15. *Em* _____ (end) *de maio.*
    a. *fins*
    b. *princípios*
    c. *primeiros*

ANSWERS
1—c; 2—c; 3—c; 4—b; 5—a; 6—b; 7—a; 8—b; 9—b;
10—b; 11—a; 12—c; 13—b; 14—c; 15—a.

LESSON 22

A. No

The word for "not"—*não*—comes before the verb:

Não vejo.	I don't see.
O senhor não vê.	You don't see.

Such negative words as the forms for "nothing," "never,"
"nobody," etc., may come after the verb, in which case *não*
is used before the verb; or they may precede the verb, in
which case *não* is not used:

Ele não diz nada.	He doesn't say anything.
Eles não trabalham nunca.	They never work.
Não vem ninguém.	Nobody is coming.

Or

Ele nada diz.	He doesn't say anything.
Eles nunca trabalham.	They never work.
Ninguém vem.	Nobody is coming.

Sim, senhor.	Yes, sir.
Isto.	Yes.
Não, senhor.	No, sir.
Ele diz que sim.	He says yes.
Ele diz que não.	He says no.

Acho que sim.	I think so.
Está bem.	Alright.
Não está bem.	It's not good.
Não é mau.	It's not bad.
Não é isso.	It's not that.
Ele não está aqui.	He's not here.
Aqui está.	Here it is.
Não é muito.	It's not very much.
Não é bastante.	It's not enough.
É bastante.	It's enough.
Não tão depressa.	Not so fast.
Não é nada.	It's nothing.
Isso não é nada.	That's nothing.
Não tem importância.	It's not important.
Não tenho tempo.	I have no time.
Não sei como nem quando.	I don't know how or when.
Não sei onde.	I don't know where.
Não sei nada.	I don't know anything.
Não sei nada disso.	I don't know anything about that.
Não desejo nada.	I don't want anything.
Nada desejo.	I don't want anything.
Não importa.	It doesn't matter.
Não me importa.	It makes no difference to me.
Não me importa nada.	It makes absolutely no difference to me.
Não me diga!	You don't say!
Não tenho nada que dizer.	I have nothing to say.
Isso não quer dizer nada.	That doesn't mean anything.
Não aconteceu nada.	Nothing happened.
Não diga a ninguém.	Don't tell anybody.
Nunca o vejo.	I never see him.
Nunca o vi.	I never saw him.

Ele nunca vem.   He never comes.
Ele nunca veio.   He never came.
Nunca vou.   I never go.
Nunca irei.   I'll never go.

B.   NEITHER . . . NOR . . .

Nem.
Nor.

Eu não disse *(nem)* sequer uma palavra.
I didn't say a word.

Nem . . . nem . . .
Neither . . . nor . . .

Nem mais nem menos.
Just so ("neither more nor less").

Nem um nem outro.
Neither one nor the other.

Nem isto nem isso.
Neither this nor that.

Nem peixe nem carne.
Neither fish nor meat.

Nem todos foram.
Not all went.

Nem bem nem mal.
So-so. Neither good nor bad.

Não posso nem desejo ir.
I can't go, nor do I want to.

Não tenho nem tempo nem dinheiro.
I have neither the time nor the money.

Ele não sabe ler nem escrever.
He can't read or write.

Não tenho cigarros nem charutos.
I don't have any cigarettes or cigars.

C. WORD STUDY

bola	ball
cheque	check (bank)
civil	civil
educação	education
esforço	effort
lógico	logical
mesa	table
omissão	omission
página	page

LESSON 23

A. ISN'T IT? AREN'T YOU? ETC.

1. Tag questions:
   In Portuguese the tag questions isn't it?, aren't you?,
   don't they?, etc. can be formed by using the expression

não é?[1] This expression can be used after either a positive or a negative statement, and it does not necessarily imply that the answers must be negative or affirmative.

Não é verdade?
Isn't that so?

Você é americano, não é?
You're an American, aren't you?

O português é fácil, não é?
Portuguese is easy, isn't it?

2. Isn't it?, didn't you?, are you?, is he?, etc. can also be expressed by *não* plus the main verb:

Você conhece a dona Maria, não conhece?
You know dona Maria, don't you?

Ele vai ficar, não vai?
He is going to stay here, isn't he?

Eles querem ficar aqui, não querem?
They want to stay here, don't they?

3. Or if the main statement is in the negative, just repeat the main verb without *não*.

Ele não quer ficar aqui, quer?
He doesn't want to stay, does he?

[1] In Brazilian speech, the expression *não é?* is often pronounced *"né?"*

4. In Portugal, if the statement is negative, the tag question can also be formed by using the expression *pois não?*[2]

Você não vai, pois não?
You're not going, are you?

Some more examples:

O senhor vem, não vem?
You'll come, won't you?

Está frio, não é?
It's cold today, isn't it?

A senhora gostou do filme, não gostou?—Gostei.
You did like the film, didn't you?—I liked it.

B. SOME, ANY, A FEW

O senhor tem algum dinheiro?
Do you have any money?

Tenho.
I have (some).

Não, não tenho.
No, I don't have any.

Ele tem dinheiro?
Does he have any money?

---

[2] In Brazil, either use *é: Você não é americano, é?* or repeat the main verb without *não*.

Ele tem um pouco.
He has some (a little).

Ele não tem.
He doesn't.

Sobrou algum dinheiro?
Is there any money left?

Fica um pouco.
There's a little left.

Quantos livros tem?
How many books do you have?

Tenho alguns.
I have a few.

Quer algumas peras?
Do you want some pears?

Dê-me algumas.
Give me a few *(fem.)*.

Dê-nos alguns.
Give us some *(masc.)*.

Dê-lhe algumas.
Give him a few *(fem.)*.

Alguns dos meus amigos.
Some of my friends.

QUIZ 19

1. *Não vejo.*	a. Neither this nor that.
2. *Não é nada.*	b. I have no time.
3. *Não me diga!*	c. I don't know where.
4. *Nunca vou.*	d. Nothing happened.
5. *Não o vi.*	e. I don't see.
6. *Acho que não.*	f. I don't know anything.
7. *Não tão depressa.*	g. It's not enough.
8. *Não sei nada.*	h. I didn't see him.
9. *Não vejo nada.*	i. You don't say!
10. *Não é bastante.*	j. He never comes.
11. *Não me importa.*	k. I see nothing.
12. *Não aconteceu nada.*	l. I'll never go.
13. *Ele nunca vem.*	m. It's nothing.
14. *Não é mau.*	n. He's not here.
15. *Nunca irei.*	o. I don't think so.
16. *Ele não está aqui.*	p. It's not bad.
17. *Ninguém vem.*	q. It makes no difference to me.
18. *Nem isto nem isso.*	r. Not so fast.
19. *Não sei onde.*	s. I never go.
20. *Não tenho tempo.*	t. No one comes.

ANSWERS

1—e; 2—m; 3—i; 4—s; 5—h; 6—o; 7—r; 8—f; 9—k;
10—g; 11—q; 12—d; 13—j; 14—p; 15—l; 16—n; 17—t;
18—a; 19—c; 20—b.

C. LIKE, AS, HOW

Como.
Like, as, how

Como eu.
Like me.

Como isso.
Like that.

Como isto.
Like this.

Como nós.
Like us.

Como os outros.
Like the others.

Este não é como esse.
This one isn't like that one.

Assim é.
That's the way it is.

Como o senhor quiser.
As you wish.

Ele não é como seu pai *(como o pai)*.[3]
He's not like his father.

Não sei como explicá-lo.
I don't know how to explain it.

É branco como a neve.
It's as white as snow.

---

[3] From now on, the material in parentheses of the recorded text will ordinarily indicate an alternate form which is the one recorded on the Continental Portuguese edition. It will be marked Ⓟ only when it is particularly characteristic of Continental Portuguese as distinguished from Brazilian usage.

Como vai?
How are you?

Como quer que seja.
However it may be.

Seja como for.
Be that as it may.

Como falo mal, ninguém me compreende.
As I speak poorly, nobody understands me.

Como? O que disse?
I beg your pardon? What did you say?

Como ela é bonita!
How pretty she is!

QUIZ 20

1. *Como o senhor quiser.*	a. He's not like his father.
2. *como os outros*	b. What did you say?
3. *como isto*	c. Give him a few.
4. *O senhor tem dinheiro?*	d. How pretty she is!
5. *alguns dos meus amigos*	e. Do you want some pears?
6. *Ele não é como seu pai.*	f. As you wish.
7. *Como? O que disse?*	g. Do you have any money?
8. *Dê-lhe algumas.*	h. like the others
9. *Como ela é bonita!*	i. like this
10. *Quer algumas peras?*	j. some of my friends

ANSWERS
1—f; 2—h; 3—i; 4—g; 5—j; 6—a; 7—b; 8—c; 9—d;
10—e.

LESSON 24

A. HAVE YOU TWO MET?

A senhora conhece o meu amigo?
Do you know my friend?

Acho que já nos conhecemos.
I believe we've met before.

Acho que não tive o prazer.
I believe I haven't had the pleasure.

Não tive o prazer de conhecê-lo.
I haven't had the pleasure of meeting you.

Acho que já se conhecem, não?
I believe you already know each other, don't you?

Claro que nos conhecemos.
Of course we know each other.

Não tive o prazer.
I haven't had the pleasure.

Desejo apresentar-lhe o meu amigo Carlos Gonçalves.
I would like to introduce my friend Charles Gonçalves.

B. HELLO, HOW ARE YOU?

Bom dia.
Good morning.

Como vai? *(Como está?)*
How are you?

Muito bem. E o senhor?
Very well. And you?

Como vão as coisas?
How is everything?

O que há de novo?
What's new?

Nada. Não há nada de novo.
Nothing. There's nothing new.

Quase nada.
Almost nothing.

Por onde você tem andando ultimamente?
Where have you been lately?

Tenho estado muito ocupada ultimamente.
I have been very busy lately.

Não deixe de telefonar-me de vez em quando.
Call me once in a while. ("Don't fail to call me once in a while.")

Por que não vem até (à) nossa casa?
Why don't you come by our house?

Vou visitá-los na próxima semana.
I'll call on you next week. ("I am going to visit you next week.")

Não (se) esqueça.
Don't forget.

Então, até a próxima semana.
Until next week then.

Passe bem.
Take it easy.

C. TAKING LEAVE

Muito prazer em conhecê-la.
Glad to have met you.

O prazer foi todo meu.
The pleasure was (all) mine.

Em breve espero vê-la de novo.
I hope to see you again soon.

Aqui tem o meu endereço e o meu telefone.
Here's my address and telephone number.

Você tem o meu endereço *(a minha direcção* Ⓟ*)*?
Do you have my address?

Não tenho. Tenha a bondade. Muito obrigada.
I don't have it. Please. Thank you.

De nada.
Don't mention it.

Quando posso lhe telefonar *(telefonar-lhe)*?
When can I call you?

Pela manhã.
In the morning.

Telefono depois de amanhã.
I'll call you the day after tomorrow.

Conto com o seu telefonema.
I'll be expecting your call.

Até breve.
See you soon.

Até já.
See you soon.

Até logo.
So long.

Até logo mais.
See you later./Until later.

Até a volta.
Until your return.

Até amanhã.
Until tomorrow.

Até sábado.
Until Saturday.

Passe bem.
Take it easy.

Adeus.
Good-bye.

QUIZ 21

1. *Até já.*
2. *Adeus.*
3. *Muito prazer em connhecê-lo.*
4. *Tem (o) meu endereço?*
5. *Muito prazer.*
6. *pela manhã*
7. *Até amanhã.*
8. *Conto com (o) seu telefonema.*
9. *Muito obrigado.*
10. *Até sábado.*

a. Do you have my address?
b. See you tomorrow.
c. I'll be expecting your call.
d. Until Saturday.
e. in the morning
f. Glad to have met you.
g. Thank you.
h. See you soon.
i. Very glad (to have met you).
j. Good-bye.

ANSWERS

1—h; 2—j; 3—f; 4—a; 5—i; 6—e; 7—b; 8—c; 9—g; 10—d.

LESSON 25

A. Visiting Someone

O senhor João Dias mora aqui?
Does Mr. João Dias live here?

Mora.
Yes, he does. ("He lives.")

Em que andar?
On what floor?

Terceiro, à esquerda.
Third floor left.

O seu João está em casa?
Is Mr. João home?

Não, senhor. Saiu.
No, sir. He's gone out.

A que horas voltará?
What time will he be back?

Não sei lhe dizer *(dizer-lhe)*.
I couldn't tell you.

Quer deixar um recado?
Do you want to leave a message?

Quero. Pode dar-me lápis e papel?
I do. Can you give me a pencil and some paper?

Volto mais tarde.
I'll be back later.

Volto hoje à noite.
I'll be back tonight.

Volto amanhã.
I'll be back tomorrow.

Volto outro dia.
I'll be back another day.

Tenha a bondade de lhe dizer *(dizer-lhe)* **que me telefone.**
Please tell him to call me.

Vou estar em casa o dia todo.
I'll be home all day.

B. MAKING FRIENDS

Bom dia, senhor. Poderia me apresentar?
Hello. May I introduce myself?

Sou Julia Adams.
I'm Julia Adams.

Muito prazer, senhora.
Pleased to meet you.

Eu sou João Silva.
I'm João Silva.

Muito prazer.
Pleased to meet you.

Está aqui de férias?
Are you here on vacation?

Sim. Vou ficar aqui por três semanas.
Yes. I'll be here for three weeks.

Que bom! Espero que goste do Brazil.
How nice! I hope you enjoy Brazil.

Obrigada. Até logo, senhor.
Thank you. So long, sir.

QUIZ 22

1. *Terceiro, à esquerda.*   a. I'll be home all day.
2. *Volto mais tarde.*   b. I hope you enjoy Brazil.
3. *Mora aqui o senhor*   c. How nice!
   João Dias?
4. *Está aqui de férias?*   d. Do you want to leave a
                                  message?
5. *Que bom!*   e. What floor?
6. *Espero que goste*   f. I'll be here for three
   do Brazil.   weeks.
7. *Em que andar?*   g. Are you here on vacation?
8. *Vou ficar aqui por*   h. Does Mr. João Dias live
   três semanas.   here?
9. *Vou estar em casa o*   i. Third floor left.
   dia todo.
10. *Quer deixar um recado?*   j. I'll come back later.

ANSWERS
1—i; 2—j; 3—h; 4—g; 5—c; 6—b; 7—e; 8—f; 9—a;
10—d.

LESSON 26

A. GETTING AROUND TOWN

Pode me dizer onde é esta rua?
Can you tell me where this street is?

Como se vai a este endereço?
How do you get to this address?

É longe?
Is it far?

Qual é o caminho mais curto para a cidade?
Which is the shortest way to the city?

Qual caminho devo tomar?
Which road should I take?

Pode me dizer *(dizer-me* ℗*)* **o caminho para a Rua da Alfândega?**
Can you tell me how to get to Alfândega Street?

A Prefeitura *(A Câmara Municipal* ℗*)* **fica perto daqui?**
Is city hall near here?

Onde há um telefone público?
Where is there a public phone?

Qual a distância daqui à estação?
How far is the station?

Ainda estamos longe da estação?
Are we still far from the station?

Táxi! Táxi!
Taxi! Taxi!

Está livre?
Are you free?

O senhor pode me levar a este endereço?
Could you take me to this address?

Estou com pressa.
I'm in a hurry.

Quanto marca o taxímetro?
How much does the meter read?

Quanto é a passagem?
How much is the fare?

O ônibus (autocarro Ⓟ) **pára aqui?**
Does the bus stop here?

O bonde (o carro eléctrico Ⓟ) **pára aqui?**
Does the streetcar stop here?

Onde devo descer?
Where should I get off?

QUIZ 23

1. *Qual é o caminho mais curto para . . . ?*   a. How far is the station?
2. *Onde há um telefone público?*   b. How do you get to . . . ?
3. *Onde é esta rua?*   c. Is it far?

4. *O senhor pode me levar a este endereço?*   d. Does the bus stop here?

5. *Qual a distância daqui à estação?*   e. Where should I get off?

6. *Fica perto daqui?*   f. Where is there a public phone?

7. *É longe?*   g. Where is this street?

8. *Onde devo descer?*   h. What's the shortest way to get to . . . ?

9. *Como se vai a . . . ?*   i. Could you take me to this address?

10. *O ônibus (autocarro Ⓟ) pára aqui?*   j. Is it near here?

ANSWERS
1—h; 2—f; 3—g; 4—i; 5—a; 6—j; 7—c; 8—e; 9—b; 10—d.

B. AT THE BOOKSTORE

Onde há uma livraria?
Where is there a bookstore?

Há uma livraria que vende livros em inglês?
Is there a bookstore that sells books in English?

Tem o livro . . . ?
Do you have the book . . . ?

Tem este livro em inglês?
Do you have this book in English?

Tem uma guia?
Do you have a guidebook?

Tem um dicionário inglês-português?
Do you have an English-Portuguese dictionary?

Tem um mapa rodoviário?
Do you have a road map?

Tem revistas?
Do you have magazines?

C. WORD STUDY

ansioso	anxious
chefe	chief
dificuldade	difficulty
doutor(-ra)	doctor
episódio	episode
futuro	future
glorioso	glorious
nervoso	nervous
período	period

LESSON 27

A. PLEASE

One of the most common ways of saying "please" is the equivalent of "Do the favor of": *Faça o favor (de)*.

Faça o favor de entrar.
Please come in.

Faça o favor de levar isto.
Please carry this.

Faça o favor de vir cedo.
Please come early.

Other polite expressions are:

1. *Faz favor* Ⓟ.
   Please ("do the favor").

   Faz favor de telefonar-me.
   Please telephone me.

   Faz favor de sentar-se.
   Please sit down.

2. *Tenha a bondade.*[1]
   Please ("have the kindness").

Tenha a bondade de preparar tudo.
Please prepare everything.

3. **Por favor.**[1]
Please.

(O) Seu bilhete, por favor.
Your ticket, please.

4. **Dá para . . .**
Is it possible . . . /Can you . . . /Could you . . . ?

Dá para você me fazer um favor?
Could you do me a favor?

Por favor, dá para você falar mais devagar?
Please speak slower.

Related expressions:

Quero lhe pedir *(pedir-lhe)* **um favor.**
I want to ask a favor of you.

Posso lhe pedir um favor?
Can I ask you a favor?

Desculpe-me.
Excuse me (for having done something).

Desculpe a demora.
Excuse my delay.

QUIZ 24

1. *Faz favor de telefonar-me.*   a. Excuse my delay.
2. *Faça o favor de vir cedo.*   b. Excuse me.

---

[1] Not recorded on the Brazilian version of the tapes.

3. *Faz favor de sentar-se.*　　c. Please come early.
4. *Desculpe a demora.*　　d. Please carry this.
5. *Desculpe-me.*　　e. Please continue until Sunday.
6. *Faça o favor de entrar.*　　f. Your ticket, please.
7. *Tenha a bondade de preparar tudo.*　　g. Please sit down.
8. *Faça o favor de levar isto.*　　h. Please come in.
9. *Seu bilhete, por favor.*　　i. Please prepare everything.
10. *Dá para continuar até domingo?*　　j. Please telephone me.

ANSWERS
1—j; 2—c; 3—g; 4—a; 5—b; 6—h; 7—i; 8—d; 9—f; 10—e.

B. SOME USEFUL EXPRESSIONS

1. *Acabar de* means "to have just":

Ele acaba de aceitar.
He just accepted.

Acabo de conseguir a chave.
I have just obtained the key.

Ele acabava de almoçar quando aparecemos.
He had just had lunch when we appeared.

2. *Ter que* or *ter de* means "to have to":

Tenho que *(Tenho de)* **apressar-me.**
I have to hurry.

Você tem de convencer-me primeiro.
You have to convince me first.

3. *Há* means "there is" or "there are":

Há muitos cachorros *(cães)* **nesta cidade.**
There are many dogs in this city.

4. *Gostaria de* means "would like to":

Gostaria de ajudar mas não posso.
I'd like to help but I can't.

REVIEW QUIZ 5

1. *O seu João está em* _____ (home).
   a. *andar*
   b. *hora*
   c. *casa*
2. *Quer deixar um* _____ (message)?
   a. *lápis*
   b. *recado*
   c. *papel*
3. *Dá para me levar a este* _____ (address).
   a. *cidade*
   b. *caminho*
   c. *endereço*
4. _____ (I need) *um selo.*
   a. *vendem*
   b. *preciso de*
   c. *acho*
5. *Não trabalham* _____ (never/ever).
   a. *amanhã*
   b. *nunca*
   c. *sábado*

6. _____ (not) *todos foram.*
    a. *nem*
    b. *nunca*
    c. *hoje*

7. *Dê-me* _____ (some).
    a. *todos*
    b. *algumas*
    c. *nada*

8. *Não tive o prazer de* _____ (meeting you).
    a. *ocupado*
    b. *chamar*
    c. *conhecê-lo*

9. *Tenha a* _____ (goodness) *de preparar tudo.*
    a. *desculpe*
    b. *bondade*
    c. *faça*

10. *Faça o* _____ (be so kind) *de entrar.*
    a. *bondade*
    b. *favor*
    c. *queira*

11. _____ (we have to) *que embarcar antes das nove.*
    a. *temos*
    b. *podemos*
    c. *vamos*

12. _____ (I've just) *de terminar o trabalho.*
    a. *chegar*
    b. *acabo*
    c. *falo*

13. _____ (I'd like) *escrever uma carta.*
    a. *gostaria de*
    b. *acaba*
    c. *vai*

14. _____ (Excuse) *a demora.*
    a. *tenha*
    b. *desculpe*
    c. *chame*

15. *Não vem* _____ (nobody).
    a. *ninguém*
    b. *nada*
    c. *outros*

ANSWERS
1—c; 2—b; 3—c; 4—b; 5—b; 6—a; 7—b; 8—c; 9—b;
10—b; 11—a; 12—b; 13—a; 14—b; 15—a.

LESSON 28

A. WHO? WHOM? WHAT? WHY? HOW?

Even though there is no change in meaning, the interrogative
words are frequently followed by the phrase *é que* for
emphasis.

    1. Who? Whom? *(Quem?):*

Quem é?	Who is it?
Não sei quem é.	I don't know who it is.
Quem *(o)* **disse?**	Who said it?
Quem disse isso?	Who said that?
De quem é esta bagagem?	Whose baggage is this?
De quem é que são essas canções?	Whose songs are those?
Para quem é que é esse brinquedo?	For whom is that toy?
A quem é que você entregou a máquina fotográfica?	To whom did you deliver the camera?

De quem você gosta?[1]	Whom do you like?
Com quem é que você brigou?	With whom did you quarrel?
Com quem falaram?	With whom did they speak?
Quem convidaram?	Whom did they invite?
Por quem é que isto foi dito?	By whom was this said?

2. What? (*Que?* or *O que?*):

Although there is no change in meaning, the use of *o que?* (with the article) seems to be preferred by most speakers.

Que é isso?	What is that?
O que é que é isto?	What is this?
Que aconteceu?	What happened?
O que é que há de novo?	What's new?
Que são?	What are they?
Que horas são?	What time is it?
Que deseja?	What do you want?
O que é que quer dizer?	What does it mean?
Que dia é hoje?	What day is it today?
O que é que ele disse?	What did he say?
O que é que você vai fazer?	What are you going to do?
Que mais?	What else (more)?
Que é feito da Maria?	What happened to Mary?
Que é que há?	What's wrong?
De que falam?	What are you talking about?
Com que pagam?	What will you pay with?
A que cinema ele foi?	To what movie theatre did he go?

[1] In Portuguese, the verb *gostar* (to like) requires the preposition *de* (of) whenever it is mentioned what is liked: *Você gosta de banana?* If no word follows the verb, the preposition is not used: *Não gosto.*

3. Why?[2] *(Por que?):*

Por que você não (*o*) **alugou?**	Why didn't you rent it?
Por que não me disse antes?	Why didn't you tell me before?
Por que é que não?	Why not?
Por que tanta pressa?	Why such a hurry?
Por que isso?	Why so?
Por que razão?	For what reason?

4. How? *(Como?):*

Como se diz em português?	How do you say it in Portuguese?
Como é que você se chama?	What is your name?
Como se escreve essa palavra?	How is that word spelled (written)?
Como vai?	How are you?
Como se cansou tão cedo?	How did you get tired so early?

B. HOW MUCH? HOW MANY? WHICH? WHERE? WHEN?

1. How Much? *(Quanto?)* How Many? *(Quantos?):*

Notice that in Portuguese there is agreement in gender as well: *Quanto? (masc.)* and *Quanta? (fem.).*

Quanto é?	How much is it?
Quantos cartões recebeu?	How many cards did you receive?

---

[2] But "because:" *porque.*

Quantas irmãs você tem?	How many sisters do you have?
Quantas vezes você foi ao Brasil?	How many times did you go to Brazil?

2. Which? *(Qual? Quais?):*

Use of these terms involves choice (which one among . . .). Notice also the agreement in number (*singular* and *plural*).

Qual o senhor deseja?	Which do you want?
Quais discos você quer comprar?	Which records do you want to buy?
Qual das cadeiras você prefere?	Which of the chairs do you prefer?
Qual é a casa do Paulo?	Which is Paul's house?
De qual é que você gosta mais?	Which one do you like better?
Quais são os melhores?	Which are the best?
Qual é que é o melhor?	Which one is the best?
Com qual dos irmãos se casou?	Which of the brothers did she marry?

3. Where? *(Onde?):*

Onde mora o seu cunhado?	Where does your brother-in-law live?
De onde *(Donde)* **ele vem?**	Where does he come from?
Para onde é que eles vão?	Where are they going?

4. When? *(Quando?):*

Quando (se) fecha a biblioteca?	When does the library close?
Quando é que aconteceu?	When did it happen?

Quando é que ele vai?	When is he going?
Não sei quando.	I don't know when.
Até quando?	Until when?
Não sei até quando.	I don't know how long (until when).
Desde quando?	Since when?
Para quando?	For when?
Para quando quiser.	For whenever you wish.

QUIZ 25

1. *Como se chama?*
2. *Quantos cartões recebeu?*
3. *Como se diz em português?*
4. *O que é que ele disse?*
5. *Quando aconteceu?*
6. *Desde quando?*
7. *Quem é?*
8. *Por que não?*

9. *Onde mora?*

10. *Como se escreve?*

a. When did it happen?
b. Since when?

c. Who is it?

d. Where does he live?
e. What's your name?
f. What did he say?
g. Why not?
h. How do you spell (write) it?

i. How many cards did you receive?

j. How do you say it in Portuguese?

ANSWERS
1—e; 2—i; 3—j; 4—f; 5—a; 6—b; 7—c; 8—g; 9—d; 10—h.

REVIEW QUIZ 6

1. *Não vejo* _____ (nothing).
    a. *ninguém*
    b. *nada*
    c. *nunca*
2. *Não vem* _____ (nobody).
    a. *ninguém*
    b. *não*
    c. *nunca*
3. *Não sabe ler* _____ (nor) *escrever.*
    a. *não*
    b. *nunca*
    c. *nem*
4. *O português é fácil* _____ (isn't it?)
    a. *não é*
    b. *não senhor*
    c. *nunca*
5. *Dê-nos* _____ (a few).
    a. *nada*
    b. *alguns*
    c. *algumas vezes*
6. *Quer* _____ (some) *peras?*
    a. *quantos*
    b. *algumas vezes*
    c. *algumas*
7. *Não é* _____ (like) *seu pai.*
    a. *como*
    b. *isto*
    c. *outros*
8. *Tenho estado muito* _____ (busy) *ultimamente.*
    a. *sempre*
    b. *ocupado*
    c. *novo*

9. *Já se* _____ (know)?
   a. *conhecido*
   b. *conhecem*
   c. *conhecê-lo*

10. *O ônibus (autocarro ℗)* _____ (stops) *aqui?*
    a. *pára*
    b. *segunda-feira*
    c. *chama*

11. *Como se vai a este* _____ (address)?
    a. *correio*
    b. *cartão*
    c. *endereço*

12. *Não há nada* _____ (new).
    a. *de novo*
    b. *nunca*
    c. *prazer*

13. *Acabo de conseguir* _____ (the key).
    a. *o dia*
    b. *a chave*
    c. *a demora*

14. _____ (what) *disse ele?*
    a. *como*
    b. *quando*
    c. *que*

15. _____ (why) *tanta pressa?*
    a. *quando*
    b. *por que*
    c. *onde*

16. _____ (how) *se diz em português?*
    a. *como*
    b. *quando*
    c. *ninguém*

17. _____ (how many) *vezes o aconselharam?*
    a. *quem*
    b. *quantas*
    c. *como*

18. _____ (who) *disse isso?*
    a. *quem*
    b. *que*
    c. *quando*

19. _____ (where) *mora o seu cunhado?*
    a. *onde*
    b. *como*
    c. *que*

20. _____ (when) *aconteceu?*
    a. *quem*
    b. *qual*
    c. *quando*

ANSWERS

1—b; 2—a; 3—c; 4—a; 5—b; 6—c; 7—a; 8—b; 9—b;
10—a; 11—c; 12—a; 13—b; 14—c; 15—b; 16—a; 17—b;
18—a; 19—a; 20—c.

LESSON 29

A. IT'S GOOD

Bom.	Good.
Muito bom.	Very good.
É muito bom.	It's very good.
É ótimo.[1]	It's excellent.
É excelente.	It's excellent.
É estupendo.	It's wonderful.
É magnífico.	It's wonderful.

[1] *óptimo* ℗.

É perfeito.	It's perfect.
Está bem.	It's alright.
Não é mau.	It's not bad.
Está bem isto?	Is this alright?
Muito bem!	Very well! Very good!
Ela é bela.	She's beautiful.
Ela é belíssima.	She's very beautiful.
Ela é muito linda.	She's very pretty.
Ela é encantadora.	She's charming.
Que bonita *(que)* ela é!	How pretty she is!
Como ela é bonita!	How pretty she is!
Que bom!	How nice!

B. IT'S NOT GOOD

Não é bom.	It's not good. It's no good.
Não é muito bom.	It's not very good.
Isso não é bom.	That's no good.
Isto não está bem.	This isn't right. It's not right. This is wrong.
Isso é mau.	That's bad.
É bastante mau.	It's pretty bad.
É péssimo.	It's very bad. It's terrible.
É muito ruim.	It's terrible.
Não vale nada.	It's no good. It's worthless.
Não serve para nada.	It's no good. It's worthless.
Não adianta.	It's no use. It's no good.
Que pena!	What a pity!
É horrível!	It's terrible!

QUIZ 26

1. *Está bem.*	a. It's excellent.
2. *Muito bem.*	b. She's very pretty.
3. *É excelente.*	c. It's worthless.
4. *Não é mau.*	d. What a pity!

5. *Isso é mau.*	e. It's no use.
6. *Que pena!*	f. It's wonderful.
7. *Ela é muito linda.*	g. It's all right.
8. *Não vale nada.*	h. That's bad.
9. *Não adianta.*	i. Very well.
10. *É estupendo.*	j. It's not bad.

ANSWERS

1—g; 2—i; 3—a; 4—j; 5—h; 6—d; 7—b; 8—c; 9—e; 10—f.

C. I LIKE IT

Gosto.	I like it.
Gosto muito.	I like it very much.
Gosto . . . Gosto de . . . [2]	I like . . . I like to . . .
Gosto dele.	I like him.
Gostamos dela.	We like her.
O senhor gosta?	Do you like it?
O senhor gosta da cor?	Do you like the color?
O senhor gosta de Portugal?	Do you like Portugal?
Eles gostam do Brasil.	They like Brazil.
Gostamos dos Estados Unidos.	We like the United States.
De qual você gosta mais?	Which one do you like more?
Gosto mais do espelho.	I like the mirror more.
O senhor acha que ela gostará da bolsa?	Do you think she will like the purse?
Não gostei do primeiro capítulo.	I didn't like the first chapter.
Eu gostaria de me deitar *(deitar-me)* cedo.	I would like to go to bed early.

[2] Not recorded in the Brazilian version of the tapes.

Os advogados não gostaram do clube.	The lawyers did not like the club.
Gostaria que eles me enviassem um convite.	I would like them to send me an invitation.
Quando quiser.	Whenever you like.
Estar com vontade de ...	To feel like ...
Estou com vontade de ir embora.	I feel like leaving.
Por que não gosta deles?	Why don't you like them?
Gosta do quarto?	Do you like the room (bedroom)?
Ela gosta de tudo.	She likes everything.

D. I DON'T LIKE IT

Não gosto.	I don't like it.
Não gosto muito.	I don't like it very much.
Ele gosta mas ela não gosta.	He likes it, but she doesn't.
Eu gosto mas (o) João não gosta.	I like it, but John doesn't.
Nós gostamos mas eles não gostam.	We like it, but they don't.
Eles não gostaram de nada.	They didn't like anything.
Ninguém gosta.	Nobody likes it.

QUIZ 27

1. *Eles não gostaram de nada.*
2. *O senhor gosta?*
3. *Gosto muito.*
4. *O senhor gosta da cor?*
5. *Quando quiser.*
6. *Eles gostariam.*
7. *Ninguém gosta.*
8. *Gostamos dela.*

a. I don't like it very much.
b. Do you like the room?
c. They would like it.
d. We like her.
e. Nobody likes it.
f. I like it very much.
g. Do you like it?
h. Whenever you like.

9. *Não gosto muito.*   i. They didn't like anything.
10. *O senhor gosta do*   j. Do you like the color?
    quarto?

ANSWERS
1—i; 2—g; 3—f; 4—j; 5—h; 6—c; 7—e; 8—d; 9—a;
10—b.

LESSON 30

A. IN, TO, FROM, FOR, ETC. (PREPOSITIONS)

Estive em Brasília.	I was in Brasilia.
Vou a Lisboa.	I am going to Lisbon.
Venho de Coimbra.	I come (am) from Coimbra.
Parto para São Paulo.	I'm leaving for São Paulo.
Cheguei até Belo Horizonte.	I got as far as Belo Horizonte.

1. To, at *(a):*

The contraction of the preposition *a* with the definite article *a (a + a = à; a + as = às)* is called *crase.*

À direita.	To the right.
À esquerda.	To the left.
Pouco a pouco.	Little by little.
A pé.	On foot.
À mão.	By hand.
Ao meio-dia.	At noon.
À meia-noite.	At midnight.
A meu ver.	In my opinion.
A que horas?	At what time?
À americana.	In the American way.
A respeito de.	Regarding, with respect to.
Ele vai à casa da Maria.	He's going to Mary's house.

Vamos ao cinema aos sábados.	We go to the movie on Saturdays.
Ele chega ao aeroporto às cinco.[1]	He arrives at the airport at five.
Ele começou a estudar.[2]	He started to study.
Ele está aprendendo a ler.	He's learning to read.

2. With *(com):*

Café com leite.	Coffee with milk.
Ela foi com o estudante.	She went with the student.
Estou com fome.	I am hungry.

3. Of, from *(de):*

The prepositicn *de* must always contract with the definite articles: *de + o(s) = do(s); de + a(s) = da(s).*

É de meu tio.	It's from my uncle.
Venho do Rio de Janeiro.	I come (am) from Rio de Janeiro.
É de pedra.	It's made of stone.
De dia e de noite.	By day and by night.
De novo.	Again.

4. In, on, at, into *(em):*

The preposition *em* must always contract with the definite articles: *em + o(s) = no(s); em + a(s) = na(s).*

Vivi em Portugal dois anos.	I lived in Portugal for two years.

---

[1] In Brazil, the verb *chegar* is usually followed by preposition *em: Chegar no aeroporto.*

[2] Certain verbs are followed by preposition *a* which is followed by another verb in the infinitive. Each instance must be learned independently.

Saio dentro de quatro dias.	I'm leaving in four days.
Em lugar de.	Instead of.
Enfim.	Finally.
Ela entrou na água.	She went into the water.
Eles estão no restaurante.	They are at the restaurant.

5. Up to, until *(até)*:

Até o Estoril.	Up to (as far as) Estoril.
Subi até o quinto andar.	I went up to the fifth floor.
Até amanhã.	Until tomorrow.
Até logo.	See you later. (See you soon.)
Até já.	See you soon.
Até a vista.	See you later.

6. From *(desde)*:

Desde aqui.	From here.
Desde que o vi.	Since I saw him.
Desde quando?	Since when?

7. About, over, on *(sobre)*:

Que disseram sobre o assunto?	What did they say about the subject?
Sobre a mesa.[3]	On the table.
Sobre o que vocês estão falando?	What are you talking about?

8. For, through *(por)*:

Sessenta milhas por hora.	Sixty miles an hour.
Eu o comprei *(comprei-o)* **por um dólar.**	I bought it for a dollar.

[3] Also: *Na mesa.*

Eu lhe dei *(dei-lhe)* **cinqüenta cruzeiros pela bolsa.**	I gave him fifty cruzeiros for the purse.
Ele me deu o seu livro pelo meu.	He gave me his book for mine.
Passamos pela Espanha.	We passed through Spain.
Ele entrou pela porta.	He came in through the door.
Eu vou por ele.	I'll go for (in place of) him.

Other expressions:

Por que?	Why?
Porque.	Because.
Por agora.	For the time being.
Pela manhã.	In the morning.
Por acaso.	By chance.
Por exemplo.	For example.
Por isso.	For that reason. Therefore.
Por meio de.	By means of.
Por causa de.	On account of.
Por fim.	Finally. At last.
Por aqui.	This way. Around here.
Está por fazer.	It's still to be done.
Por atacado.	Wholesale.
Por certo.	Certainly.
Por assim dizer.	So to speak.
Por conseguinte.	Consequently. Therefore.
Por bem ou por mal.	For better or for worse.
Por escrito.	In writing.
Por Deus!	For heaven's sake!
Por enquanto.	For the time being.
Por pouco.	Almost.
Por interessante que seja.	However interesting it may be.
Por volta das duas.	Around two o'clock.

9. For, in order to *(para)*:

Para indicates direction, purpose:

Para ir lá.	To go there.
Uma estante para livros.	A bookcase ("a stand for books").
Ele partiu para Belém.	He left for Belém.
A carta é para ela.	The letter is for her.
A lição para amanhã.	The lesson for tomorrow.
Para ele é fácil.	It's easy for him.
Não serve para nada.	It's worthless. It's not good for anything.
Para lá e para cá.	Back and forth.
Para onde eles foram?	Where did they go?
Para que você (*o*) faz?	Why do you do it? (For what reason do you do it?)
Para sempre.	Forever. For always.
Descrevo com detalhes para que compreendam bem.	I am describing it in detail so that they may understand it well.
Estamos prontos para a viagem.	We are ready for the trip.

With *estar* it means "about to":

Estamos para sair.	We are about to leave. We are leaving.

B. WORD STUDY

ângulo	angle
causa	cause
convicção	conviction
distância	distance
efeito	effect

instante	instant
obscuro	obscure
proprietário(-ria)	proprietor
qualidade	quality

QUIZ 28

1. *ao meio-dia*	a. on foot
2. *pouco a pouco*	b. in my opinion
3. *à direita*	c. I come from Rio de Janeiro.
4. *à americana*	d. It's made of stone.
5. *com*	e. by day and by night
6. *a pé*	f. again
7. *Venho do Rio de Janeiro.*	g. on the table
8. *É de pedra.*	h. to the right
9. *a respeito de*	i. for example
10. *de novo*	j. little by little
11. *por exemplo*	k. until tomorrow
12. *de dia e de noite*	l. at noon
13. *à esquerda*	m. since I saw him
14. *a meu ver*	n. in the American way
15. *até o Estoril*	o. with
16. *por assim dizer*	p. instead of
17. *sobre a mesa*	q. to the left
18. *até amanhã*	r. regarding
19. *em lugar de*	s. as far as Estoril
20. *desde que o vi*	t. so to speak

ANSWERS

1—l; 2—j; 3—h; 4—n; 5—o; 6—a; 7—c; 8—d; 9—r; 10—f; 11—i; 12—e; 13—q; 14—b; 15—s; 16—t; 17—g; 18—k; 19—p; 20—m.

QUIZ 29

1. *por acaso*	a. I bought it for a dollar.
2. *por volta das duas*	b. sixty miles an hour
3. *Passamos pela Espanha.*	c. certainly
4. *por agora*	d. for that reason
5. *Eu o comprei por um dólar.*	e. around here
6. *por isso*	f. For heaven's sake!
7. *sessenta milhas por hora*	g. at last
8. *por certo*	h. by chance
9. *Até logo.*	i. It's still to be done.
10. *Por Deus!*	j. for the time being
11. *por fim*	k. See you soon.
12. *Ele entrou pela porta.*	l. around two o'clock
13. *por aqui*	m. so to speak
14. *por assim dizer*	n. He came in through the door.
15. *Está por fazer.*	o. We passed through Spain.

ANSWERS

1—h; 2—l; 3—o; 4—j; 5—a; 6—d; 7—b; 8—c; 9—k; 10—f; 11—g; 12—n; 13—e; 14—m; 15—i.

QUIZ 30

1. *A carta é para ela.*	a. a bookcase
2. *Não serve para nada.*	b. The lesson is due tomorrow.
3. *A lição é para amanhã.*	c. to go there
4. *Estamos para sair.*	d. He left for Belém.
5. *para sempre*	e. Where did they go?
6. *uma estante para livros*	f. We are ready for the trip.

7. *para ir lá*   g. The letter is for her.
8. *Ele partiu para Belém.*   h. forever
9. *Estamos prontos para a*   i. It's worthless.
   viagem.
10. *Para onde eles foram?*   j. We are about to leave.

ANSWERS
1—g; 2—i; 3—b; 4—j; 5—h; 6—a; 7—c; 8—d; 9—f;
10—e.

LESSON 31

A. ON THE ROAD

Por favor.
Excuse me. Please.

Como se chama esta cidade?
What is the name of this town?

A que distância estamos de Porto Alegre?
How far are we from Porto Alegre?

Quantos quilômetros são daqui a Sintra?
How many kilometers is it from here to Sintra?

Fica a dez quilômetros daqui.
It's ten kilometers from here.

Como se vai daqui a Braga?
How do you (does one) get to Braga from here?

Siga este caminho.
Follow this road.

Você pode me dizer como faço para ir até este endereço
*(esta direcção Ⓟ)***?**
Can you tell me how I can get to this address?

Sabe onde fica este lugar?
Do you know where this place is?

Como se chama esta rua?
What is the name of this street?

Pode dizer-me onde fica esta rua?
Can you tell me where this street is?

Onde é a Rua da Liberdade?
Where is Liberdade Street (Liberty Street)?

Fica longe daqui?
Is it far from here?

Fica perto?
Is it near?

É a terceira rua à direita.
It's the third street on the right.

Passe por aqui.
Go this way.

Siga sempre em frente.
Go straight ahead.

Siga até a esquina e dobre *(vire Ⓟ)* **à esquerda.**
Go to the corner and turn left.

Dobre *(Vire Ⓟ)* **à direita.**
Turn right.

Pode me dizer onde há uma garagem?
Can you tell me where there's a garage?

Como posso ir à estrada principal?
How can I get to the main highway?

Onde é o posto policial *(a esquadra* Ⓟ*)*?
Where is the police station?

B. Bus, Subway, Train

Onde fica o ponto de ônibus?
Where is the bus stop?

Onde fica a estação rodoviária?
Where is the bus station?

Qual ônibus tomo para ir ao Rio de Janeiro?
Which bus do I take to go to Rio de Janeiro?

Qual ônibus tomo para ir ao aeroporto?
Which bus do I take to go to the airport?

Quanto é a passagem?
How much is the fare?

Onde devo descer?
Where do I get off?

A estação fica perto daqui?
Is the station near from here?

Onde posso comprar uma ficha?
Where can I buy a token?

Onde fica a estação da estrada *(do caminho* Ⓟ*)* **de ferro?**
Where is the train station?

Qual é o trem *(o comboio* Ⓟ*)* **para a capital?**
Which is the train to the capital?

De que plataforma sai?
From which platform does it leave?

Onde está o guichê *(guichet* Ⓟ*)* **de informações?**
Where is the information desk?

O senhor podia me dar o horário dos trens?
Could you give me the train schedule?

Gostaria de uma passagem.
I'd like a ticket.

Este trem pára em Minas?
Does this train stop in Minas?

A que horas chega em Brasília?
At what time does it arrive in Brasilia?

É melhor descer em qual estação?
At which station is it better to get off?

A que horas sai?
What time does it leave?

Acaba de sair.
It just left.

Vai sair agora.
It's going to leave now.

A que horas sai o próximo trem *(comboio* Ⓟ*)***?**
What time does the next train leave?

Tem carro dormitório? *(Tem carruagem cama?* Ⓟ*)*
Does it have a sleeper?

Não, mas tem carro *(vagão)* **restaurante e carro para fumar** *(fumadores* Ⓟ*)*.
No, but it has a diner and a smoking car.

Onde fica o guichê de passagens *(a bilheteira* Ⓟ*)*?
Where is the ticket window?

Por favor, uma passagem para São Paulo.
A ticket to São Paulo, please.

Simples ou de ida e volta?
One way or round trip?

De ida e volta; é mais barato, não é?
Round trip; it's cheaper, isn't it?

É. De primeira ou (de) segunda classe?
Yes, it is. First or second class?

De primeira. Quanto é?
First-class. How much is it?

Tenho pouca bagagem. Só duas malas.
I have only a little baggage. Just two bags.

C. AT THE AIRPORT

A que horas tem vôo na segunda?
What time do you have flights on Monday?

Eu prefiro o vôo das 21 horas.[1]
I prefer the 9:00 P.M. flight.

Temos que estar no aeroporto duas horas antes da partida.
We must be at the airport two hours before departure.

Qual companhia de aviação?
Which airline?

Quero um lugar junto da janela.
I want a seat by the window.

Há um vôo sem escala?
Is there a direct flight?

O vôo faz escala no Rio e em Recife.
The flight stops in Rio and Recife.

Temos que trocar de avião?
Do we have to change planes?

Primeiro temos que passar pela alfândega.
First we have to go through customs.

Quanto tempo demoramos aqui?
How long are we stopping here?

Onde posso pôr a bagagem de mão?
Where can I put the carry-on luggage?

Este lugar está ocupado?
Is this seat taken?

---

[1] Offices, airports, railroads, and other public services use the 24-hour system.

Com licença!
Pardon me! Allow me! Excuse me!

D. WORD STUDY

aeromoça	stewardess
ataque	attack
aventura	adventure
confortável	comfortable
coragem	courage
independência	independence
língua	language
mensagem	message
opinião	opinion
silêncio	silence

LESSON 32

A. WRITING AND MAILING LETTERS

Gostaria de escrever uma carta.
I'd like to write a letter.

O senhor teria um lápis para me emprestar?
Would you have a pencil that I could borrow?

O senhor tem *(uma)* caneta?
Do you have a pen?

Você pode me dar algum papel?
Can you give me some paper?

Aqui tem papel e uma caneta.
Here's some paper and a pen.

Não tenho envelopes.
I don't have any envelopes.

Nem selos.
Or stamps.

Desejo mandar uma carta aérea *(uma carta por avião).*
I want to send an airmail letter.

Onde é o correio?
Where is the post office?

Na esquina.
On the corner.

Vou ao correio.
I'm going to the post office.

Tem selos?
Do you have any stamps?

Onde vendem selos?
Where do they sell stamps?

Quero enviar este cartão postal.
I want to send this postcard.

Preciso de um selo para carta aérea *(selo de correio aéreo).*
I need an airmail stamp.

Quanto é o porte?
How much is the postage?

Quanto custa para enviar este pacote por via aérea?
How much is it to send this package airmail?

B. FAXES AND E-MAIL

Eu lhe mando pelo fax.
I'll send you a fax.

Gostaria de passar um fax.
I'd like to send a fax.

Quanto custa por página?
How much is it per page?

Preciso enviar um correio eletrônico.
I need to send an e-mail.

Posso entrar na Internet?
Can I get on the Internet?

Você tem um site?
Do you have a website?

Onde está o computador?
Where is the computer?

C. TELEPHONING

Fazer um telefonema:
To make a telephone call:

Alô *(Está Ⓟ)*! De onde fala?
Hello! Who is this?

Aqui é três-meia-cinco, um-meia-dois-nove.[1]
It's 365-1629.

É engano.
It's the wrong number.

Disquei *(Marquei Ⓟ)* o número errado.[2]
I dialed the wrong number.

Está ocupado *(impedido Ⓟ)*.
It's busy.

Está tocando *(a tocar Ⓟ)*.
It's ringing.

Ninguém atende.
Nobody's there.

Há um telefone aqui?
Is there a telephone here?

Onde posso telefonar?
Where can I make a phone call?

---

[1] In Brazil, the form *meia* (=*meia dúzia:* half dozen) is used instead of *seis* in order to avoid mistaking it with *três*.
[2] In Portugal: *marcar* (to dial).

Dá licença para o usar o telefone?
May I use your phone?

Poderia usar a lista telefônica, por favor?[3]
Could I use the telephone book, please?

Você sabe onde há uma cabine telefônica?[4]
Do you know where there's a telephone booth?

No vestíbulo do hotel.
In the hotel lobby.

O senhor tem ficha de telefone?
Do you have tokens for telephone calls?

Quero uma ficha, por favor.
I want a phone token, please.

Quero fazer um telefonema interurbano.
I want to make a long-distance call.

Telefonista, quanto custa um telefonema para Lisboa?
Operator, how much is a phone call to Lisbon?

É ele mesmo./É ela mesma. *(É o próprio./É a própria.* Ⓟ)
This is he./This is she.

Um momento, por favor!
Just a moment, please!

Com quem estou falando?
With whom am I speaking?

---

[3] *telefónica* Ⓟ.
[4] In Portugal: *cabina telefónica.*

Com a dona Laura.
With Laura.

Gostaria de falar com o seu Paulo.
I'd like to speak to Mr. Paulo.

O senhor quer deixar um recado?
Do you want to leave a message?

Sim.
Yes.

LESSON 33

A. WHAT'S YOUR NAME?

Como o senhor se chama?
What is your name?

Chamo-me João Martins.
My name is João Martins.

Como ele se chama?
What is his name?

Ele se chama (*Chama-se*) **Carlos Magalhães.**
His name is Carlos Magalhães.

Como ela se chama?
What is her name?

Ela se chama *(Ela chama-se)* **Maria Fernandes.**
Her name is Maria Fernandes.

Como eles se chamam?
What are their names?

Ele se chama *(chama-se)* **José Campos e ela Ana Coelho.**
His name is José Campos, and hers is Ana Coelho.

Qual é o nome dele?
What is his name?

O nome dele é Carlos.
His name is Carlos.

Qual é o seu nome de família?
What is his last name?

É Silva.
It's Silva.

B.   WHERE ARE YOU FROM?

Donde é o senhor?
Where are you from?

Sou de Lisboa.
I'm from Lisbon.

Sou de Nova Iorque.
I'm from New York.

Onde o senhor nasceu?
Where were you born?

Nasci em Coimbra.
I was born in Coimbra.

Onde mora?
Where do you live?

Moro nos Estados Unidos.
I live in the United States.

C. HOW OLD ARE YOU?

Quantos anos o senhor tem? *(Quantos anos tem?)*
How old are you?

Tenho vinte e quatro anos.
I am twenty-four years old.

Eu faço vinte e cinco anos em setembro.
I'll be twenty-five in September.

Quando é o seu aniversário?
When is your birthday?

O meu aniversário é daqui a duas semanas.
My birthday is in two weeks.

Eu nasci no dia dezenove *(dezanove* Ⓟ*)* **de agosto de mil novecentos e sessenta e seis.**
I was born August 19, 1966.

O meu irmão mais velho tem dezessete *(dezassete* Ⓟ*)* **anos.**
My older brother is seventeen.

O mais novo tem quinze anos.
The younger one is fifteen.

Ele estuda na universidade.
He's at the university.

Ele é estudante na Faculdade de Medicina.
He studies at the School of Medicine.

Ele está no último ano do curso de segundo-grau (*ano do liceu* ℗).
He's in the last year of high school.

Minha irmã ainda está na escola de primeiro-grau (*escola primária* ℗).
My sister still goes to elementary (primary) school.

D. PROFESSIONS

Onde você trabalha?
Where do you work?

Qual é a sua profissão?
What is your profession?

O que faz?
What do you do?

Sou empresário.
I'm a businessman.

Sou empresária.
I'm a businesswoman.

O que o seu pai faz?
What does your father do?

O que o sua mãe faz?
What does your mother do?

É advogado.
He's a lawyer.

É advogada.
She's a lawyer.

É arquiteto *(arquitecto)*.
He's an architect.

É professora.
She's a teacher.

É professora universitária.
She's a university professor.

É médico.
He's a doctor.

É médica.
She's a doctor.

É jornalista.
He's/she's a journalist.

É fazendeiro Ⓑ *(lavrador)*.
He's a farmer.

E. FAMILY MATTERS

Você tem parentes aqui?
Do you have any relatives here?

De onde sua família é?
Where is your family from?

Minha família veio de Portugal.
My family came from Portugal.

Toda a sua família mora aqui?
Does all your family live here?

Toda a família menos os meus avós.
All my family except my grandparents.

O meu avô nasceu em Portugal e a minha avó nos Açores.
My grandfather was born in Portugal and my grandmother
in the Azores.

Os meus pais são estrangeiros.
My parents are foreigners.

A dona Elizabeth é parente da sua mãe?
Is Elizabeth related to your mother?

Sim.
Yes.

O meu tio é engenheiro.
My uncle is an engineer.

A minha tia é enfermeira.
My aunt is a nurse.

A minha prima é funcionária pública.
My cousin is a government employee.

Eu tenho muitos primos.
I have lots of cousins.

Quantos irmãos você tem?
How many brothers do you have?

Tenho um irmão e uma irmã.
I have one brother and one sister.

O meu sogro e sogra são aposentados.
My father-in-law and mother-in-law are retired.

O meu genro está desempregado.
My son-in-law is unemployed.

A nossa nora trabalha em um banco.
Our daughter-in-law works for a bank.

O meu sobrinho ainda é um bebê.
My nephew is still a baby.

A minha filha está tomando conta das crianças.
My daughter is taking care of the children.

O neto dele é casado?
Is his grandson married?

Eu sou a neta mais velha.
I am the oldest granddaughter.

A nossa cunhada é solteira.
Our sister-in-law is single.

Eu sou divorciado.
I am divorced.

O namorado dela tem duas irmãs.
Her boyfriend has two sisters.

A noiva do meu primo está na Faculdade de Direito.
My cousin's fiancée is in Law School.

O meu noivo é filho único.
My fiancé is an only child.

A minha filha ficou noiva.
My daughter got engaged.

Quando vocês vão se casar?
When are you getting married?

Nós vamos nos casar no ano que vem.
We are getting married next year.

O casamento vai ser em maio *(Maio* Ⓟ*).*
The wedding is going to be in May.

O esposo dela morreu.
Her husband died/is deceased.

Meus pais são falecidos.
My parents are deceased.

A mãe dele é viúva.
His mother is a widow.

F. WORD STUDY

cômico	comic
detalhe	detail
empregado	employee
juízo	judgment
músculo	muscle
parque	park
restaurante	restaurant
rosa	rose

LESSON 34

A. SHOPPING: *COMPRAS*

1. **Quanto custa isto?**
   How much is this?
2. **Dez cruzeiros** *(euros Ⓟ).*
   Ten cruzeiros (euros).
3. **É muito caro. Não tem alguma coisa mais barata?**
   That's pretty expensive. Don't you have anything cheaper?
4. **Do mesmo gênero?**[1]
   Of the same kind?
5. **Do mesmo ou de outro parecido.**
   Of the same or something similar.
6. **Mais barato.**
   Less expensive.

[1] *género* Ⓟ.

7. **Não faz diferença!**
It doesn't matter!

8. **Qual é o preço mínimo?**
What is the lowest price?

9. **Não dá para fazer por menos?**
Can't you charge less?

10. **Qual é o desconto se eu levar três?**
What is the discount if I take three?

11. **Depende do preço.**
That depends on the price.

12. **O senhor podia me mostrar outra coisa?**
Could you show me something else?

13. **Gosto mais do que do outro.**
I like it better than the other one.

14. **Eu fico com este.**
I'll take this.

15. **E este outro, é mais barato ou mais caro?**
How about this one; is it cheaper or more expensive?

16. **É mais caro.**
It's more expensive.

17. **Não tem mais alguma coisa em estoque** *(em existência* Ⓟ*)*?
Don't you have anything else in stock?

18. **Em breve espero receber novos estilos.** *(Espero receber em breve novos modelos.* Ⓟ*)*
I'm hoping to receive some new styles soon.

19. **Para quando?**
How soon?

20. **De um dia para o outro. Pode passar (por aqui) lá pelo fim da semana?**
Any day now. Can you drop in toward the end of the week?

21. **Posso. . . . E qual é o preço disto?**
Yes, I can. . . . What's the price of this?

22. **Cinco cruzeiros** *(euros* Ⓟ*)* **o par.**
Five cruzeiros (euros) a pair.

23. **Quero uma dúzia.**
I'd like to have a dozen.

24. *Quer levar consigo Ⓟ?*
Will you take them with you?

25. **Prefiro[2] comprar uns artigos regionais.**
I'd rather buy some local crafts.

26. **Aquela é muito bonita.**
That one is very pretty (something *fem.*).

27. **Você gosta deste?**
Do you like this one (something *masc.*)?

28. **Vou dar de presente para . . .** (or *Vou dá-lo . . .*)
I'm going to give it as a gift to . . .

29. **Ainda não decidi.**
I haven't decided yet.

30. **Qual é o tamanho?**
What size is it?

31. **É muito pequeno. Não tem maior?**
It's too small. Isn't there a larger one?

32. **É muito grande. Não tem menor?[3]**
It's too big. Isn't there a smaller one?

33. **De outra cor.**
In another color.

34. **Posso trocar depois?** (or *Posso trocá-lo . . .*)
Can I exchange it later?

35. **Tem garantia?**
Does it have a warranty?

36. **Não preciso de mais nada.**
I don't need anything else.

37. **O que mais?**
What else?

---

[2] *Prefíro* is from *preferir*, a radical-changing verb. See grammar summary, radical-changing verbs in Section 39.
[3] In Portugal: *mais pequeno*.

NOTES

1. [4]*Quanto custa isto?* ("How much does this cost?")[5] How much is this? You can also say: *Quanto é?* How much is it? *Por quanto se vende isto?* ("At/for how much is this sold?") How much is this? *Por quanto se vendem os limões?* ("For how much are the lemons sold?") How much are the lemons? *Quanto lhe custaram as calças?* ("How much did the trousers cost to you?") How much did your trousers cost?

2. The real is the currency unit of Brazil; formerly it was the cruzeiro. Its value has varied greatly due to steep inflation. The escudo is the currency unit of Portugal.

3. *É muito caro.* ("It's very expensive.") That's pretty expensive. *Isto é muito caro.* This is very high (expensive). *Barato* cheap. *Mais barato* ("more cheap") Cheaper. (See Section 17 of the grammar summary.) *Muito barato* very cheap.

4. *Gênero, tipo, modelo* kind, type, sort, class, model.

11. *Depender de* to depend on.

15. *E este outro.* "And this other one."

18. *Em breve* in brief; in a short time.

19. *Para quando?* "For when?"

20. *De um dia para o outro.* "From one day to the other." *Passar (por aqui)* to pass (by here, to stop in).

21. *Posso* I can. In answer to a question, often just the verb will be repeated without "yes" or "no." *Pode passar por aqui? Posso. Pode vir amanhã?* Can you come tomorrow? *Não posso.* No, I can't. ("I can't.")

24. *Consigo* is a combination which comes from *com* (with) and *si* (oneself, yourself, etc.). One also hears *com o senhor* or *com a senhora* for "with you."

25. *Prefiro . . .* I prefer that, I'd prefer that, or I'd rather . . .

---

[4] Numbers refer to the sentences above.
[5] Words in quotation marks are literal translations.

QUIZ 31

1. *É muito* _____ (expensive).
   a. *custa*
   b. *isto*
   c. *caro*
2. *Não tem alguma coisa mais* _____ (cheap)?
   a. *gênero*
   b. *preço*
   c. *barata*
3. *Do* _____ (same) *tipo*.
   a. *alguma coisa*
   b. *mesmo*
   c. *mais*
4. *Quero* _____ (exchange) *este presente*.
   a. *ficar*
   b. *trocar*
   c. *levar*
5. *Gosto* _____ (more) *do que do outro*.
   a. *custa*
   b. *mais*
   c. *mesmo*
6. *Não* _____ (have) *mais alguma coisa*?
   a. *tem*
   b. *caro*
   c. *outro*
7. *Espero* _____ (receive) *novos estilos (novos modelos)*.
   a. *custar*
   b. *levar*
   c. *receber*
8. *Para* _____ (when)?
   a. *estoque*
   b. *caro*
   c. *quando*

9. *O que você quer* _____ (else)?
   a. *mais*
   b. *melhor*
   c. *menos*

ANSWERS
1—c; 2—c; 3—b; 4—b; 5—b; 6—a; 7—c; 8—c; 9—a.

B.   GENERAL SHOPPING EXPRESSIONS

Desculpe-me.
Excuse me.

Gostaria de comprar . . .
I'd like to buy . . .

Gostaria de comprar lembranças.
I'd like to buy souvenirs.

Só estou olhando.
I'm just looking.

Quanto custa isto?
How much is this?

É um pouco caro!
It's pretty expensive!

É o preço final?
Is that the final price?

O meu tamanho é . . .
My size is . . .

Vou comprar.
I'll take it.

Aceita cheques de viagem?
Do you take traveler's checks?

LESSON 35

A. BREAKFAST (*O Café da Manhã* Ⓑ[1]
[*O Pequeno Almoço* Ⓟ])

1. P:[2] **Você está com fome? (Você tem fome?)**
   P: Are you hungry?
2. M: **Estou.** *(Tenho.)*
   M: Yes, I am.
3. P: **Estou morrendo de fome.**
   P: I'm starving.
4. P: **Garçom! Garçom!** *(Empregado! Empregado!* Ⓟ)
   P: Waiter! Waiter!
5. G: **Às suas ordens. Que desejam?**
   G: At your service. What would you like?

[1] In Brazil, breakfast *(o café da manhã)* is usually very light. The main meals are: lunch *(o almoço),* which is heavier than dinner *(o jantar). Tomar um lanche* or *fazer um lanche* basically means to eat a sandwich or a snack.
[2] *P.* stands here for *Pedro* (Peter); *M.* for *Maria* (Mary); *G.* for *Garçom* (Waiter).

6. P: **Desejamos o café da manhã** *(o pequeno almoço* Ⓟ*).*
   P: We'd like breakfast.

7. M: **Que pode nos servir** *(servir-nos)*?
   M: What do you have?

8. G: **Café com leite, chá, chocolate . . .**
   G: Coffee with milk, tea, chocolate . . .

9. P: **O que servem com o café?**
   P: What do you serve with the coffee?

10. G: **Pão, torradas . . .**
    G: Bread, toast . . .

11. M: **E manteiga?**
    M: And butter?

12. G: **Sim, também.**
    G: Yes, also.

13. P: **Quero uma xícara** *(chávena* Ⓟ*)* **de café com leite, e pão.**
    P: I'd like a cup of coffee with milk, and some bread (rolls).

14. P: **Maria, o que você quer?** *(Maria, o que quer?)*
    P: Mary, what do you want?

15. M: **Acho que vou tomar um suco de laranja.**
    M: I think that I'm going to drink an orange juice.

16. P: **Eu só quero um copo de água mineral, por favor.**
    P: I just want a glass of mineral water, please.

17. P: **Eu quero um pouco de gelo, por favor.**
    P: I want some ice, please.

18. P: **O que mais você vai pedir?**
    P: What else are you going to order?

19. M: **Chá e um ovo quente.**
    M: Tea and a soft-boiled egg.

20. P: **Garçom, o senhor podia me trazer um guarda-napo, por favor.**
    P: Waiter, could you bring me a napkin, please.

21. M: **E para mim um garfo, por favor.**
    M: And a fork for me, please.

22. P: **Tenha a bondade de nos trazer** *(trazer-nos)* **mais açúcar.**
    P: Please bring us some more sugar.
23. M: **E um cafezinho** *(bica* ℗*)* **também.**
    M: And an expresso as well.
24. M: **E depois, a conta ... Aqui tem, garçom, fique com o troco.**
    M: And then, the check. . . . Here you are, waiter. Keep the change.
25. G: **Muito obrigado, senhora.**
    G: Thank you, madam.

NOTES

1. *Você está com fome?* ("Are you with hunger?") *Você tem fome?* ("Do you have hunger?") Are you hungry?
2. *Estou morrendo de fome/de sede.* (Lit. "I'm dying of hunger/thirst.")
4. *Garçon* and *garção* are also used.
5. *Às suas ordens.* ("At you orders.") At your service. *Que desejam?* ("What do you want?") What would you like?
6. *O café da manhã* ("The coffee of the morning") Breakfast. (Used in Brazil, where it is also shortened to *o café.*) *O pequeno almoço* ("The small lunch") and *o primeiro almoço* ("The first lunch") Breakfast. (Used in Portugal.)
7. "What can you serve us?" The *nos* may come before the infinitive *servir,* or after it, joined with a hyphen (see Section 19 of the grammar summary).
10. *Pão* is bread, but in a general sense it can also include rolls. *Pãozinho* means roll, plural *pãezinhos.*

13. In Portugal, coffee with milk is called *garoto*.
19. *Ovo* egg. *Ovos quentes* soft-boiled eggs. *Ovos estrelados* fried eggs. *Ovos mexidos* scrambled eggs. *Ovos duros* hard-boiled eggs.
22. "Have the kindness to bring me more sugar."
24. *Fique com o troco.* ("Remain with the change.") Keep the change. The verb *ficar* (to stay, remain) is used in a variety of expressions with an extension of meaning, often being the equivalent of "to be." *Ficou em casa.* He stayed home. *Onde fica?* Where is it? *Fico convencido.* I am convinced. *Eles ficam em pé.* They are standing. *Esse paletó lhe fica bem.* That jacket looks good on you. *Fiquei doente.* I became ill. *Ela ficou zangada.* She was (became) angry.
25. "Much obliged."

QUIZ 32

1. _____ (We want) *o café da manhã (o pequeno almoço) para três pessoas.*
   a. *desjamos*
   b. *conservamos*
   c. *fome*
2. _____ (and) *manteiga?*
   a. *a*
   b. *e*
   c. *ovo*
3. *Quero o* _____ (same).
   a. *muito*
   b. *mesmo*
   c. *servem*
4. *O que* _____ (do you want)?
   a. *tenho*
   b. *tem*
   c. *quer*

5. *Eu não quero* _____ (much).
   a. *fome*
   b. *mesmo*
   c. *muita coisa*
6. *Podia* _____ (bring me) *um guardanapo.*
   a. *costume*
   b. *me trazer (trazer-me)*
   c. *mesmo*
7. *E* _____ (then, later) *a conta.*
   a. *amanhã*
   b. *garfo*
   c. *depois*

ANSWERS
1—a; 2—b; 3—b; 4—c; 5—c; 6—b; 7—c.

B. A SAMPLE MENU
(*O Cardápio* [*Ementa* Ⓟ])

Canja ou sopa de cebola	Chicken-rice soup or onion soup
Omelete (Omeleta Ⓟ)	Omelet
Bacalhau	Cod
Frango assado	Roast chicken
Costeletas grelhadas	Grilled chops
Bife com batatas fritas	Steak with fried potatoes
Salada de alface com tomate	Lettuce and tomato salad
Queijo e frutas	Cheese and fruit
Café	Coffee

LESSON 36

A. APARTMENT HUNTING
(*Procurando Apartamento*)

1. **Venho ver o apartamento.**
   I've come to see ("I come to see") the apartment.
2. **Qual deles?**
   Which one?
3. **Aquele que está para alugar.**
   The one which is for rent.
4. **Tem ⑧ (*há*) dois.**
   There are two.
5. **O senhor pode me dar (*dar-me* ℗) alguns detalhes
   (*algumas informações* ℗)?**
   Can you describe them?
6. **O do quinto andar não tem mobília.**
   The one on the fifth floor is unfurnished.
7. **E o outro?**
   And the other one?
8. **O do segundo andar é mobiliado.**
   The one on the second floor is furnished.
9. **Quantos quartos (*divisões* ℗) têm?**
   How many rooms do they have?
10. **O do quinto andar tem quatro quartos (*divisões* ℗),
    cozinha e banheiro (*casa de banho* ℗).**
    The one on the fifth floor has four bedrooms, a
    kitchen, and a bathroom.
11. **Dá para a rua?**
    Does it face the street?
12. **Não, dá para o pátio.**
    No, it faces the courtyard.

13. **E o do segundo andar?**
And the one on the second floor?

14. **O do segundo andar tem um quarto, sala de estar, e sala de jantar.**
The one on the second floor has a bedroom, a living room, and a dining room.

15. **Também dá para o pátio?**
Does it also look out on the courtyard?

16. **Não, dá para a rua.**
No, it faces the street.

17. **Quanto é o aluguel** *(a renda* Ⓟ*)*?
How much is the rent?

18. **O aluguel do maior é vinte e cinco mil cruzeiros por mês, mais a água e o gás.** *(A renda do maior é mil e quinhentos euros por mês, além da água e do gás.* Ⓟ*)*
The larger one rents for twenty-five thousand cruzeiros a month, plus water and gas. (The larger one rents for fifteen hundred euros a month, besides water and gas. Ⓟ)

19. **E o apartamento mobiliado?**
And the furnished apartment?

20. **Este se aluga por quarenta mil cruzeiros por mês, tudo incluído.** *(Este aluga-se por três mil escudos, tudo incluído.* Ⓟ*)*
That one rents for forty thousand cruzeiros everything included. (That one rents for three thousand euros, everything included. Ⓟ)

21. **Como é a mobília?**
How is the furniture?

22. **Os móveis são modernos e estão em boas condições.**
It's modern furniture and it's in excellent condition.

23. **Estão incluídos a roupa de cama e o serviço de mesa?**
Are bed linens and silverware included?

24. **A senhora achará tudo o que precisar, até utensílios de cozinha.**
You'll find everything you need, even kitchen utensils.

25. **É preciso assinar um contrato?**
Is it necessary to sign a lease?

26. **Para isso a senhora terá que falar com o administrador.**
You'll have to speak to the renting agent about that.

27. **Quais são as condições?**
What are the terms?

28. **Um mês adiantado e outro de depósito.**
One month's rent in advance and another as a deposit.

29. **É tudo?**
Is that all?

30. **Naturalmente, a senhora terá que dar referências.**
Of course, you will have to give references.

31. **A propósito, tem elevador?**
By the way, is there an elevator?

32. **Não, não tem.**
No, there isn't.

33. **É pena.**
That's too bad.

34. **Além disso, o prédio é muito moderno.**
Aside from that, the building is very modern.

35. **Que quer dizer com isso?**
What do you mean?

36. **Tem aquecimento central e ar condicionado.**
There's central heating and air conditioning.

37. **Tem água quente?**
Is there hot water?

38. **Naturalmente. Os banheiros foram remodelados recentemente.** *(As casas de banho foram remodeladas recentemente.* Ⓟ*)*
Of course! The bathrooms were remodeled recently.

39. **Podemos ver os apartamentos?**
May we see the apartments?

40. **Só pela manhã.**
   Only in the morning.
41. **Muito bem. Venho amanhã pela manhã. Muito obrigada.**
   Very well. I'll come tomorrow morning. Thank you very much.
42. **De nada. Às suas ordens.**
   Don't mention it. At your service.

NOTES

2. "Which of them?"
3. *Aquele* "that one." *Alugar* to rent, to lease, to let, to hire out.
5. "Can you give me some details (some information)?"
6. "The one of the fifth floor does not have furniture." *Móveis* also means furniture.
9. *Peças* has a variety of meanings. Here it means "rooms" in the sense of units. The word also means piece, portion, section, a play (theater), etc. *Quarto* and *sala* are used for rooms of the house. *Quarto* will often have the meaning of bedroom or sleeping quarters. *Divisão* (division) can mean "room" in Portugal.
10. *Banho* bath. *Banheiro* Ⓑ bathroom, *banheira* bathtub, *chuveiro* shower, *tomar banho de chuveiro* to take a shower. *Casa* (house) can mean "room" in Portugal: *casa de banho* bathroom.
11. *Dá* is from the verb *dar* to give.
13. "And the one of the second floor?"
14. *Quarto* bedroom; also *quarto de dormir*. Some times *o living* is heard for living room.
18. "The rent of the larger one is . . ."
20. "This one is rented for . . ."
22. "The furniture is modern . . ." Notice that *mobília* takes a singular verb; *móveis* takes a plural verb; *móvel* is the singular form.

23. "Are (there) included bed linens and table service?"
26. "For that you will have to speak . . ."
27. *Quais* is the plural of *qual,* what, which.
33. *Pena* also means pain, sorrow, pity.
35. *Querer dizer* to mean. "What do you mean with that?"
36. *Escada de serviço* service stairway.
38. *Remodelados* or *reformados* remodeled.
40. "Can we see . . ."
42. *Venho* from the verb *vir,* "I come."
43. "For nothing. At your orders."

QUIZ 33

1. _____ (I come) *ver o apartamento.*
   a. *vem*
   b. *venho*
   c. *como*
2. *Aquele que* _____ (is) *para alugar.*
   a. *ver*
   b. *este*
   c. *está*
3. _____ (there are) *dois.*
   a. *tem (há)*
   b. *venho (vem)*
   c. *lá*
4. *Não tem* _____ (furniture).
   a. *andar*
   b. *banheiro*
   c. *mobília*
5. _____ (how many) *peças (divisões) têm?*
   a. *como*
   b. *quantas*
   c. *muitas*

6. *Dá para a* _____ (street)?
   a. *cozinha*
   b. *pátio*
   c. *rua*
7. _____ (also) *dá para o pátio?*
   a. *também*
   b. *outro*
   c. *rua*
8. _____ (what) *são as condições?*
   a. *quais*
   b. *quando*
   c. *onde*
9. *A senhora* _____ (will find) *tudo o que precisar.*
   a. *andar*
   b. *terá*
   c. *achará*
10. *O prédio é* _____ (very) *moderno.*
    a. *manhã*
    b. *muito*
    c. *mobiliado*

ANSWERS
1—b; 2—c; 3—a; 4—c; 5—b; 6—c; 7—a; 8—a; 9—c;
10—b.

B. To Have: *TER*

1. I have, etc.:

tenho	*temos*
(tens)	*(tendes)*
tem	*têm*[1]

[1] The singular *(tem)* and plural *(têm)* forms are pronounced alike. However, in the written form the circumflex accent is required in order to differentiate them.

Tenho um belo jardim.	I have a pretty garden.
Não tenho nada.	I don't have anything.
O senhor tem?	Do you have it?
Não tenho.	I don't have (it).
Tenho tempo.	I have time.
Não tenho dinheiro.	I don't have any money.
Não tenho filhos.	I don't have any children.
Ele não tem amigos.	He doesn't have any friends.
Tenho fome. *(Estou com fome.)*[2]	I'm hungry.
Tenho sede. *(Estou com sede.)*	I'm thirsty.
Tenho sono. *(Estou com sono.)*	I'm sleepy.
Tenho frio. *(Estou com frio.)*	I'm cold.
Tenho razão.	I'm right.
Ele não tem razão.	He's not right.
Eles não têm razão.	They're wrong.
O senhor tem um cachimbo?	Do you have a pipe?
Não tenho. Não fumo.	I don't have (any). I don't smoke.
A fazenda tem muitos animais?	Does the farm have many animals?
Tem. Tem gado, cavalos, e carneiros.	Yes, it has. It has cattle, horses, and sheep.
Tenho vinte anos.	I'm twenty years old.
Tenho dor de cabeça. *(Estou com dor de cabeça.)*	I have a headache.

[2] In this section, the form in parentheses is usually more common in Brazil.

Ela tem dor de dente. *(Ela está com dor de dente or dentes.)*	She has a toothache.
O que é que você tem?	What's the matter with you?
Não tenho nada.	Nothing's the matter with me.
Eles têm pressa. *(Eles estão com pressa.)*	They're in a hurry.
Elas não tiveram bom êxito.	They were not successful.
Tenha a bondade de avisar-me.	Please inform me.
Tenha cuidado.	Be careful.
O senhor tem a palavra.	You have the floor.
Tenho saudades de minha terra.	I miss my country.
Tenho sorte. *(Estou com sorte.)*	I'm lucky.
Não tem importância.	It doesn't matter.

2. *Ter que* or *ter de* both mean "to have to":

Tenho que ir hoje.	I have to go today.
O senhor tem que acreditar.	You have to believe.
Os meninos têm de brincar.	The children have to play.
Ela tem de indagar.	She has to inquire.

3. Do I have it?

Eu tenho?	Do I have it?
O senhor tem?	Do you have it?
Ele tem?	Does he have it?
Ela tem?	Does she have it?
Nós temos?	Do we have it?
Os senhores têm?	Do you have it?
Eles *(elas)* **têm?**	Do they have it?

4. Don't I have it?

Eu não tenho?	Don't I have it?
O senhor não tem?	Don't you have it?
Ele não tem?	Doesn't he have it?
Ela não tem?	Doesn't she have it?
Nós não temos?	Don't we have it?
Os senhores não têm?	Don't you have it?
Eles *(elas)* não têm?	Don't they have it?

QUIZ 34

1.	*Não tenho dinheiro.*	a.	I have a headache.
2.	*Não tenho nada.*	b.	Don't you have it?
3.	*Ele não tem razão.*	c.	I don't have it.
4.	*Tenho sono.*	d.	I'm cold.
5.	*Ele tem?*	e.	They're in a hurry.
6.	*Eu não tenho.*	f.	I don't have any money.
7.	*Tenho fome.*	g.	Does he have it?
8.	*Tenho frio.*	h.	He's wrong.
9.	*Tenho vinte anos.*	i.	I'm thirsty.
10.	*O senhor não tem?*	j.	Be careful.
11.	*Tenho que ir hoje.*	k.	I don't have anything.
12.	*Eles têm pressa.*	l.	I'm sleepy.
13.	*Tenho sede.*	m.	I'm hungry.
14.	*Tenho dor de cabeça.*	n.	I have to go today.
15.	*Tenha cuidado.*	o.	I'm twenty years old.

ANSWERS
1—f; 2—k; 3—h; 4—l; 5—g; 6—c; 7—m; 8—d; 9—o;
10—b; 11—n; 12—e; 13—i; 14—a; 15—j.

C. There Is/Are, To Have (Auxiliary Verb): *Haver*

1. *Haver* is not used to translate "to have" in the sense of "to possess" (*ter* is used for this meaning). *Há*, the third person singular, is used to translate the meanings of "there is" or "there are" (though *tem* is often used in this sense, especially in Brazil):

Há um bom hotel perto do aeroporto (or *Tem . . .*)
There is a good hotel near the airport.

Há muitos estrangeiros nesta cidade? (or *Tem . . .*)
Are there many foreigners in this city?

Não há uma festa amanhã.
There isn't a party tomorrow.

2. "There was" and "There were" can be translated by the preterit *houve* (when telling about a past fact) or by the imperfect *havia* (more as a narration about a situation or a state in the past):

Houve um incêndio aqui.
There was a fire here.

Havia muita gente quando eu cheguei.
There were many people when I arrived.

Não havia tempo para mais nada.
There wasn't time for anything else.

3. *Haverá* means "there will be":

A que horas haverá outro vôo?
At what time will there be another flight?

Não haverá mais tempo para isto.
There will not be more time for this.

4. *Há* is used in many idiomatic expressions, mostly expressions of time:

Há quanto tempo?
How long ago?

Há pouco tempo.
Not long ago.

Há muito tempo.
A long time ago.

Fui ao Brasil há cinco anos.
I went to Brazil five years ago.

Há dois dias que estamos no Rio.
We have been in Rio for two days.

Eles telefonaram há três horas.
They called three hours ago.

Há uma semana que não vejo a Maria.
I haven't seen Maria for a week.

5. Other expressions:

O que é que há?
What's going on?/What's happening?/What's up?

O que há de novo?
What's new?

Não há nada de novo.
There is nothing new.

Não há de quê.
Not at all. You're welcome. Don't mention it.

Haja o que houver.
Come what may.

D. TO DO, TO MAKE: *FAZER*

faço	*fazemos*
(fazes)	*(fazeis)*
faz	*fazem*

Que vai fazer?	What are you going to do?
Como se faz isto?	How do you do this?
Ela fez a cama.	She made the bed.

1. The third person singular of *fazer* is used in some
   expressions about the weather:

Faz bom tempo.	The weather is good.
Ontem fez mau tempo.	Yesterday the weather was bad.
Aqui nunca faz frio.	It's never cold here.
Faz calor no verão?	Is it warm in the summer?

2. *Fazer* is used at times instead of *haver* in expressions
   of time:

Faz tempo que ele não me fala.	He hasn't spoken to me for some time.
Faz três dias que não (o) vejo.	I haven't seen him for three days.

3. Other uses of *fazer:*

Agora vocês podem fazer perguntas.	Now you can ask questions.
Faça o favor de cobrir tudo.	Please cover everything.
É preciso fazer fila?	Is it necessary to stand in line?
Ele ainda não fez a barba.	He doesn't shave yet.
Quando nos vai fazer uma visita?	When are you going to visit us?
Não faz mal.	It doesn't matter.
Vamos fazer uma viagem no verão.	We're going to take a trip in the summer.
Ele fez dezoito anos ontem.	He turned eighteen yesterday.
Eles vão fazer compras amanhã de manhã.	They are going shopping tomorrow morning.

QUIZ 35

1. *Há uma festa amanhã.*
2. *Que vai fazer?*
3. *Faz bom tempo.*
4. *Há dois dias que não me falam.*
5. *Faça o favor.*
6. *Faz frio.*
7. *Haja o que houver.*

a. Three hours ago.
b. It's cold.
c. Come what may.
d. She made the bed.
e. What are you going to do?
f. Please.
g. There is a party tomorrow.

8. *Ela fez a cama.*   h. The weather is good.
9. *Como se faz isto?*   i. They haven't spoken to
                              me for two days.
10. *Há três horas.*   j. How do you do this?

ANSWERS
1—g; 2—e; 3—h; 4—i; 5—f; 6—b; 7—c; 8—d; 9—j;
10—a.

LESSON 37

A. **COULD YOU GIVE ME SOME INFORMATION?**
  *(Podia me Dar [Dar-me] Algumas
  Informações?)*

1. **Boa tarde.**
   Good afternoon.
2. **Boa tarde. Em que posso servi-lo?**
   Good afternoon. What can I do for you?
3. **Podia me dar** *(dar-me)* **algumas informações?**
   Could you give me some information?
4. **Com muito prazer.**
   Gladly. ("With much pleasure.")
5. **Não conheço a cidade e não posso me orientar**
   (orientar-me).
   I don't know the city and I can't find my way around.
6. *(Pois)*, **é muito simples.**
   (Well), it's quite simple.
7. **É que eu não sou daqui.**
   It's just that I'm not from here.

•

8. **Nesse caso eu lhe mostro (mostro-lhe) a cidade.**
   In that case I'll show you the town.

9. **Agradeço muito.**
   I'm very grateful to you.

10. **Vê aquele prédio grande na esquina?**
    Do you see that large building on the corner?

11. **Aquele da bandeira?**
    The one with the flag?

12. **Precisamente. É o correio. Em frente dele, do outro
    lado da rua . . .**
    That's right. ("Exactly.") That's the post office. Opposite
    it, on the other side of the street . . .

13. **Onde?**
    Where?

14. **Lá** *(Acolá* Ⓟ)**. O senhor vê aquele outro prédio com
    o relógio?**
    Over there. Do you see that other building with the
    clock?

15. **Ah sim, vejo.**
    Oh, yes, I see it.

16. **É a Prefeitura.** *(É a Câmara Municipal.* Ⓟ)
    That's City Hall.

17. **Vejo . . . A propósito, em que rua estamos?**
    I see . . . By the way, what street are we on?

18. **Estamos na rua principal da cidade.**
    We're on the city's main street.

19. **Onde fica a delegacia de polícia** *(a esquadra* Ⓟ)**?**
    Where is the police station?

20. **No fim da rua. Siga sempre em frente.**
    At the end of the street. Go straight ahead.

21. **E se não acerto?**
    What if I don't find it?

22. **Vai acertar. É um prédio grande com uma grade de
    ferro em redor . . . O senhor vê aquela loja?**
    You'll find it. It's a big building with an iron fence
    around it . . . Do you see that store?

23. **Que loja? Aquela à direita?**
Which store? The one on the right?

24. **Sim, aquela que tem um globo verde na vitrîna** *(montra Ⓟ).*
Yes, the one with a green globe in the window.

25. **É uma barbearia?**
Is it a barbershop?

26. **Não, é uma farmácia. Há um médico na casa ao lado. Tem o nome na porta.**
No, it's a pharmacy. A doctor lives in the house next door. His name's on the door.
("There's a doctor in the house at the side. He has the name on the door.")

27. **Ele tem o consultório na mesma casa em que mora?**
Does he have his office in his home? ("Does he have the office in the same house in which he lives ['dwells']?")

28. **Tem, mas pela manhã está no hospital.**
Yes, he does, but in the morning he is at the hospital.

29. **Onde é o hospital?**
Where is the hospital?

30. **O hospital fica a duas quadras** *(dois quarteirões)* **daqui, um pouco antes de chegar à rodovia** *(estrada).*
The hospital is two blocks from here, just before ("a little before") you come to the highway.

31. **Como posso voltar ao** *(a)* **meu hotel?**
How can I get back to my hotel?

32. **Venha aqui. O senhor está vendo, é lá perto do . . .**
(Venha aqui, o senhor está a ver, acolá perto do . . .)
Come over here. You see it there, next to the . . .

33. **. . . cinema.**
. . . movie theatre.

34. **Exato** *(Exacto Ⓟ).*
That's right.

35. **Já sei.**
I know. ("I already know.")

36. **Por que não compra um guia?**
    Why don't you buy a guidebook?

37. **Boa idéia** *(ideia* ℗*)*. **Onde posso comprar** *(comprálo)*?
    Good idea. Where can I buy (one)?

38. **Na estação ou em qualquer banca** *(quiosque* ℗*)* **de jornais.**
    In the station or at any newspaper stand.

39. **A estação é longe daqui?**
    Is the station far from here?

40. **A estação fica na Praça Mauá.**
    The station is on Mauá Square.

41. **Onde há uma banca** *(um quiosque)* **de jornais por aqui?**
    Where is there a newsstand near here?

42. **Há uma (um) na esquina.**
    There's one on the corner.

43. **Fico-lhe muito grato.**
    Thank you very much. ("I remain much obliged to you.")

44. **Não há de quê. Foi um prazer poder ser-lhe útil.**
    Don't mention it. ("There is nothing for which to be grateful.") I'm very glad to have been of some assistance. ("It was a pleasure to be able to be useful to you.")

45. **Tive muita sorte em encontrá-lo. O senhor conhece muito bem a cidade.**
    I was very lucky to meet you. You know the city very well.

46. **Não é de admirar. Sou o prefeito** *(administrador do conselho)*.
    That's not surprising. I'm the mayor.

NOTES

Title: *Não sou daqui.* I'm a stranger. ("I'm not from here.")   •

2. "Good afternoon. In what can I serve you?" *Posso* I can, from *poder* to be able.

3. *Podia?* Could you?; from *poder.*[1] *Poderia* could also be used.

5. *Orientar-se* to orient oneself, to get one's bearings, to find one's way.

11. "That one of the flag?"

15. *Vejo.* I see; from *ver* to see.[1]

31. *Voltar* to return.

34. "Exactly."

44. *Foi.* It was; from *ser* to be.[1]

45. "I had much luck in meeting you."

46. *Não é de admirar.* ("It is not to cause surprise.") It's not surprising.

QUIZ 36

1. *É a* _____ (City Hall).
   a. *simples*
   b. *Prefeitura (Cámara Municipal Ⓟ)*
   c. *cidade*

2. *Eu lhe mostro a* _____ (city).
   a. *correio*
   b. *cidade*
   c. *caso*

3. *Aquele prédio grande na* _____ (corner).
   a. *esquina*
   b. *correio*
   c. *rua*

---

[1] For these and other irregular verbs see section 40 of the grammar summary.

4. *É o* _____ (post office).
   a. *prédio*
   b. *correio*
   c. *Prefeitura (Cámara Municipal ℗)*
5. *O senhor vê aquela* _____ (store)?
   a. *direita*
   b. *loja*
   c. *barbearia*
6. *Há um* _____ (doctor) *na casa ao lado.*
   a. *médico*
   b. *farmácia*
   c. *nome*
7. *Tem o nome na* _____ (door).
   a. *mesma*
   b. *porta*
   c. *consultório*
8. *Ele tem o consultório na mesma* _____ (house) *em que mora?*
   a. *porta*
   b. *lado*
   c. *casa*
9. *Um pouco* _____ (before) *de chegar à rodovia.*
   a. *barbearia*
   b. *antes*
   c. *jornais*
10. *Onde* _____ (can I) *comprar?*
    a. *posso*
    b. *conheço*
    c. *vejo*

ANSWERS
1—b; 2—b; 3—a; 4—b; 5—b; 6—a; 7—b; 8—c; 9—b;
10—a.

B. To Know: *Conhecer, Saber*

conheço	*sei*
(conheces)	*(sabes)*
conhece	*sabe*
conhecemos	*sabemos*
conhecem	*sabem*

Conhecer is used with the meaning of "to be familiar/acquainted with something or somebody."

Você conhece São Paulo?	Do you know São Paulo?
Conheço o pai dele muito bem.	I know his father very well.

Saber means "to have knowledge."

Não sei o nome dela.	I don't know her name.
Vocês sabem onde ela mora?	Do you know where she lives?
Você sabe as horas?	Do you know the time?
Não sei quem é o seu pai.	I don't know who your father is.

It is also used in such constructions as "to know how," "can":

Eu sei nadar.	I can swim.
Tu sabes falar inglês?	Can you speak English?
Não sei dirigir (*conduzir* Ⓟ).	I can't drive.

C. MORE ABOUT THE USE OF PORTUGUESE VERBS

1. In Portuguese, the infinitive is used after a preposition (whereas in English, prepositions are followed by a present participle):

Ele saiu sem dizer nada.
He left without saying anything.

Depois de comer, vou dormir.
After eating, I am going to sleep.

Fechei as portas antes de sair.
I closed the doors before leaving.

2. The infinitive can be used as the subject of the sentence. Notice that in English there are two ways to express the same idea:

Ver é crer.
To see is to believe./Seeing is believing.

Viajar só, *(sozinho)* **tem suas vantagens.**
To travel alone has its advantages./Traveling alone has . . .

3. Certain verbs govern the infinitive without a preposition. Among these are: *dever* (to have to), *querer* (to want), *poder* (to be able to), *precisar* (to need), *decidir* (to decide), *tentar* (to try), *saber* (to know), *esperar* (to hope/wait), *deixar* (to allow), *preferir* (to prefer).

Você deve ficar aqui.   You must stay here.
Ela espera ir ao Brasil. She hopes to go to Brazil.

Prefiro fazer isto.	I prefer to do this.
Quero comer.	I want to eat.
Precisamos ir.	We need to go.

4. Certain verbs are followed by a preposition before an infinitive. Some require *a;* others take *de, em,* or *por.* There is no rule for determining which preposition follows any verb. The proper preposition should be learned individually. Among the most common are: *começar a* (to start to), *pensar em* (to think of), *acabar de* (to finish), *lembrar-se de* (to remember), *aprender a* (to learn to), *gostar de* (to like), *aconselhar a* (to advise), *parar de* (to stop), *cuidar de* (to take care of), *insistir em* (to insist on), etc.

Para onde ele pensa em ir?	Where does he think about going to?
Ele acaba de chegar.	He just arrived.
O que você gostaria de fazer?	What would you like to do?
Ele está aprendendo a tocar piano.	He's learning how to play the piano.
Quando ele começou a trabalhar?	When did he start working?

5. The equivalent to the English "have to"/"ought to"/"must" in Portuguese is *ter que* (or *ter de*) followed by the infinitive:

Temos que partir cedo.	We have to leave early.
Tenho de estudar mais.	I have to study more.
Ela tem que comer agora.	She must eat now.

LESSON 38

A. THE MEDIA AND COMMUNICATIONS
(Meios de Communicação)

1. **Hugo:[1] Eu não queria que você comprasse o jornal de hoje.**
   Hugo: I wish you wouldn't buy today's paper.

2. **Gabriela: Por que não? O que aconteceu?**
   Gabriela: Why not? What happened?

3. **H: As manchetes dos jornais trazem notícias chocantes. A primeira página traz notícias sobre desastres, roubos, assassinatos, estupros, guerras, e secas—nada mais.**
   H: The newspaper headlines bring shocking news. The front page has news about disasters, robberies, murders, rapes, wars, and droughts—nothing else.

4. **G: Seria melhor que não houvesse tais notícias, mas elas representam fatos da vida real.**
   G: It would be better if there weren't any such news, but these are facts of life.

5. **H: Se pelo menos pudessemos nos basear nas experiências do passado!**
   H: If only we could learn from the past!

6. **G: Talvez não devessemos ler a primeira página ou os editoriais, assim evitaríamos as notícias chocantes.**
   G: Maybe we shouldn't read the first page or the editorials; that way we'd avoid the shocking news.

7. **H: Tão pouco me interessam as seçoes de finanças, esportes, crítica de livros, e os classificados.**
   H: The financial pages, sports, book reviews, and classified sections don't interest me much.

8. **G: Poderia divertirlhe com as palavras cruzadas, a parte cômica, ou a coluna social.**

G: You could entertain yourself with the crossword puzzle and the comic strips or the gossip column.

9. **H: É melhor não comprar o jornal, não o ler.**

H: It's better not to buy the paper . . . not to read it.

10. **G: A culpa não é só da emprensa. Os satélites e as faxes também nos permitem saber todas as tragédias do mundo com grande rapidez. Mas há sempre algo interessante, e estou certa de que haverá boas notícias também!**

G: It's not just the fault of the press. Satellites and fax machines allow us to find out about all the world's misfortunes very quickly. But there's always something interesting, and I'm sure that there will be good news, too!

B. AT THE AIRPORT
(No Aeroporto)

1. **Francisca: Com licença, Sr., aqui estão nossas passagens, passaportes, e vistos.**

Francisca: Excuse me, sir, here are our tickets, passports, and visas.

2. **Enrique: Desculpe, Senhora, mas este passaporte não é seu. Ele pertence a uma jovem.**

Enrique: Pardon me, madam. This passport isn't yours. It belongs to a young girl.

3. **F: Não é meu? Meu Deus! Desculpe, eu me enganei. Nossa filha não está viajando conosco. Um momento! Bem, aqui está, este é o meu passaporte.**

F: It isn't mine? Shoot! I'm sorry, I made a mistake. Our daughter isn't traveling with us. One moment. Okay, here it is, this is my passport.

4. **E: O vôo está atrasado. Sairá do portão 23 às oito e meia. Você quer despachar a bagagem?**

E: Your flight is late. It will leave from gate 23 at 8:30.
Do you want to check your bags?

5. **F: A minha não, mas a dele sim.**
   F: Mine, no, but his, yes.

6. **E: Aqui está o recibo. Siga à direita, passe pela
   segurança, e depois terá você que fazer uma
   declaração à alfandega.**
   E: Here's your receipt. Go to the right, pass through
   security, and then you will have to make a customs
   declaration.

7. **F: Queremos escolher assentos na seção de não-
   fumantes.**
   F: We want to sit in the non-smoking section.

8. **E: No portão de embarque haverá um agente que
   lhe indicará os assentos. Boa viagem!**
   E: At the departure gate there'll be an agent who will
   show you your seats. Have a good trip!

QUIZ 37

1. De que eles estão falando?
   a. *a guerra*
   b. *o jornal*
   c. *a emprensa*

2. *De onde deveriamos aprender?*
   a. *do futuro*
   b. *do presente*
   c. *do passado*

3. *Como nos chegam as notícias?*
   a. *pelos classificados*
   b. *via satélite*
   c. *por telefone*

4. *A primeira página apresenta* _____.
   a. *esportes*
   b. *fatos*
   c. *notícias*
5. *Um jornal tem varias* _____.
   a. *acidentes/disastres*
   b. *seções*
   c. *títulos cabeçalhos*
6. *De quem é o passaporte?*
   a. *da menina*
   b. *da senhora*
   c. *do homem*
7. *Onde eles querem se sentar?*
   a. *na primeira classe*
   b. *na seção de fumantes*
   c. *na seção de não-fumantes*
8. *O vôo está* _____ .
   a. *atrasado*
   b. *aquí*
   c. *adiantado*
9. *Teremos que passar pela* _____.
   a. *esquerda*
   b. *bagagem*
   c. *segurança*
10. *Nossa filha não* _____ *conosco.*
   a. *come*
   b. *trabalha*
   c. *viaja*

ANSWERS
1—b; 2—c; 3—b; 4—c; 5—b; 6—a; 7—c; 8—a; 9—c;
10—c.

B. THE MOST COMMON VERBS AND THEIR MOST COMMON FORMS

1. To do, to make *(fazer):*

	PRESENT	PAST	FUTURE
eu	*faço*	*fiz*	*farei*
(tu) (sing.)	*(fazes)*	*(fizeste)*	*(farás)*
você, ele, ela	*faz*	*fez*	*fará*
nós	*fazemos*	*fizemos*	*faremos*
(vós) (pl.)	*(fazeis)*	*(fizestes)*	*(fareis)*
vocês, eles, elas	*fazem*	*fizeram*	*farão*

IMPERATIVE

Familiar:	Polite:
Faz! (sing.)	*Faça! (sing.)*
	Façam! (pl.)

Eu mesmo o fiz.	I made/did it myself.
Eles farão muitas promessas.	They will make many promises.
Ela o faz de algodão.	She is making it (out) of cotton.
Faça o mais cedo possível.	Do (it) as soon as possible.

2. To have *(haver;* auxiliary verb, usually replaced by *ter* today):

	PRESENT	PAST	FUTURE
eu	*hei*	*houve*	*haverei*
(tu) (sing.)	*(hás)*	*(houveste)*	*(haverás)*
você, ele, ela	*há*	*houve*	*haverá*
nós	*havemos*	*houvemos*	*haveremos*
(vós) (pl.)	*(haveis)*	*(houvestes)*	*(havereis)*
vocês, eles, elas	*hão*	*houveram*	*haverão*

IMPERATIVE

Familiar:	Polite:
(Há!) (sing.)	*Haja! (sing.)*
	Hajam! (pl.)

O que é que havia aqui antes?	What was here before?
Não há estrelas no céu.	There are no stars in the sky.
Elas não haviam favorecido isso.	They *(fem.)* had not favored that.
Não houve guerra nesse ano.	There was no war that year.

3. To go *(ir):*

	PRESENT	PAST	FUTURE
eu	*vou*	*fui*	*irei*
(tu) (sing.)	*(vais)*	*(foste)*	*(irás)*
você, ele, ela	*vai*	*foi*	*irá*
nós	*vamos*	*fomos*	*iremos*
(vós) (pl.)	*(ides)*	*(fostes)*	*(ireis)*
vocês, eles, elas	*vão*	*foram*	*irão*

IMPERATIVE

Familiar:	Polite:
Vai! (sing.)	*Vá! (sing.)*
	Vão (pl.)

Vou ao Brasil no verão.	I am going to Brazil in the summer.
Ele vai sozinho.	He's going by himself.
Eu vou jogar tênis amanhã.	I'm going to play tennis tomorrow. (This construction is often used to express future actions.)

Ele foi vê-la.	He went to see her.
Vamos!	Let's go!
Vá com ela.	Go with her.

4. To come *(vir):*

IMPERATIVE

	PRESENT	PAST	FUTURE
eu	*venho*	*vim*	*virei*
(tu) (sing.)	*(vens)*	*(vieste)*	*(virás)*
você, ele, ela	*vem*	*veio*	*virá*
nós	*vimos*	*viemos*	*viremos*
(vós) (pl.)	*(vindes)*	*(viestes)*	*(vireis)*
vocês, eles, elas	*vêm*	*vieram*	*virão*

Familiar:	Polite:
Vem! (sing.)	*Venha! (sing.)*
	Venham! (pl.)

Familiar:	Polite:
Vem comigo?	Are you coming with me?
Ninguém veio.	Nobody came.
Eles vêm todos os dias.	They come every day.
Ela virá às duas horas.	She will come at two o'clock.
Venham comigo.	Come with me.

5. To believe *(crer):*

	PRESENT	PAST	FUTURE
eu	*creio*	*cri*	*crerei*
(tu) (sing.)	*(crês)*	*(creste)*	*(crerás)*
você, ele, ela	*crê*	*creu*	*crerá*

nós	cremos	cremos	creremos
(vós) (pl.)	(credes)	(crestes)	(crereis)
vocês, eles, elas	crêem	creram	crerão

IMPERATIVE

Familiar:	Polite
Crê! (sing.)	Creia! (sing.)
	Creiam! (pl.)

| Ele não crê em nada. | He doesn't believe in anything. |

6. To give (dar):

	PRESENT	PAST	FUTURE
eu	dou	dei	darei
(tu) (sing.)	(dás)	(deste)	(darás)
você, ele, ela	dá	deu	dará
nós	damos	demos	daremos
(vós) (pl.)	(dais)	(destes)	(dareis)
vocês, eles, elas	dão	deram	darão

IMPERATIVE

Familiar:	Polite:
Dá! (sing.)	Dê! (sing.)
	Dêem! (pl.)

Ele me deu essa lâmpada.	He gave me that lamp.
Quando você vai me dar resposta?	When are you going to give me an answer?
Dê-lhe o título.	Give him the title.

7. To have *(ter):*

	PRESENT	PAST	FUTURE
eu	*tenho*	*tive*	*terei*
(tu) (sing.)	*(tens)*	*(tiveste)*	*(terás)*
você, ele, ela	*tem*	*teve*	*terá*
nós	*temos*	*tivemos*	*teremos*
(vós) (pl.)	*(tendes)*	*(tivestes)*	*(tereis)*
vocês, eles, elas	*têm*	*tiveram*	*terão*

IMPERATIVE

Familiar:	Polite:
Tem! (sing.)	*Tenha! (sing.)*
	Tenham! (pl.)

Ela tem muitos vestidos nôvos.	She has many new dresses.
Alguém tem que representar a escola.	Somebody has to represent the school.
Tiveram outra crise.	They had another crisis.
Tenha cuidado!	Be careful!

8. To say *(dizer):*

	PRESENT	PAST	FUTURE
eu	*digo*	*disse*	*direi*
(tu) (sing.)	*(dizes)*	*(disseste)*	*(dirás)*
você, ele, ela	*diz*	*disse*	*dirá*
nós	*dizemos*	*dissemos*	*diremos*
(vós) (pl.)	*(dizeis)*	*(dissestes)*	*(direis)*
vocês, eles, elas	*dizem*	*disseram*	*dirão*

IMPERATIVE

Familiar:	Polite:
Diz! (sing.)	*Diga! (sing.)*
	Digam! (pl.)

Dizem que ele tem muitas dívidas.	They say he has many debts.
Ela disse que tinha certas dúvidas.	She said she had certain doubts.
Que dirá ela amanhã?	What will she say tomorrow? I wonder what she will say tomorrow.
Diga-me a verdade.	Tell me the truth.

9. To put *(pôr):*

	PRESENT	PAST	FUTURE
eu	*ponho*	*pus*	*porei*
(tu) (sing.)	*(pões)*	*(puseste)*	*(porás)*
você, ele, ela	*põe*	*pôs*	*porá*
nós	*pomos*	*pusemos*	*poremos*
(vós) (pl.)	*(pondes)*	*(pusestes)*	*(poreis)*
vocês, eles, elas	*põem*	*puseram*	*porão*

IMPERATIVE

Familiar:	Polite:
Põe! (sing.)	*Ponha! (sing.)*
	Ponham! (pl.)

Onde o senhor pôs as instruções?	Where did you put the instructions?
Ponha a lenha aqui.	Put the wood here.

Vamos pôr as revistas na mesa.

We are going to put the magazines on the table.

Ele não porá nada na cadeira.

He will not put anything on the chair.

10. To wish, to want *(querer):*

	PRESENT	PAST	FUTURE
eu	*quero*	*quis*	*quererei*
(tu) (sing.)	*(queres)*	*(quiseste)*	*(quererás)*
você, ele, ela	*quer*	*quis*	*quererá*
nós	*queremos*	*quisemos*	*quereremos*
vós (pl.)	*(quereis)*	*(quisestes)*	*(querereis)*
vocês, eles, elas	*querem*	*quiseram*	*quererão*

IMPERATIVE

Familiar:	Polite:
Quer! (sing.)	*Queira! (sing.)*
	Queiram! (pl.)

Quero permanecer aqui. I want to stay here.

Não quiseram perdoar-nos. They wouldn't (didn't want to) pardon us.

11. To bring *(trazer):*

	PRESENT	PAST	FUTURE
eu	*trago*	*trouxe*[3]	*trarei*
(tu) (sing.)	*(trazes)*[4]	*(trouxeste)*	*(trarás)*
você, ele, ela	*traz*	*trouxe*	*trará*

nós	trazemos	trouxemos	traremos
(vós) (pl.)	(trazeis)	(trouxestes)	(trareis)
vocês, eles, elas	trazem	trouxeram	trarão

IMPERATIVE

Familiar:	Polite:
Traz! (sing.)	*Traga! (sing.)*
	Tragam! (pl.)

Que história triste nos traz hoje?	What sad story are you bringing us today?
Ele viajou por Portugal mas não me trouxe nada.	He traveled through Portugal but he didn't bring me anything.
Traga para cá!	Bring it here!

12. To leave *(sair)*:

	PRESENT	PAST	FUTURE
eu	saio	saí	sairei
(tu) (sing.)	(sais)	(saíste)	(sairás)
você, ele, ela	sai	saiu	sairá
nós	saímos	saímos	sairemos
(vós) (pl.)	(saís)	(saístes)	(saireis)
vocês, eles, elas	saem	saíram	sairão

IMPERATIVE

Familiar:	Polite:
Saí! (sing.)	*Saia! (sing.)*
	Saiam! (pl.)

Saio agora.	I'm leaving now.
Ela saiu por aqui.	She went out this way.

13. To see *(ver):*

	PRESENT	PAST	FUTURE
eu	*vejo*	*vi*	*verei*
(tu) (sing.)	*(vês)*	*(viste)*	*(verás)*
você, ele, ela	*vê*	*viu*	*verá*
nós	*vemos*	*vimos*	*veremos*
(vós) (pl.)	*(vedes)*	*(vistes)*	*(vereis)*
vocês, eles, elas	*vêem*	*viram*	*verão*

IMPERATIVE

Familiar:	Polite:
Vê! (sing.)	*Veja! (sing.)*
	Vejam! (pl.)

Ele não vê bem sem os óculos.	He can't see well without his glasses.
Mas eu os vi ontem!	But I saw them yesterday!
O senhor verá que o que digo é verdade.	You'll see that what I say is true.

14. To know *(saber):*

	PRESENT	PAST	FUTURE
eu	*sei*	*soube*	*saberei*
(tu) (sing.)	*(sabes)*	*(soubeste)*	*(saberás)*
você, ele, ela	*sabe*	*soube*	*saberá*

	PRESENT	PAST	FUTURE
nós	*sabemos*	*soubemos*	*saberemos*
(vós) (pl.)	*(sabeis)*	*(soubestes)*	*(sabereis)*
vocês, eles, elas	*sabem*	*souberam*	*saberão*

Familiar:	Polite:
Sabe! (sing.)	*Saiba! (sing.)*
	Saibam! (pl.)

Sei que a vida lá está cara.	I know that living there is expensive.
Eu soube o segredo ontem.	I found out (learned) the secret yesterday.
Os senhores saberão o valor mais tarde.	You will know (find out) its value later.

15. To be able to *(poder)*:

	PRESENT	PAST	FUTURE
eu	*posso*	*pude*	*poderei*
(tu) (sing.)	*(podes)*	*(pudeste)*	*(poderás)*
você, ele, ela	*pode*	*pôde*	*poderá*
nós	*podemos*	*pudemos*	*poderemos*
(vós) (pl.)	*(podeis)*	*(pudestes)*	*(podereis)*
vocês, eles, elas	*podem*	*puderam*	*poderão*

Familiar:	Polite:
Pode! (sing.)	*Possa! (sing.)*
	Possam! (pl.)

Não pode chover mais.	It can't rain any more.
Poderei escolher o melhor?	Will I be able to pick the best one?
Posso ligar agora?	Can I connect it (turn it on) now?

LESSON 39

A. What's in a Name?

Como ele se chama?
What's his name?

Ele se chama *(Chama-se)* **João Coutinho.**
His name is João (John) Coutinho.

Como se chama a jovem que está com ele?
What's the name of the young lady with him?

Ela se chama Maria Campos. *(Chama-se Maria Campos.)*
Her name is Maria (Mary) Campos.

Como o pai dela se chama?
What's her father's name?

O pai dela se chama *(chama-se)* **Carlos Campos.**
His name is Carlos (Charles) Campos.

Mas eu o conheço *(conheço-o)***! Ele é juiz, não é?**
Why, I know him! He's a judge, isn't he?

É. E você conhece a esposa dele, a dona Ana?
That's right. And do you know his wife, Dona Ana?

Não conheço, mas o João Campos deve ser irmão dessa jovem.
I don't know her, but João (John) Campos must be that girl's brother.

---

[3] In these forms *x* is pronounced like *s* in see.
[4] No difference in pronunciation between singular and plural forms.

Você está certa. *(Tem razão.)* **Todos nós lhe chamamos Joãozinho. E ela tem outro irmão, Chico.**
You're right. We all call him Joãozinho (Johnny). And she has another brother, Chico.

Ah, sim! Francisco.
Of course! Francisco (Francis).

Mas mais interessante ainda é que a Maria tem duas irmãs, uma mais velha e a outra mais nova, e ambas são bonitas.
But even more interesting is the fact that Maria has two sisters, one older and one younger than she is, and both of them are pretty.

Não me diga! Como se chamam?
You don't say! What are their names?

A mais velha é Isabel Gomes, quer dizer, é casada. Casou com o senhor Gomes.
The older one is Isabel Gomes, that is, she is married. She married Mr. Gomes.

O senhor Eduardo Gomes?
Mr. Eduardo (Edward) Gomes?

Esse mesmo.
That's right.

E a irmã mais nova?
How about the younger sister?

A Teresinha? É uma beleza.
Theresa ("little Theresa")? She's a beauty.

Diga-me mais.
Tell me more.

Tem onze anos. E ...
She's eleven years old. And ...

Chega. Vamos tomar um cafezinho.
That's enough. Let's go get some coffee.

B. NOTES ON PORTUGUESE NAMES

Chamar-se is a reflexive verb, literally "to call oneself."

eu me chamo	*nós nos chamamos*
(tu te chamas)	*(vós vos chamais)*
ele se chama	*eles se chamam*

See Lesson 15, Part E, and Item 5 of Section 18 of the grammar summary.

Dona and the first name are often used to refer to a married woman. Thus, *a senhora Campos,* Mrs. Campos, would often be referred to by those who know her as *Dona Ana.* (In Portugal, *a Sra. D. Ana* is used.) *Dona* can also be used with unmarried and even young ladies.

Jovem refers to a young person, masculine or feminine. Modifying words will make the reference clearer: *irmão dessa jovem* brother of that young girl; *irmão desse jovem* brother of that young man.

Você está certo.	You are right.
Tem razão.	You are right.
Não me diga!	("Don't tell me!")
	You don't say!
Esse mesmo.	The same one.
E a irmã mais nova?	And the younger sister?

LESSON 40

A. Fun in Portuguese

Uma Perda de Pouca Importância

(A Minor Loss)

—Tenha a bondade de me dar *(dar-me)* "A Liberdade."
Não tenho troco. Pode trocar esta nota?[1]
—O senhor me paga *(O senhor paga)* amanhã—diz a
vendedora.
—E se eu morrer esta noite?
—Ora! A perda não seria grande.

"Please give me a copy of *Liberty*. I don't have any
change. Can you change this bill?"
"You can pay me tomorrow," says the vendor.
"What if I should die tonight?"
"Oh, it wouldn't be a great loss."

Uma Lição de Etiqueta

(A Lesson in Etiquette)

Pedro e João vão a um restaurante para jantar. Ambos
pedem um bife. O garçom *(empregado* Ⓟ*)* os serve *(serve-
os)*. Quando Pedro tira para si o maior bife *(bife maior)*,
João, zangado, diz *(diz-lhe)*:
—Que maneiras *(que)* você tem! Foi o primeiro a se
servir *(servir-se)* e tirou o maior.

---

[1] Notice how Portuguese punctuation in dialogues differs from English: (1)
there are no quotation marks and (2) each change of speaker is indicated by
a dash (see Item 1 of Section 3 of the grammar summary).

Pedro responde:
—Se você estivesse em (no) meu lugar, qual teria tirado?
—O menor *(mais pequeno* Ⓟ*)*, **naturalmente.**
—Então, por que se queixa? Não o tem aí?

Peter and John go to a restaurant for dinner. They both order steak. The waiter serves them. When Peter grabs the bigger steak, John says to him angrily:

"What bad manners you have! You helped yourself first and you took the bigger piece."

Peter answers:

"If you had been in my place, which would you have taken?"

"The smaller one, of course."

"Then what are you complaining about? You have it, don't you?"

NOTES
Perda loss.
De pouca importância of little importance.
Tenha a bondade. Please. ("Have the kindness.")
O senhor (me) paga amanhã. "You pay (me) tomorrow."
E se eu morrer esta noite? And if I die tonight? *Morrer* is a form of the future subjunctive (see Items 3 and 4 of Section 29 of the grammar summary).
A perda não seria grande. The loss would not be great. *Seria* is the conditional of the verb *ser* (see Section 32 of the grammar summary).

Jantar to have dinner; dinner.
Pedem they ask for; from *pedir* (to ask for).
Foi o primeiro a se servir (servir-se) "You were the first in serving yourself."
Se você estivesse em (no) meu lugar, qual teria tirado? "If you had been in my place, which would you have taken?"
Estivesse is the imperfect subjunctive of *estar* (to be) (see

Item 2, Section 29 and Item 3, Section 33 of the grammar summary). *Teria tirado* is the perfect conditional of *tirar* (to take) (see Item 3, Section 32 of the grammar summary). *Então, por que se queixa? Não o tem aí?* Then, why do you complain? Don't you have it there?

Um Otimista[2]

(An Optimist)

O chefe de uma (duma) firma comercial importante, olhando uma ficha de pedido de emprego, fica surpreso *(surpreendido ℗)* ao notar que o candidato não tinha muita experiência, e pedia um ordenado excessivo.

—Não acha—perguntou perplexo—que está pedindo *(está a pedir ℗)* um ordenado excessivo em vista da sua pouca experiência?
—Pelo contrário—respondeu o pretendente—um trabalho do qual não se sabe absolutamente nada é mais difícil e deve merecer um pagamento melhor.

The head of an important firm, looking at an application, is astonished on noticing that the applicant for the position, although lacking experience, is asking for an excessive salary.

Rather puzzled, he asks him: "Don't you think you're asking for too high a salary, considering the little experience you have?"

"On the contrary," replies the applicant. "Work that one knows nothing about is more difficult and should be better paid."

[2] *optimista ℗.*

NOTES

Olhando looking; from *olhar* (to look).

Fica surpreso (surpreendido) is ("remains") surprised, astonished.

Não acha? Don't you think? *Achar* (to find) also has taken on the meaning of "to believe, to think."

Respondeu and *perguntou* are past tense forms of *responder* and *perguntar.*

O Espírito Prático

(The Practical Mind)

Um comerciante apareceu um dia na casa dum fazendeiro *(lavrador* Ⓟ) e pediu um quilo de manteiga. O fazendeiro *(lavrador* Ⓟ) respondeu que trocaria esse quilo de manteiga por um par de meias de lã.

Quando o comerciante contou o fato[3] à mulher *(à sua esposa* Ⓟ), ela propôs o seguinte:

—Temos uma colcha de lã; eu a desfaço *(desfaço-a* Ⓟ) e dela farei um par de meias.

Assim fez, e o comerciante deu o par de meias e recebeu um quilo de manteiga. Desde então, quando o comerciante precisava de manteiga, a sua mulher desfazia um pouco da colcha e tricotava umas meias. Mas chegou um dia em que só tinha lã para uma única meia. O comerciante a levou *(levou-a* Ⓟ) ao fazendeiro *(lavrador* Ⓟ), pedindo meio quilo de manteiga.

—Não—respondeu o fazendeiro *(lavrador)*—dou-lhe um quilo. A minha mulher desfaz as meias para uma colcha que está fazendo *(a fazer* Ⓟ). Só precisa desta meia para acabá-la.

[3] *facto* Ⓟ.

A merchant went to the house of a farmer and asked him for a kilogram of butter. The farmer answered that he would exchange it for a pair of woolen socks.

When the merchant told his wife about it, she proposed: "We have an afghan; I'll unravel it and I'll make a pair of socks."

She did so and the merchant gave the pair of socks in exchange for the kilogram of butter. From then on, when the merchant needed butter, his wife unraveled some of the afghan and knitted some socks. But one day she had just enough wool for one sock. The merchant took it to the farmer and asked him for half a kilogram of butter.

"No," said the farmer, "I'll give you a kilogram. My wife unravels the socks for an afghan she is making. All she needs is this one sock to finish it."

NOTES

O espírito the spirit, mind.

Trocaria he would exchange; from *trocar* (to exchange, change).

Propôs she proposed; from *propôr* (to propose, suggest).

Desfaço I'll unravel; from *desfazer* (to unravel, undo).

Farei I'll make; from *fazer* (to make, do).

Levou he took; from *levar* (to take away/along).

Um pouco de a little of.

Tinha she had; from *ter* (to have).

Pedindo asking; from *pedir* (to ask for).

Dou I'll give; from *dar* (to give).

Acabá-la to finish it; a combination of *acabar* (to finish) and *a* "it," referring to the afghan.

B. Important Signs

Homens or *Cavalheiros*	Men
Senhoras or *Damas*	Women
Lavatório	Lavatory

O banheiro[4]	Bathroom/Restroom
Água quente/fria	Hot/Cold Water
Fechado	Closed
Aberto	Open
É proibido fumar	No Smoking
É proibido entrar	No Admittance
Bata	Knock
Toque a compainha	Ring Bell
Curva	Curve
Pare!	Stop!
Siga!	Go!
Cuidado! Atenção!	Look Out! Attention!
Perigo!	Danger!
Devagar!	Slow!
Desvio	Detour
Cautela!	Caution!
Conserve a sua direita	Keep to the Right
Siga pela direita	Keep to the Right
Ponte	Bridge
É proibido estacionar	No Parking
Câmbio	(Money) Exchange
Informações	Information
Sala de espera	Waiting Room
Vagão	Freight Car
Ferrovia	Railroad
Expresso or *Rápido*	Express
Parada (Paragem ℗)	Stop (bus, streetcar, etc.)
A estação ferroviária	Train Station
A estação rodoviária	Bus Station
O aeroporto	Airport
O porto	Port/Harbor
Em conserto	Under Repair
Caixa (x = sh)	Cashier

[4] In Brazil, sometimes public restrooms display a "W.C." sign at the door.

Entrada	Entrance
Saída	Exit
Quartos mobiliados	Furnished Rooms
Apartamentos	Apartments
A pensão	Boarding house
A delegacia de polícia	Police Station
O posto de gasolina	Gas Station
O museu	Museum
O correio	Post Office
A livraria	Bookstore
A papelaria	Stationery Store
O salão de beleza	Beauty Shop
A barbearia	Barbershop
A lavanderia (lavandaria Ⓟ)	Laundry
O supermercado	Supermarket
A padaria	Bakery
A farmácia	Pharmacy
O teatro	Theater
A peça de teatro	A Play
O cinema	Movie Theater
A praça de touros	Bullring
A boite[5]	Nightclub
O café e bar	Tavern/Bar
Fazer Cooper Ⓑ	Jogging
O golfe (golfo Ⓟ)	Golf
O tênis	Tennis
A ginástica	Gymnastics
O futebol	Soccer
O futebol americano	Football
O beisebol	Baseball
O basquetebol	Basketball
O time (a equipa Ⓟ)	Team
O jogo	Match

[5] French word *boîte*, pronounced *bwat*.

O ginásio	Gymnasium
O estádio	Stadium
O clube	Club
O campo de golfe	Golf Course
A quadra de tênis	Tennis Court
A piscina	Swimming Pool
A pista	Track
O taco para golfe	Golf Club (stick)
O armário com cadeado	Locker
O vestiário	Locker Room

QUIZ 38

1. *Entrada*	a. No Smoking
2. *Desvio*	b. Express
3. *Devagar!*	c. No Parking
4. *Fechado*	d. Open
5. *Aberto*	e. Exit
6. *É proibido fumar*	f. Stop!
7. *Expresso*	g. Detour
8. *É proibido estacionar*	h. Entrance
9. *Saída*	i. Closed
10. *Pare!*	j. Slow!

ANSWERS
1—h; 2—g; 3—j; 4—i; 5—d; 6—a; 7—b; 8—c; 9—e; 10—f.

FINAL QUIZ
When you get 100% on this quiz you have mastered the course.

1. *Faça o favor de* _____ (tell me) *onde é a estação.*
   a. *diga-me*
   b. *me dizer (dizer-me)*
   c. *me trazer (trazer-me)*

2. _____ (can) *me dizer (dizer-me) onde é o correio?*
   a. *pode*
   b. *tem*
   c. *custa*

3. *Onde* _____ (is there) *um bom restaurante?*
   a. *faz*
   b. *há*
   c. *hoje*

4. _____ (bring me) *um pouco de pão.*
   a. *conhecê-la*
   b. *servi-lo*
   c. *traga-me*

5. _____ (I need) *presunto.*
   a. *preciso de*
   b. *tem*
   c. *ninguém*

6. _____ (I would like) *um pouco mais de carne.*
   a. *traga-me*
   b. *preciso de*
   c. *gostaria de*

7. *Vou* _____ (to introduce you) *a meu amigo.*
   a. *apresentá-lo*
   b. *o prazer*
   c. *vê-lo*

8. *Onde* _____ (is) *o livro?*
   a. *está*
   b. *é*
   c. *este*

9. *Tenha* _____ (the goodness) *de falar mais devagar.*
   a. *a bondade*
   b. *o favor*
   c. *o prazer*

10. _____ (we speak) *português.*
    a. *falam*
    b. *ficamos*
    c. *falamos*

11. _____ (Go) *lá.*
    a. *vá*
    b. *fale*
    c. *venho*

12. _____ (Come) *cá.*
    a. *venha*
    b. *comigo*
    c. *vamos*

13. *Como se* _____ (call) *o senhor?*
    a. *charuto*
    b. *chama*
    c. *chover*

14. *Que dia da* _____ (week) *é hoje?*
    a. *semana*
    b. *mês*
    c. *ano*

15. *Que* _____ (time) *são?*
    a. *horas*
    b. *agora*
    c. *tempo*

16. *Não* _____ (I have) *cigarros.*
    a. *tempo*
    b. *tenho*
    c. *ter*

17. *O senhor* _____ (don't want) *carne?*
    a. *não fica*
    b. *não compra*
    c. *não quer*

18. _____ (Please) *de escrever o nome aqui.*
    a. *comprar*
    b. *faça o favor*
    c. *por certo*

19. _____ (There were) *muitos livros na livraria.*
    a. *há*
    b. *havia*
    c. *lá*

20. _____ (I prefer) *esta*.
    a. *prefiro*
    b. *prefere*
    c. *prefira*
21. *Vamos* _____ (to have dinner).
    a. *jantar*
    b. *almoçar*
    c. *mostrar*
22. *São* _____ (2:15).
    a. *duas e meia*
    b. *duas e quinze*
    c. *duas e cinco*
23. *Venha* _____ (tomorrow morning).
    a. *ontem pela manhã*
    b. *amanhã pela manhã*
    c. *amanhã ao meio-dia*
24. *Em que* _____ (can I) *servi-lo?*
    a. *pode*
    b. *chamo*
    c. *posso*
25. *Não* _____ (has) *importância*.
    a. *tenha*
    b. *tem*
    c. *houve*

ANSWERS
1—b; 2—a; 3—b; 4—c; 5—a; 6—c; 7—a; 8—a; 9—a;
10—c; 11—b; 12—a; 13—b; 14—a; 15—a; 16—b;
17—c; 18—b; 19—b; 20—a; 21—a; 22—b; 23—b;
24—c; 25—b.

SUMMARY OF PORTUGUESE GRAMMAR

1. THE ALPHABET

LETTER	NAME	LETTER	NAME	LETTER	NAME
a	*a*	j	*jota*	s	*esse*
b	*bê*	k	*ka*	t	*tê*
c	*cê*	l	*ele*	u	*u*
d	*dê*	m	*eme*	v	*vê*
e	*é*	n	*ene*	w	*dobliu*
f	*efe*	o	*ó*	x	*xis*
g	*gê*	p	*pê*	y	*ipsilão*
h	*agá*	q	*quê*	z	*zê*
i	*i*	r	*erre*		

2. PRONUNCIATION

SIMPLE VOWELS[1]

a 1. In a stressed position it is "open" as in *ah* or *father.*
   2. In unstressed positions and in the case of the article *a* and its plural *as* (the) it tends to be more "closed" like the final *a* in *America* (this is particularly true in Portugal and in general with unstressed final *a*).

e 1. "Open" as in *best; é* has this sound.
   2. "Closed" somewhat between the sound of *a* in *case* and *e* in *fez; ê* has this sound, as does nasal *e.*
   3. Variations occur in different areas:
    a. In a final unstressed position: In Brazil it varies between the sound of *i* in *did* and the *i* in *machine;* in Portugal it is often clipped sharply, being like a mute *e,* or it is dropped.

[1] Also see Lessons 1 and 3 of the conversation manual.

b. Stressed *e* before *j, ch, lh, nh* in Portugal can have the sound of final *a* in *America,* or of closed *e.*

c. In an unstressed position it is sometimes pronounced as *e* in *be* in parts of Brazil, as mute *e* in Portugal, or as *i* in *did* in both.

i   As *i* in *machine.*

o   1. "Open" as *o* in *off; ó* has this sound.

     2. "Closed" as in *rose; ô* has this sound and so does nasal *o.*

     3. In an unstressed position and in the case of the definite article *o, os* (the) it is also pronounced like *oo* in *boot;* this is heard quite regularly in Portugal, but less consistently in Brazil.

u   Approximates *u* in *rule.*

VOWEL COMBINATIONS[2]

ai   *ai* in *aisle.*
au   *ou* in *out.*
ei   *ey* in *they.*
éi   similar sound with open *e.*[3]
eu   *ey* of *they* plus *u* of *lute.*
éu   similar but with open *e.*
ia   *ya* in *yard.*
ié   *ye* in *yes.*
ie   similar but with close *e.*
io   *yo* in *yoke.*
iu   *e* plus *u* of *lute.*
oi   *oy* in *boy.*
ói   similar but with open *o.*
ou   *ou* in *soul.*
ua   *wah,* as *ua* in *quadrangle.*
ué   *we* in *wet.*
ui   *we* (if main stress is on *u,* however, like *u* of *lute* plus *e*).
uo   *wo* in *woe,* or as *uó.*

---

[2] Also see Lesson 3.

[3] The sound indicated in *éi* may also be given in the case of *ei* in some cases. This is also true of other members of the pairs given.

CONSONANTS[4]

Those consonants not mentioned are approximately like English.

c   Before *a, o,* and *u,* and before another consonant like *c* in *cut.*

c   Before *e* and *i* like *c* in *center.*

ch   As *ch* in *machine.*

d   As *d* in *dog;* it is pronounced forcefully in Rio de Janeiro and with some speakers (especially before *e* or *i*) it approximates the *j* in *just.*

g   Before *e* and *i* somewhat like *s* in *measure.*

g   Otherwise like *g* in *go.*

h   Not pronounced.

j   Like a soft *j* (see *g* above).

l   Formed with the tongue forward, the tip near the upper teeth.

l   In final position is quite soft.

lh   Like *lli* in *million.*

m   In initial position in a word or syllable, like English *m;* in final position in a syllable or word it tends to nasalize the preceding vowel; this nasal quality is especially strong in Brazil, but it may be slight or even absent in Continental Portuguese. (Lips should not be closed in pronouncing *m* at the end of a word.)[5]

n   In initial position like English *n;* in final position as for *m,* above.[5]

nh   As *ni* in *onion.*[5]

qu   Before *a* or *o* like *qu* in *quota.*

qu   Before *e* or *i* usually like *k.*

---

[4] Also see Lessons 1, 2, 3.
[5] Also see Lesson 4.

r   Pronounced by tapping the tip of the tongue against
    the gum ridge back of the upper teeth; initial *r* and
    rr are trilled with the tongue vibrating in this posi-
    tion; this pronunciation is heard in Portugal and in
    São Paulo. In Rio de Janeiro and in some other parts
    of Brazil *r* is pronounced back in the mouth (simi-
    lar to a French back *r*), initial *r* like a cross between
    h and German *ch*.

s   Between vowels is *z*, as *s* in *rose*.

s   Before a voiced consonant (a consonant sound pro-
    duced with a vibration of the cords, as *b, d, ge, gi,
    j, l, m, n, r, v, z*) tends to be as *z* in *azure*.

s   Before a voiceless consonant (a consonant sound pro-
    duced without a vibration of the vocal cords, as
    hard *c* and hard *g, f, p, qu, t*), and in the final posi-
    tion is pronounced as *s* in *see* in São Paulo and by
    some *cariocas*, and as *sh* in *shine* in Portugal and by
    some *cariocas*.

s   In initial position, or after a consonant, as *s* in *see*.

ss As *ss* in *passage*.

t   Much like English *t;* before *e* or *i* it is pronounced
    very forcefully by some *cariocas*, being palatalized
    and approximating the *ch* in *church*.

x   Like *z* in some words *(exame);* like *sh* in some words
    (caixa); like *s* in *see* in some words *(máximo);* like
    x in *wax* in some words *(táxi)*.

z   Is generally like *z* in *zeal;* however, in final position or
    before a voiceless consonant *s* is also heard in
    Brazil, *sh* is the common pronunciation in Portugal
    and is also used by some *cariocas;* before a voiced
    consonant it is like *z* in *azure* in Portugal and with
    some *cariocas*.

STRESS

1. Words ending in -a, -e, or -o (or in one of these vowels and -s, -m, or -ns) are stressed on the next to the last syllable:

casa	house
estudante	student
jovem	young

2. Words ending in a nasal vowel or diphthong (two vowels pronounced in union) are stressed on the last syllable:

papel	paper
manhã	morning
descansei	I rested

3. Words not following the above rules have a written accent mark that indicates the stressed syllable:

café	coffee
América	America
Itália	Italy
difícil	difficult
órfão	orphan

3. PUNCTUATION

In general, Portuguese punctuation is similar to English. Some differences are:

1. The dash is used in dialogues to indicate the words of the speakers:

—*Como vai o senhor?*
—*Muito bem, obrigado.*

2. Capitals are not used as frequently as in English. They are not used with adjectives of nationality, the days of the week and the months (except that in Portugal the months and the seasons are capitalized), nor is the pronoun *eu* (I) capitalized:

Eles são russos.	They are Russians.
Ela chegará na quinta.	She will arrive on Thursday.
Comprei o tapete em setembro (Setembro ℗).	I bought the carpet in September.

3. Suspension points (. . .) are used more frequently than in English to indicate interruption, etc.

4. Notice the variance from English in the use of the decimal point:

3.000.000 de habitantes	3,000,000 inhabitants
5.289 metros	5,289 meters
R$8.300,00	8,300 reais
1.800$00	1,800 escudos (Portugal)

4. SOME ORTHOGRAPHIC SIGNS

1. The tilde *(til)* (˜) over a vowel indicates a nasal sound:

posição	position

2. The dieresis *(trema)* (¨) is used in Brazil but not in Portugal in modern spelling over the letter *u* when it occurs after *q* or *g* and before *e* or *i* and is pronounced:

eloqüente (eloquente ℗)	eloquent

3. The cedilla *(cedilha)* is used with *c (ç)* when it is pronounced *s* before *a, o,* or *u:*

pedaço   piece, bit

4. Written accent marks are used to indicate the stressed syllable in words not following the regular rules (see Section 2 of the grammar summary). They also help distinguish between words spelled alike but with different meanings and between different forms of the same verb:

pôr to put   *por* for, by
pôde he was able, could   *pode* he is able, can
pára he stops   *para* for, to

The circumflex accent *(acento circunflexo)* (ˆ) is used over stressed closed *e* and *o;* the acute accent *(acento agudo)* (´) is used over stressed open *a, e,* and *o:*

conhecê-lo to know him   *câmera* camera
avô grandfather   *avó* grandmother
célebre famous   *fé* faith

The acute accent is used over stressed *i* or *u* when not combined with the preceding vowel:

país country   *pais* parents
saúde health   *saída* departure

The grave accent *(acento grave)* (`) indicates the contraction of preposition *a* with the definite articles *a* and/or *as.* Also, the same combination happens when the prepositions are followed by the demonstratives *aquele, aquela,* and *aquilo.* It is important to observe that in speech there is no distinction in stress between *a* and *à*. The listener will be able to tell from the semantic context that a contraction has occurred.

ir (a):   *Ele vai a + a biblioteca = Ele vai à biblioteca.*

go (to):   He's going to + the library = He's going to the library.

Vamos a + aqueles parques = Vamos àqueles parques.
     Let's go to those parks.

dar (a):   *Ele deu o livro a + as meninas = Ele deu o livro às meninas.*

give (to):   He gave the book to + the girls = He gave the book to the girls.

A final note about written accents:

Notice that the circumflex or acute accent is dropped when suffixes such as *-mente, -zinho, -íssimo,* etc. are added to a word because there is a change in the stressed syllable:

café—cafezinho	small cup of coffee
só—somente	only
útil—utilíssimo	very useful
câmera—camerazinha	little camera
ângulo—angulozinho	little angle

The grave accent indicates a combination of *a* and a word beginning with *a* (demonstratives, as *aquele,* etc.) or with the definite article *a:*

àqueles to those   *à* to the

5. SYLLABLE DIVISION

1. A single consonant goes with the following vowel:

a-fi-nal   finally

2. Two similar consonants usually split:

in-ter-rom-per   to interrupt

   ch, lh, nh do not split:

bor-ra-cha   rubber, eraser
o-re-lha   ear
so-nhar   to dream

3. Two vowels that are pronounced separately are split:

vi-ú-va   widow
ca-ir   to fall
vo-ar   to fly

6. THE DEFINITE ARTICLE

	SINGULAR	PLURAL
Masculine	*o*	*os*
Feminine	*a*	*as*

SINGULAR
o menino   the boy
a menina   the girl

PLURAL
os meninos   the boys
as meninas   the girls

The definite article is also used:

1. With abstract nouns:

A verdade vale mais que o dinheiro.	Truth is worth more than money.

2. With nouns used in a general sense:

A mulher brasileira veste (-se) bem.	Brazilian women dress well.
As mulheres americanas vestem (-se) bem.	American women dress well.
O óleo é muito útil.	Oil is very useful.

3. With the names of languages (except when immediately after *falar, de,* or *em;* the article is often not used with languages in some situations):

O português é fácil.	Portuguese is easy.
Falo inglês.	I speak English.
Tenho um livro de espanhol.	I have a Spanish book.

4. With expressions of time:

a semana passada	last week
às duas horas	at two o'clock

5. With days of the week:

na segunda-feira	on Monday

6. With the seasons:

a primavera (*Primavera* Ⓟ)	spring

7. With the names of most countries[7] and with other geo-
graphical names. On the other hand, names of most
cities do not require the use of articles.[8]

o Brasil	Brazil
a Itália	Italy
a África	Africa

8. With first names at times:

o Carlos	Charles

9. With titles or other words modifying a proper noun:

Ele jantou com o professor Silva.	He dined with Professor Silva.
O senhor Ramos não está em casa.	Mr. Ramos is not home.

10. With possessive pronouns and adjectives (Brazil uses
the article less with possessive adjectives than does
Portugal):

Este não é (o) meu lenço; é o seu.	This is not my handkerchief; it's yours.

11. With parts of the body and articles of clothing instead
of the possessive form:

O menino lavou as mãos.	The boy washed his hands.
Ela perdeu as luvas.	She lost her gloves.

---

[7] Main exceptions that do not need an article: *Portugal, Moçambique, Angola, Cuba, Israel, Porto Rico.*
[8] Main exceptions that need an article: *o Rio de Janeiro, o Porto.*

7. THE INDEFINITE ARTICLE

	SINGULAR	PLURAL
Masculine	*um*	uns
Feminine	*uma*	umas

SINGULAR

um homem	a man
uma mulher	a woman

PLURAL

uns homens	some (a few) men
umas mulheres	some (a few) women

The indefinite article is omitted:

1. Before a noun of occupation, nationality, etc. coming after the verb, especially if the noun is not modified:

Ele é capitão.	He is a captain.
Ela é aluna.	She is a student.

2. Before *cem* (a hundred) and *mil* (a thousand):

cem entrevistas	a hundred interviews
mil esperanças	a thousand hopes

3. In certain expressions:

Ele saiu sem chapéu.	He left without a hat.

8. CONTRACTIONS

1. Contractions of *de* with the definite article (*o/a* and its other forms):

de + o = do	*de + os = dos*	of the, from the
de + a = da	*de + as = das*	
a + o = ao	*a + os = aos*	to the
a + a = às	*a + as = às*	
em + o = no	*em + os = nos*	in the, on the
em + a = na	*em + as = nas*	
por + o = pelo	*por + os = pelos*	by, through the
por + a = pela	*por + as = pelas*	

do menino	*dos meninos*	of the boy, of the boys
da menina	*das meninas*	of the girl, of the girls
ao menino	*aos meninos*	to the boy, to the boys
à menina	*às meninas*	to the girl, to the girls
no lago	*nos lagos*	in (on) the lake, in the lakes
na pátria	*nas pátrias*	in the fatherland, in the fatherlands
pelo menino	*pelos meninos*	by the boy, by the boys
pela praça	*pela praça*	through the square, through the squares

2. Contractions of *de* and *em* with the indefinite article (*um* and its other forms) are optional, both contracted and noncontracted forms being used:

de um artigo or *dum artigo*	of an article
de uma árvore or *duma árvore*	of a tree
em umas aldeias or *numas aldeias*	in some villages

Por never makes contractions with indefinite articles.

De and *em* combine with the demonstrative forms (see Section 24 of the grammar summary):

daquela	of that one
naquele	in that one

3. The preposition *a* combines with the initial *a* of the demonstratives *aquele,* etc. and with the definite article *a:*

àquela	to that one
à baía	to the bay

9. DAYS OF THE WEEK

The days of the week are not capitalized. *Sábado* (Saturday) and *domingo* (Sunday) are masculine; the other days are feminine. The article is generally used except after *ser:*

segunda-feira or *segunda*	Monday
terça-feira or *terça*	Tuesday
quarta-feira or *quarta*	Wednesday
quinta-feira or *quinta*	Thursday
sexta-feira or *sexta*	Friday
sábado	Saturday
domingo	Sunday
Vou vê-lo na segunda.	I am going to see him Monday.
Hoje é terça.	Today is Tuesday.

"On Monday," "on Mondays," etc.:

na segunda-feira	on Monday
nas segundas-feiras	on Mondays

10. THE NAMES OF THE MONTHS

The names of the months are masculine and usually are not capitalized in Brazil (but they are in Portugal: *Janeiro*, etc.). They are usually used without the definite article:

janeiro	January
fevereiro	February
março	March
abril	April
maio	May
junho	June
julho	July
agosto	August
setembro	September
outubro	October
novembro	November
dezembro	December

11. THE NAMES OF THE SEASONS

a primavera	spring
o verão	summer
o outono	autumn
o inverno	winter

The names of the seasons are usually not capitalized in Brazil (but they are in Portugal). They are usually used with the definite article:

Ninguém vai lá no inverno.   Nobody goes there in the winter.

12. MASCULINE AND FEMININE

Nouns referring to males are masculine; nouns referring to females are feminine:

o pai	the father	*a mãe*	the mother
o filho	the son	*a filha*	the daughter
o homem	the man	*a mulher*	the woman
o leão	the lion	*a leoa*	the lioness

The masculine plural of certain nouns can include both genders:

os pais	the parents, the father and mother
os irmãos	the brothers, the brother and sister, the brothers and sisters

MASCULINE NOUNS

Nouns ending in diphthongs (vowel combinations pronounced together), *-m* (but not *-em*), *-s*, and *-o* are usually masculine:

o grau	the degree
o elogio	the praise
o dom	the gift
o lápis	the pencil
um abraço	an embrace, hug

Names of months, seas, rivers, mountains, and letters of the alphabet are generally masculine:

Janeiro é o primeiro mês.	January is the first month.
o Atlântico	the Atlantic

| *o Amazonas* | the Amazon (River) |
| *o dê* | the *d* |

FEMININE NOUNS

Nouns ending in *-a, -ie, -em, -ade, -ede,* and *-ice* are usually feminine:

a boca	the mouth
a ordem	the order
a amizade	friendship
a parede	the wall
a velhice	old age

Common exceptions:

| *o homem* | the man |

A good number of words ending in *-a* (or *-ma*), especially words of Greek origin, are masculine:

o programa	the program
o problema	the problem
o cinema	the cinema
o drama	the drama
o clima	the climate
o dia	the day
o mapa	the map
o idioma	the language

-a is added to some nouns ending in *-r:*

leitor	reader	*leitora*
director[9]	director	*diretora*[9]
orador	speaker, orator	*oradora*

---

[9] *director, directora* Ⓟ.

Names of islands and continents are usually feminine:

a Europa	Europe
a Sicília	Sicily
a América	America

13. THE PLURAL

1. Nouns ending in a vowel (including nasal vowels), or in a diphthong, usually add *s* to form the plural:

um ato[10]	one act	*dois atos*[10]	two acts
a maçã	the apple	*as maçãs*	the apples
a lei	the law	*as leis*	the laws

2. Words ending in -*ão* form the plural with -*ões:*

a ambição	ambition	*as ambições*	ambitions
o avião	airplane	*os aviões*	airplanes
a posição	position	*as posições*	positions

However, there are a few exceptions to the above rule, and these words should be learned individually. Some change -*ão* to -*ães* in the plural:

o capitão	*os capitães*	the captain(s)
o alemão	*os alemães*	the German(s)
o pão	*os pães*	the bread(s)
o cão	*os cães*	the dog(s)

---

[10] *acto, actos* Ⓟ.

Others by just adding an -s:

o irmão	os irmãos	brother(s)
a mão	as mãos	hand(s)
o cidadão	os cidadãos	citizen(s)
o órfão	os órfãos	orphan(s)
o grão	os grãos	grain(s)

3. Words that end in -m change the "m" into "n" before adding -s. This change has no effect on the pronunciation:

o homem	man	os homens	men
o fim	end	os fins	end
jovem	young	jovens	young (adj.)
bom	good	bons	good (adj.)

4. Words ending in -r, -z, and -s add -es:

o doutor	doctor	os doutores	doctors
a luz	light	as luzes	lights
o mês	month	os meses	months

Words ending in unstressed -s retain the same form in the plural:

o ônibus	os ônibus	the bus(es)
o lápis	os lápis	the pencil(s)
o campus	os campus	the campus(es)
simples	simples	simple (adj.)

5. Words ending in -l drop the "l" and add -is. Note that the endings -éis and -óis bear a written accent:

a capital	as capitais	capital(s)
o jornal	os jornais	newspaper(s)

o papel	*os papéis*	paper(s)
o hotel	*os hotéis*	hotel(s)
espanhol	*espanhóis*	Spanish (adj.)
azul	*azuis*	blue (adj.)

Words ending in -*il* drop the "l" and add -*s:*

o barril	*os barris*	barrel(s)
civil	*civis*	civil (adj.)

But, a few words ending in unstressed -*il* have irregular plurals in -*eis:*

fácil	*fáceis*	easy (adj.)
difícil	*difíceis*	difficult (adj.)
útil	*úteis*	useful (adj.)
fútil	*fúteis*	futile (adj.)

14. THE POSSESSIVE

1. English -'*s* or -*s'* is translated by *de* "of ":

o neto de Dona Maria	Dona Maria's grandson

2. Possessive adjectives and pronouns agree in number and gender with the object possessed. The possessive adjective usually comes before the word it modifies:

meu livro	my book
meus livros	my books
minha sobrinha	my niece
minhas sobrinhas	my nieces

Note: See Lesson 14, Parts E and F, in the conversation manual.

3. In conversation *seu* tends to refer to the person spoken to and thus translates "your." However, *seu* can also be used to translate "his," "her," "their." For greater clarity the prepositional form with *de* may be used:

Eles falaram de seu amigo.
They spoke of your (his, her, their) friend.

Eles falaram do amigo dele/do amigo dela/do amigo deles.
They spoke of his friend/or her friend/of their friend.

15. ADJECTIVES

1. Singular and plural:

SINGULAR
um menino alto   a tall boy
uma menina alta   a tall girl

PLURAL
dois meninos altos   two tall boys
duas meninas altas   two tall girls

Notice that the adjective agrees with the noun it modifies in gender and number.

2. Feminine endings:
   a. *-a* is substituted for the *-o* of the masculine form:

MASCULINE		FEMININE
antigo	old, ancient	*antiga*
rico	rich	*rica*
baixo	short, low	*baixa*

b. The masculine form ends in *-u*, the feminine in *-a:*

MASCULINE		FEMININE
nu	nude, bare	*nua*
mau	bad	*má*

c. No change if the masculine form ends in *-e:*

MASCULINE		FEMININE
contente	happy, content	*contente*

Common exceptions:

este	this	*esta*
aquele	that	*aquela*

d. *-ã* is substituted for the *-ão* of the masculine form:

MASCULINE		FEMININE
alemão	German	*alemã*
cristão	Christian	*cristã*

Common exception: augmentatives (see Section 23 in the grammar summary), in which *-ona* replaces *-ão:*

bonitão	handsome, pretty	*bonitona*

e. Adjectives ending in a consonant tend to have the same form for the masculine and the feminine:

MASCULINE		FEMININE
capaz	capable	*capaz*
comum	common	*comum*
formidável	formidable	*formidável*
simples	simple	*simples*

Examples:

Ela não é capaz de fazê-lo.
She is not able to do it.

A lição é muito simples.
The lesson is quite simple.

Common exceptions:

adjectives of nationality, *-a* usually being added to the masculine form:

francês	French	*francesa*
português	Portuguese	*portuguesa*

3. *Santo* is used before names beginning with a vowel and before *Tomás* and *Gral,* and *São* is used before most other names; *Santa* is used before feminine names:

Santo Antônio[11]	Saint Anthony
o Santo Gral	the Holy Grail
São Paulo	Saint Paul
São Francisco	Saint Francis
Santa Bárbara	Saint Barbara

16. POSITION OF ADJECTIVES

1. Descriptive adjectives (which tend to distinguish persons or things from others of the same type or class) and adjectives of nationality usually come after the noun they modify:

uma casa branca	a white house
uma anedota engraçada	a funny anecdote, joke

[11] *António* Ⓟ.

um bairro residencial	a residential district, suburb
romances contemporâneos	contemporary novels

2. Adjectives that indicate a characteristic quality of the type or class usually precede the noun:

o poderoso ditador	the powerful dictator
a melhor cidade	the best city

3. Limiting adjectives, such as the demonstrative adjectives, possessive adjectives, numerals, and adjectives of quantity, usually precede the noun they modify:

este conselho	this advice
nossa conversa	our conversation
a primeira decisão	the first decision
dez dedos	ten fingers
muitas lutas	many struggles

4. Some adjectives have a different meaning according to their position. After the noun modified they have their literal (usual) meaning, and before the noun they have a figurative (extended meaning):

um homem pobre	a poor (financially) man
um pobre homem	a poor (to be pitied) man
presentes caros	expensive gifts
meu caro amigo	my dear friend
a cidade toda	all the city
toda cidade	every city
um carro novo	a new car (a brand new one)
um novo carro	a new car (a different one)
uma grande cidade	a great city
uma cidade grande	a big city
meu amigo velho	my old (not young) friend
meu velho amigo	my old (longstanding) friend

17. COMPARISON

1. Regular comparison:

fácil	easy
mais fácil	easier
menos fácil	less easy
o mais fácil	the easier, the easiest
o menos fácil	the less easy, the least easy

2. Irregular comparison:

bom	good	*melhor*	better, best
mau	bad	*pior*	worse, worst
ruim	bad	*pior*	worse, worst
muito	much	*mais*	more, most
pouco	little	*menos*	less, least
grande	big, large	*maior*	bigger, biggest
pequeno	small	*menor*	smaller, smallest
bem	well	*melhor*	better, best
mal	badly	*pior*	worse, worst

Este livro é bom mas o outro é melhor.	This book is good but the other is better.

3. "More (less) . . . than . . ." = *mais (menos) . . . que . . .*

O português é mais fácil que o inglês.	Portuguese is easier than English.
Ele é mais inteligente do que parece.	He is more intelligent than he looks.

4. "As . . . as . . ." = *tão . . . quanto . . .*

a. Before an adjective or adverb:

Tão fácil quanto . . .　　　　As easy as . . .
Ela fala português tão　　　She speaks Portuguese as well
　bem quanto ele.　　　　　　as he does.

b. Before a noun the proper form of *tanto* is used:

Este teatro não tem tantas　This theatre does not have as
　entradas quanto aquele.　　many entrances as that one.

5. Before numerals *mais de* and *menos de* are used:

Eles têm mais de duzentas　They have more than two
　vacas.　　　　　　　　　　hundred cows.

6. An adjective may be qualified as to degree with a modifying word:

Ela está cansada.　　　　　She is tired.
Ela está muito cansada.　　She is very tired.

The meaning "very" is also given by adding the proper form of *íssimo* to a word (this cannot always be done):

Ela está cansadíssima.　　　She is very tired.
Estamos cansadíssimos.　　　We are very tired.

18. PRONOUNS

Pronouns have varying forms depending on whether they are:

1. The subject of a verb
2. Used after a preposition
3. The object of a verb
4. Used as indirect objects
5. Used with reflexive verbs
6. Used to join parts of a sentence (relative pronouns)

1. Pronouns as the subject of a verb:

SINGULAR

eu	I
(tu)	(you) *(familiar)*
ele	he
ela	she
o senhor	you *(masc., polite)*
a senhora	you *(fem., polite)*
você	you *(friendly)*

PLURAL

nós	we
(vos)[12]	(you)
eles	they *(masc.)*
elas	they *(fem.)*
os senhores	you *(masc., polite)*
as senhoras	you *(fem., polite)*
vocês	you *(friendly)*

SINGULAR

eu falo	I speak
(tu falas)	(you speak) *(familiar)*

[12] Rarely used. See Lesson 8.

SINGULAR

ele fala	he speaks
ela fala	she speaks
o senhor fala	you speak *(masc., polite)*
a senhora fala	you speak *(fem., polite)*
você fala	you speak *(friendly)*

PLURAL

nós falamos	we speak
(vós falais)	(you speak)
eles falam	they speak *(masc.)*
elas falam	they speak *(fem.)*
os senhores falam	you speak *(masc., polite)*
as senhoras falam	you speak *(fem., polite)*
vocês falam	you speak *(friendly)*

2. Pronouns used after prepositions:

para mim	for me
(para ti)	(for you) *(familiar)*
para ele	for him
para ela	for her
para o senhor	for you *(masc., polite)*
para a senhora	for you *(fem., polite)*
para você	for you *(friendly)*

para nós	for us
(para vós)	(for you)
para eles	for them *(masc.)*
para elas	for them *(fem.)*
para os senhores	for you *(masc., polite)*
para as senhoras	for you *(fem., polite)*
para vocês	for you *(friendly)*

Notice that the form of the pronoun used after a preposition is the same as the form of the pronoun used before a verb as subject, except for *mim* (me) and *ti* (you, *familiar*).

There is a special form for "with me," *comigo*, "with us," *conosco*, "with you" (*familiar*), *contigo*, and "with you, with him, with her," etc., *consigo*, although the latter form is not used frequently, *com o senhor, com ele*, etc., being preferred.

3. Pronouns used as direct objects:

me	me
te	you *(familiar)*
o	him
a	her
o	you (*masc.*, *polite* and *friendly*)
a	you (*fem.*, *polite* and *friendly*)
nos	us
(vos)	(you)
os	them *(masc.)*
as	them *(fem.)*
os	you (*masc.*, *polite* and *friendly*)
as	you (*fem.*, *polite* and *friendly*)

4. Pronouns as indirect objects:

me	to me
te	to you *(familiar)*
lhe	to him, her, you (*polite* and *friendly*)
nos	to us
(vos)	(to you)
lhes	to them (*masc.* and *fem.*) to you (*polite* and *friendly*)

Note that the subject pronouns *nós* and *vós* and the forms used after prepositions have the accent mark, that the direct and indirect object pronouns that correspond do not have the accent mark and are pronounced differently.

Inasmuch as *lhe* and *lhes* can have several meanings, a prepositional form can be used for clarity:

Eu lhe mandei uma carta.	I sent him (or her, you) a letter.
Eu mandei a ela uma carta.	I sent her a letter.

5. Reflexive pronouns are used with reflexive verbs to indicate an action the subject performs upon itself:

me	myself
te	yourself *(familiar)*
se	himself, herself, yourself *(polite* and *friendly)*
nos	ourselves
vos	yourselves
se	themselves, yourselves *(polite* and *friendly)*

For more information and examples, see Lesson 15.

6. Relative pronouns are used more in Portuguese than in English, for they are normally required, even in cases where English usage is optional (see first example below). *Que* is by far the most common form used for "that," "which," and even for "who," and "whom," although *quem* may be used for the last two. Both these forms are invariable, not changing for gender or number:

Ela disse que viria mais tarde.	She said (that) she would come later.
Ele não é o homem que me falou ontem.	He is not the man who spoke to me yesterday.

19. POSITION OF PRONOUNS

The position of object pronouns is not a fixed one, and variations will be noted in different areas. The following rules are given as a general guide.

1. Object pronouns usually follow the verb and are attached to the verb with a hyphen:

    a. In commands:

Prometa-me isso.	Promise me that.

    b. With a present participle:

oferecendo-nos mais	offering us more

    c. To avoid beginning a sentence with an object pronoun:

Abracei-o.	I embraced him.

Note: In popular speech Brazilians put the pronoun before the verb in these cases:

Me deu o livro.	He gave me the book.
Me faz um favor.	Do me a favor.

2. Object pronouns may come before or after the verb:

a. If the sentence begins with a pronoun or noun subject:

Ele me perdoou.	He pardoned me.
Ele perdoou-me.	He pardoned me.

b. With infinitives:

Ela veio para me dizer a verdade.	She came to tell me the truth.
Ela veio para dizer-me a verdade.	She came to tell me the truth.

In these cases, Brazil tends to prefer the position BEFORE the verb, and Portugal AFTER the verb.

Remember that if the direct object pronouns *o, a, os,* or *as* follow an infinitive, the *-r* of the infinitive is dropped, and the letter "l" is added to the object pronoun (*lo, la, los,* and *las*). The *-ar* and *-er* verbs bear a written accent (*á* and *ê,* respectively):

Vou comprá-lo.	I'm going to buy it.
Precisamos vê-los.	We must see them.
Quero abri-lo.	I want to open it.

3. In negative sentences and negative commands, the object pronouns precede the verb; in most other cases they tend to come before the verb:

Não o traduzimos.	We did not translate it.
Não me escreva mais.	Don't write me anymore.
Eles decidiram que nos mandariam o dinheiro.	They decided that they would send us the money.
Onde o vimos?	Where did we see him?

4. If two object pronouns, one direct and the other indirect, are used as objects of the same verb, the indirect comes before the direct object. This would cause the following contractions:

me + o, a, os, as = mo, ma, mos, mas
(te + o, a, os, as = to, ta, tos, tas)
lhe + o, a, os, as = lho, lha, lhos, lhas
nos + o, a, os, as = no-lo, no-la, no-los, no-las
(vos + o, a, os, as = vo-lo, vo-la, vo-los, vo-las)
lhes + o, a, os, as = lho, lha, lhos, lhas

Note: These contractions are usually avoided and are *never* used in Brazil. Contractions can be avoided:

a. By using the prepositional form for the indirect object:

Eu lho dei.   I gave it to him.
Eu o dei a ele.   I gave it to him.

b. In conversation, especially in Brazil, by sometimes omitting the direct object pronoun:

Eu lhe dei.   I gave (it) to him.
Eu dei a ele.   I gave (it) to him.

5. If a direct object pronoun comes after a verb form ending in *-r*, *-s*, or *-z*, this last letter is dropped and *l-* is prefixed to the direct object form:

Ele fê-lo.   He did it. (The verb is *fez* from
                                   fazer.)
Ela vai comprá-los.   She is going to buy them.
                                   (The verb is comprar and the
                                   pronoun is *os*.)

Note: In conversation these combinations, except after an infinitive, are avoided:

Ele o fez.   He did it.

If a direct object pronoun comes after a verb form that ends in a nasal sound (a vowel plus *m*), *n-* is prefixed to the object pronoun:

Eles abandonaram-no.   They abandoned him.

Note: These combinations are also avoided in conversation:

a. By placing the pronoun before the verb:

Eles o abandonaram.   They abandoned him.

b. By omitting the pronoun, if the meaning is clear (reference just having been made to the object, for example):

Eles abandonaram.   They abandoned (him).

20. SOME CONJUNCTIONS

ainda que	although
assim que	as soon as
até que	until
como	as, since
conforme	as
de maneira que	so, so that
depois que	after
e	and
embora	although

logo que	as soon as
mas	but
ou	or
para que	so that, in order that
porque	because
quando	when
se	if
segundo	as, according to
a menos que	unless

1. And *(e):*

Ele é alto e magro.	He is tall and thin.

2. But *(mas):*

Quero ir mas não posso.	I want to go but I can't.

3. Or *(ou):*

Mais ou menos.	More or less.
Cinco ou seis dólares.	Five or six dollars.

4. Because *(porque):*

Gosto dele porque é muito simpático.	I like him because he is very nice.

21. QUESTION WORDS

1. *Quê?*[13] or *O quê?*[13] "What?"
   Que é que . . . ? (with normal word order)

---

[13] When alone, or in an emphatic position, as at the end of a sentence, these forms have an accent mark.

Que disse ele? Que é que ele disse?	What did he say?
2. *Por quê?*	"Why?"
Por que ela não chegou antes das nove?	Why didn't she arrive before nine?
3. *Como?*	"How?"
Como se diz em português?	How do you say (it) in Portuguese?
4. *Quanto? Quanta?*	"How much?"
Quanto dinheiro temos?	How much money do we have?
Quantas irmãs João tem?	How many sisters does John have?
5. *Qual? Quais?*	"Which?" "What?"
Qual é o seu?	Which one is yours?
Quais são os seus?	Which ones are yours?
6. *Quem?*	"Who?"
Quem veio com ela?	Who came with her?
7. *Onde?*	"Where?"
Onde estão os livros?	Where are the books?

8. *Quando?*   "When?"

Quando aconteceu?   When did it happen?

22. ADVERBS

1. Some Portuguese adverbs are formed by adding
   -mente to the feminine singular form of the adjective;
   this corresponds to the English ending *-ly:*

exclusivamente   exclusively

If there are two or more adverbs with this same ending,
-mente is given only with the last one:

clara e concisamente   clearly and concisely

If the word has a written accent, the accent is dropped
after adding *-mente:*

só—somente   only
fácil—facilmente   easily
último—ultimamente   lately

Adverbs are generally compared like adjectives (see
Section 17 of the grammar summary).

POSITIVE	*claramente*	clearly
COMPARATIVE	*mais claramente*	more clearly
SUPERLATIVE	*o mais claramente*	the most clearly

2. Irregular comparatives:

bem	well	*melhor*	better, best
mal	badly	*pior*	worse, worst

muito	much	*mais*	more, most
pouco	little	*menos*	less, least

3. Adverbs and prepositions:

Many adverbs become prepositions when *de* is added:

ADVERB		PREPOSITION	
depois	afterward	*depois de*	after
antes	formerly	*antes de*	before

Other words that act similarly: *atrás* (behind); *debaixo* (under); *longe* (far); *mais* (more); *menos* (less); *perto* (near).

When *que* is added to some of these, they act as conjunctions:

Depois que eles chegarem falaremos.	After they arrive, we'll talk.

4. Adverbs of time:

hoje	today
ontem	yesterday
amanhã	tomorrow
cedo	early
tarde	late
muitas vezes	often
sempre	always
nunca	never
depois	afterward
antes	before, formerly
depressa	quickly
devagar	slowly

imediatamente	immediately
raramente	seldom, rarely
agora	now

5. Adverbs of place:

aqui	here
cá	here (motion)
aí	there
ali	there (farther away)
lá (acolá)	there (more remote)
adiante	forward, ahead
atrás	behind
dentro	inside
fora	outside
debaixo (x = sh)	below, down
perto	near
longe	far
abaixo (x = sh)	below, under
acima	above

6. Adverbs of quantity:

muito	very, much
pouco	little
mais	more
menos	less
quanto	how much
tão	so
tanto	so much
demais, muito	too much
só, somente	only
apenas	only, hardly
quase	almost
bastante	enough

7. Adverbs expressing affirmation:

sim	yes
também	also
verdadeiramente	truly
certamente	truly, certainly
claro	certainly, of course
pois não!	certainly, of course!

8. Adverbs expressing negation:

não	no, not
nunca	never
já não	no longer, not now
ainda não	not yet
nem	nor
nem . . . nem	neither . . . nor

9. "Here" and "there":

Aqui (here) refers to something near the speaker.

Aí (there) refers to something near the person spoken to.

Cá (here) expresses motion toward the speaker.

Ali (there) refers to something away from the speaker and from the person spoken to.

Lá (acolá) (there) refers to something more remote.

See Lesson 13 in the conversational manual for examples.

23. DIMINUTIVES AND AUGMENTATIVES

1. Certain endings, such as *-inho, -ote, -ete,* and *-ilho* imply smallness, daintiness, or even affection:

um pouco	a little
um pouquinho	a little bit
gato	cat
gatinha	kitten
sabão	soap
sabonete	a bar of soap
velho	old man
velhinho	little old man
avô	grandfather
avozinho	(dear) grandfather
avó	grandmother
avozinha	(dear) grandmother
cedo	soon
cedinho	quite soon

Remember that circumflex and acute accents are dropped since there is also a shift of stress:

pé—pezinho	little feet
café—cafezinho	demitasse (small cup of coffee)
árvore—arvorezinha	little tree
prêmio (prémio ℗) *—premiozinho*	little prize

2. Certain endings, such as *-ão, -arrão,* and *-aço* indicate large size, but they can also be uncomplimentary, indicating clumsiness, etc.:

gato	cat	*gatão*	big cat
homem	man	*homenzarrão*	very large man

casa	house	*casarão*	large house, mansion
drama	drama, play	*dramalhão*	melodrama
mulher	woman	*mulheraça*	big woman
mulher	woman	*mulherona*	big woman

3. Note: Although you should notice the difference in meaning given by these endings, you should be careful in using them and be sure you know the form and meaning before employing words with these endings.

24. DEMONSTRATIVES

1. Demonstrative adjectives:

MASCULINE	FEMININE	
este	*esta*	this
esse	*essa*	that
aquele	*aquela*	that (farther removed)
estes	*estas*	these
esses	*essas*	those
aqueles	*aquelas*	those (farther removed)

a. Portuguese demonstrative adjectives usually precede the nouns they modify and agree with them in gender and number:

este menino	this boy
aqueles vizinhos	those neighbors

b. *Esse* and *aquele* both mean "that." *Esse* refers to something near to or related to the person spoken to; *aquele* refers to something more remote:

Não gosto desse livro.   I don't like that book (near you
                                         or mentioned by you).

É aquele senhor que   He's that gentleman who
  chegou ontem.   arrived yesterday.

2. Demonstrative pronouns:

a. The same forms are also used as demonstrative pronouns:

Não quero este sem aquele.   I don't want this one without
                                that one.

b. *Este* and *aquele* also mean "the latter" and "the
former":

Acabam de chegar o   The ambassador and his
  embaixador (x = sh) e (o)   secretary just arrived.
  seu secretário.

Este é jovem e aquele é   The former is old and the
  velho.   latter is young.

Notice that the order in Portuguese is the opposite of
the English order: *este . . . aquele* ("the latter . . . the
former").

c. There are also some neuter forms:

isto	this, this (one)
isso	that, that (one) (near person spoken to, or mentioned by him)
aquilo	that, that (one) (farther removed)

The neuter forms are more general, referring to an idea
or statement or referring to an object or several items in
a general way, more as "this" than "this one" or "these":

Isto é melhor que (or do que) aquilo.	This is better than that.

3. Contractions of demonstrative forms:
   a. With the preposition *a:*

àquele	*àqueles*	*àquela*	*àquelas*	*àquilo*

   b. With the preposition *de:*

deste	*destes*	*desta*	*destas*	*disto*
desse	*desses*	*dessa*	*dessas*	*disso*
daquele	*daqueles*	*daquela*	*daquelas*	*daquilo*

   c. With the preposition *em:*

neste	*nestes*	*nesta*	*nestas*	*nisto*
nesse	*nesses*	*nessa*	*nessas*	*nisso*
naquele	*naqueles*	*naquela*	*naquelas*	*naquilo*

25. INDEFINITE ADJECTIVES AND PRONOUNS

todos	all
tal (tais, pl.)	such (a)
outro	another, other
alguém	somebody, someone
ninguém	nobody, no one
alguma coisa	something
nenhum	no one, none
algum	some
vários	several, some
nada	nothing
cada	each, every
tudo	all, everything
tanto	as much

certo	certain, a certain
mais	more
menos	less
qualquer	any, whatever, whoever
os demais	the rest

The adjectives above generally vary in form to agree with the word modified; *tal (tais), alguém, ninguém, nada, cada, tudo, mais,* and *menos* have only these forms.

26. NEGATION

Não (not) comes before the verb:

| *Não falo italiano.* | I don't speak Italian. |

There are two forms for "nothing," "never," "nobody," etc., one with and one without *não:*

Não vejo nada.	I don't see anything.
Não vou nunca.	I never go.
Não vem ninguém.	Nobody is coming. No one comes.

Note: This is the form used more often.

Or:

Nada vejo.	I don't see anything.
Nunca vou.	I never go.
Ninguém vem.	Nobody is coming. No one comes.

Also see Lesson 22 in the conversational manual.

27. WORD ORDER

1. The usual order tends to be subject—verb—adverb—object:

João comprou lá os livros de português. John bought the Portuguese books there.

2. The tendency in Portuguese is to put the longer member of the sentence (or the emphasized part, at times) last:

João viu os seus amigos no restaurante espanhol que é na esquina. John saw his friends in the Spanish restaurant that is on the corner.

3. To ask a question, the same word order as for a statement can be used; this is the more common form in conversation:

João comprou lá os livros de português? Did John buy his Portuguese books there?

A change of intonation indicates the difference between a statement and a question.

A question can also be formed by adding *É que* in front of a statement.

4. Adjectives come right after forms of the verb *ser:*

É tarde?   Is it late?
É bom?   Is it good?
A lição é fácil?   Is the lesson easy?

28. THE TENSES OF VERBS

Portuguese verbs are generally organized in three classes or conjugations according to their endings:

-ar:	I—*falar*
-er:	II—*aprender*
-ir:	III—*partir*

1. In the present tense, regular verbs have the following endings added to the stem of the verb (the infinitive minus the last two letters):

I	II	III
-o	*-o*	*-o*
(-as)	*(-es)*	*(-es)*
-a	*-e*	*-e*
-amos	*-emos*	*-imos*
(-ais)	*(-eis)*	*(-is)*
-am	*-em*	*-em*

falar to speak	*aprender* to learn	*partir* to leave
falo	*aprendo*	*parto*
(falas)	*(aprendes)*	*(partes)*
fala	*aprende*	*parte*
falamos	*aprendemos*	*partimos*
(falais)	*(aprendeis)*	*(partis)*
falam	*aprendem*	*partem*

The present can be translated in several ways:

Falo português.
I speak Portuguese.
I am speaking Portuguese.
I do speak Portuguese.

2. In the imperfect tense, regular verbs have the following endings added to the stem of the verb:

I	II AND III
-ava	-ia
(-avas)	(-ias)
-ava	-ia
-ávamos	-íamos
(-áveis)	(-íeis)
-avam	-iam

The imperfect is used:

a. To indicate continued or customary action or physical, mental, emotional states in the past, as well as past conditions such as weather, time, and age:

Quando eu era estudante, morava aqui.
When I was a student, I used to live here.

Ele não estava em casa.
He was not at home.

Ele sempre me telefonava.
He always used to call me.

Fazia muito calor.
It was very hot.

Eram cinco e meia da manhã.
It was 5:30 A.M.

b. To indicate an action in progress at the time of another past action, or two actions in progress simultaneously:

Eu dormia quando você telefonou.
I was sleeping when you called me.

Eu dormia enquanto ele falava no telefone.
I was sleeping while he was talking on the phone.

    c. Mostly in spoken language, for the conditional (expressed in English by "would"):

Eu queria ficar aqui, mas ela disse que ia embora.
I'd like to stay here, but she said she'd go.

Eu podia ir com ele.
I'd be able to go with him.

    There are four verbs in Portuguese that are irregular in the imperfect: *pôr, ser, ter, vir* (to put, to be, to have, to come):

pôr—punha, (punhas), punha, púnhamos, (púnheis), punham
ser—era, (eras), era, éramos, (éreis), eram
ter—tinha, (tinhas), tinha, tínhamos, (tínheis), tinham
vir—vinha, (vinhas), vinha, vínhamos, (vínheis), vinham

    3. The future of regular verbs is formed by adding the endings *-ei, (-ás), -á, -emos, (-eis), -ão* to the full infinitive:

falar to speak	*aprender* to learn	*partir* to leave
falarei	*aprenderei*	*partirei*
(falarás)	*(aprenderás)*	*(partirás)*
falará	*apprenderá*	*partirá*
falaremos	*aprenderemos*	*partiremos*
(falareis)	*(aprendereis)*	*(partireis)*
falarão	*aprenderão*	*partirão*

There are three verbs that are irregular in the future: *dizer, fazer, trazer* (to say, to do, to bring).

dizer—direi, (dirás), dirá, diremos, (direis), dirão
fazer—farei, (farás), fará, faremos, (fareis), farão
trazer—trarei, (trarás), trará, traremos, (trareis), trarão

The future generally expresses a future action:

Chegarei às nove.	I'll arrive at nine.

Sometimes it expresses conjecture or probability in the present:

Que horas serão?	What time can it be?
Serão sete horas.	It must be seven o'clock.
Ele provavelmente estará em casa.	He's probably home.

4. The preterit (also called simple past tense) of regular verbs is formed by adding the following endings to the stem of the verb:

I	II	III
-ei	*-i*	*-i*
(-aste)	*(-este)*	*(-iste)*
-ou	*-eu*	*-iu*
-amos (-ámos ℗*)*	*-emos*	*-imos*
(-astes)	*(-estes)*	*(-istes)*
-aram	*-eram*	*-iram*

Note that the first person plural of regular verbs has the same form in the present and in the preterit.[14]

---

[14] In Portugal, there is an accent in the preterit: *-ámos.*

Nós estudamos muito.	We study a lot (today).
Nós estudamos (*estudámos* Ⓟ) *ontem.*	We studied yesterday.

For phonetic reasons, there are a few spelling changes in the first person singular of some verbs:

a. Verbs ending in *-car* change the "c" to "qu" before the ending *-ei:*

Explicar (to explain)	*eu expliquei*
Praticar (to practice)	*eu pratiquei*

b. Verbs ending in *-çar* change the "ç" to "c" before the ending *-ei:*

Dançar (to dance)	*eu dancei*
Almoçar (to eat lunch)	*eu almocei*

c. Verbs ending in *-gar* change the "g" to "gu" before the ending *-ei:*

Pagar (to pay)	*eu paguei*
Chegar (to arrive)	*eu cheguei*

The preterit expresses an action completed in the past with emphasis on the fact rather than on the duration, repetition, or description:

Carlos falou comigo ontem.	Charles spoke to me yesterday.
Ele me disse (*disse-me* Ⓟ) *tudo.*	He told me everything.
Fomos ao cinema.	We went to the movies.
Ela nos viu (*viu-nos* Ⓟ).	She saw us.
Escrevi uma carta.	I wrote a letter.
Choveu todo o dia.	It rained all day.

Ficaram lá dois meses.   They stayed there two months.

It is important to observe that the simple past (preterit) in Portuguese is the tense that indicates the same idea expressed by the present perfect in English. Sometimes the verb is preceded by the adverb *já* (already):

Você já comeu?	Have you eaten?
Ele já saiu.	He has already left.
Eles me disseram isto.	They have told me this.
Você leu este livro?	Have you read this book?
Ele vendeu muitos livros.	He has sold many books.
Onde você foi?	Where have you gone to?

5. The perfect tenses are formed with the simple tenses of *ter* (*haver* may occur in literary style) and the past participle of the main verb (see Section 35 of the grammar summary). Most perfect tenses in English correspond to the perfect tenses in Portuguese; however, some distinctions must be observed carefully.

a. The present perfect in Portuguese often expresses a situation that requires the progressive form of the present perfect in English:

Nós temos estudado português.
We have been studying Portuguese.

O que é que você tem feito?
What have you been doing?

Não tenho ido ao parque ultimamente.
I haven't been going to the park lately.

Remember that the English present perfect is translated by the simple past in Portuguese:

I have studied Portuguese.   *Eu estudei português.*
I have already gone to Brazil.   *Eu já fui ao Brasil.*

    b. The pluperfect or past perfect is formed with the imperfect of *ter* or *haver* and the past participle of the main verb. It is used as in English and implies an action that took place prior to the main action of the statement. It translates "had + past participle" in English:

Quando eu cheguei, ele já tinha partido.
When I arrived, he had already left.

Esqueci que você tinha comprado o presente.
I forgot that you had bought the gift.

    c. The future perfect is formed with the future of *ter* (rarely *haver*) and the past participle of the main verb. It is used to express a future action that will take place before another future action:

Quando eu chegar, ele já terá partido.
When I arrive, he will already have left.

    Sometimes it indicates probability:

Eles já terão chegado.
They probably have already arrived.

29. THE SUBJUNCTIVE

The tenses given in the preceding section are called tenses of the indicative mode. There is another set of tenses for the subjunctive mode. The subjunctive mode expresses, among other things, hypothetical states or actions, feelings, a command, a suggestion, or a wish of the speaker. The subjunctive is used in a dependent clause introduced by a conjunction, most frequently *que* (except in sentences with *talvez* and in indirect commands; see Items c and e below). In Portuguese there are present, imperfect, and future forms of the subjunctive.

1. The present subjunctive is formed by removing the final *-o* of the first person singular of the present indicative (*eu* form) and then adding the following endings to the stem:

   Conjugation I: *-e, (-es), -e, -emos, (-eis), -em*

falar (to speak)—present indicative: *eu falo*

Pres. subj.: *que eu fale,*
              que você fale
              que ele/ela fale
              que nós falemos
              que vocês falem
              que eles/elas falem

   Conjugation II and III: *-a, (as), -a, -amos, (-ais), -am*

ter (have)—*eu tenho*   Pres. subj.: *tenha, tenhamos,*
                                            tenham
vir (come)—*eu venho*   Pres. subj.: *venha, venhamos,*
                                            venham
pôr (put)—*eu ponho*   Pres. subj.: *ponha, ponhamos,*
                                            ponham

   There are seven verbs that have irregular forms and do not follow the above rule:[15]

---

[15] Except for *querer*, these verbs do not have a final *-o* in the "eu" form.

ser: seja, sejamos, sejam
estar: esteja, estejamos, estejam
haver: haja, hajamos, hajam
ir: vá, vamos, vão
dar: dê, demos, dêem
saber: saiba, saibamos, saibam
querer: queira, queiramos, queiram

Uses of the present subjunctive:

a. The present subjunctive is used after any verb or phrase that expresses the imposing of desire, request, permission, approval, disapproval, etc. of one person (or persons) upon another. Some of these verbs of volition are: *querer* (to want), *proibir* (to forbid), *aconselhar* (to advise), *esperar* (to hope), *permitir* (to permit, allow), *insistir* (to insist), *exigir* (to require), *desejar* (to wish), *pedir* (to ask, demand), *preferir* (to prefer), *sugerir* (to suggest), etc.:

Eu quero que ele venha cedo.	I want him to come early (lit., I want that he comes early).
Nós esperamos que eles façam isto.	We hope that they do this.
O que você quer que eu diga?	What do you want me to say?
Aconselho que você vá lá.	I advise you to go there.

Note that at times the subjunctive is used in Portuguese when we would use the infinitive in English.

b. After verbs or expressions of emotion (to be happy, to be sorry, etc.):

Sinto muito que ela não possa vir.	I am very sorry that she can't come.

Estou contente que ela venha.	I am happy that she is coming.
Estou com medo que ela não venha.	I'm afraid she won't come.
Lamento que ela não venha.	I regret that she can't come.

c. After verbs or expressions of doubt or denial; likewise, after verbs in the **negative** that express an opinion or thought:

Duvido que eles estejam em casa.	I doubt they are at home.
Não acho que seja verdade.	I don't believe it is true.
Não é certo que ela venha.	It's not sure/definite that she will come.
Pode ser que ela queira.	Maybe (It can be that) she wants it.

Note that the adverb *talvez* (perhaps) expresses possibility or doubt; as such, it requires the subjunctive, and *que* (that) is not used:

Talvez eles não o conheçam.	Perhaps they don't know him.
Talvez ela vá ao Brasil o ano que vem.	Perhaps she will go to Brazil next year.

However, if the verb in the main clause expresses certainty, the indicative is used instead of the subjunctive:

Estou certo que ela vem.	I'm sure that she's coming.
Eu acho que é verdade.	I believe it is true.

d. After most impersonal expressions (except those that express certainty):

É pouco provável que ele o faça.	It's hardly probable that he will do it.
É importante que tragamos dinheiro.	It's important that we bring money.
É melhor que ela não fume.	It's better that she doesn't smoke.
É necessário que você me ajude.	It's necessary that you help me.
É preferível que ele não fume.	It's preferable that he doesn't smoke.

Note: If the statement is general and there is no specific need to use a subject for the second verb, the infinitive can be used by eliminating the conjunction *que:*

É possível fazê-lo.	It's possible to do it.
É preciso chegar cedo.	It's necessary to arrive early.
É necessario ajudar o professor.	It's necessary to help the teacher.
É melhor não fumar aqui.	It's better not to smoke here.

e. In indirect commands (expressed by the expression "Let . . ." or "Let's . . ." in English):

Não digamos mais.	Let's not say any more.
Que eles venham cedo.	Let them come early.
Que ele vá!	Let him go!
Que ele pague a conta.	Let him pay the bill.
Comamos!	Let's eat.
Vejamos . . .	Let's see . . .
Vamos!	Let's go!

f. The subjunctive is also used when the antecedent of the word *que* is not known. Words such as *alguém, ninguém, nenhum, um,* etc., imply indefinite things, and because there is doubt, the subjunctive is needed:

Não conheço nenhum hotel que seja mais barato.
I don't know any hotel that is cheaper.

Há alguém aqui que possa me ajudar?
Is there anyone here who could help me?

Quero um livro que me explique isto.
I want a book that will explain this to me.

But, if the subject is something definite, the indicative is used:

Conheço o hotel barato.	I know the cheap hotel.
Aquele moço pode lhe ajudar.	That young man can help you.
Este livro explica bem isto.	This book explains this well.

g. The subjunctive is always used following certain adverbial conjunctions:

CONCESSION

embora	although
se bem que	although, even if
ainda que	although, even if
nem que	even if
mesmo que	even if

TIME

antes que	before
até que	until

CONDITIONS

sem que	without
a menos que	unless

PURPOSE

para que	in order that
a fim de que	in order that
de maneira que	so that

Embora não tenha dinheiro, irei.
Although I don't have money, I will go.

Mesmo que faça frio, nós iremos.
Even if it's cold, we'll go.

Vou comprar um antes que vendam todos.
I'm going to buy one before they sell them all.

Para que aprendamos bem, temos que praticar.
In order for us to learn (it) well, we have to practice (it).

Vamos ficar aqui até que eles retornem.
We are going to stay here until they come back.

2. In the imperfect subjunctive, there is just one set of endings for all the conjugations. The stem is derived by removing the letters *-ram* from the third person plural of the preterit and by adding the following endings:

-sse, (-sses), -sse, -ssemos, (-sseis), -ssem

falar (to speak)—preterit: *eles falaram*

Impf. subj.:   *que eu falasse*
             que você falasse
             que ele/ela falasse
             que nós falássemos
             que vocês falassem
             que eles/elas falassem

ter (have)—*eles tiveram*   *tivesse, tivéssemos, tivessem*
vir (come)—*eles vieram*   *viesse, viéssemos, viessem*
pôr (put)—*eles puseram*   *pusesse, puséssemos, pusessem*

Uses of the imperfect subjunctive:

a. The imperfect subjunctive is used in the dependent clause instead of the present or future subjunctive if the verb of the main clause is in a past tense or in the conditional. Since the circumstances still denote a hypothetical state of affairs, its use is basically a matter of sequence of tenses:

Eu queria que ela ficasse.
I wanted her to stay (lit., I wanted that she stayed).

Embora estudasse muito, aprendi pouco.
Although I studied a lot, I learned little.

Talvez ele fosse lá ontem.
Perhaps he went there yesterday.

Eu compraria esta casa se tivesse dinheiro.
I would buy this house if I had money.

Se eu fosse você, não iria.
If I were you, I wouldn't go.

3. In the future subjunctive there is just one set of endings for all the conjugations. The form is also derived by removing the letters *-ram* from the third person plural of the preterit and by the following endings to the stem:

-r, (-res), -r, -rmos, (-rdes), -rem

falar (to speak)—preterit: *eles falaram*

eu falar
você falar
ele/ela falar
nós falarmos
vocês falarem
eles/elas falarem

ter (have)—*eles tiveram*	Fut. subj.: *tiver, tivermos, tiverem*
vir (come)—*eles vieram*	Fut. subj.: *vier, viermos, vierem*
pôr (put)—*eles puseram*	Fut. subj.: *puser, pusermos, puserem*

Uses of the future subjunctive:

a. The future subjunctive is a peculiarity of Portuguese. It is required in situations in which the uncertainty of future actions is implied. It is used when words that imply uncertainty such as *se* (if), *quando* (when), *assim que* (as soon as), *logo que* (as soon as), and *depois que* (after) introduce a dependent clause. Note that these words refer primarily to a condition that "may" exist:

Eu vou (or *irei*) *se você quiser.*
I will go if you want me to.

Eu lhe pagarei quando puder.
I will pay when I can.

Eu lhe telefonarei quando chegar em casa.
I will call you up when I arrive at home.

Assim que tivermos dinheiro, viremos.
As soon as we have money, we will come.

Eu lhe mando o livro se ele me mandar o dinheiro.
I will send him the book if he sends me the money.

Depois que vocês acabarem de comer, venham para cá.
After you finish eating, come here.

> b. The future subjunctive is also used with the "ever" expressions: whatever *(o que)*, whenever *(quando)*, whoever *(quem)*, wherever *(onde)*:

Faça o que puder.
Do whatever you can.

Vá onde quiser.
Go wherever you want.

Estude quando tiver tempo.
Study whenever you have time.

4. Finally, it is important to observe that the choice between the present or future subjunctive in the dependent clause does not depend exactly on the tense of the main clause. Rather, the choice depends on certain conditions such as doubt, the use of impersonal expressions, or the use of specific expressions such as *embora* (although), *talvez* (perhaps), etc. In these cases the dependent clause requires the present subjunctive even if the verb in the main clause is in the future, or even if the action referred to will take place in the future:

Será preciso que você fique.
It will be necessary for you to stay. (It will be necessary that you stay.)

Estou contente que ele não venha o ano que vem.
I am happy that he will not come next year.

Ele comprará o carro embora não tenha dinheiro.
He will buy the car although he doesn't have money.

Eu proibirei que você vá.
I will forbid you to go. (I will forbid that you go.)

Talvez ele faça isto o ano que vem.
Perhaps he will do this next year.

> Likewise, the future subjunctive must be used following those words mentioned previously *(se, quando, assim/logo que, depois que)* whenever they refer to an uncertain action even if the verb in the main clause is in the present tense:

Eu faço isto se tiver tempo.
I do this if I have time.

Eu dou o livro para ele quando puder.
I will give the book to him when I can.

Você pode vir comigo se tiver tempo.
You can come with me if you have time.

Compro se quiser.
I buy (it) if I want to.

Venha quando puder.
Come when you can.

5. A few aspects of the past subjunctive in reference to the future subjunctive:

After *quando* (when), *assim que/logo que* (as soon as), and *depois que* (after), the past subjunctive is used only if the verb in the main clause is the conditional tense. Remember that the statement must imply a hypothesis in order for the subjunctive to be used:

Eu lhe compraria o carro quando tivesse dinheiro.
I'd buy you the car if I had the money. (I didn't buy it.)

Ele não ficaria aqui depois que você chegasse.
He would not stay here after your arrival (hypothesis).

However, if the verb in the main clause is the simple past, those words must be followed by a tense in the indicative mood since the clause expresses an accepted fact and no longer a hypothesis:

Eu comprei quando tinha dinheiro.
I bought (it) when I had money. (I did buy.)

Eu fui assim que pude.
I went as soon as I was able to. (I did go.)

Ele saiu depois que você chegou.
He left after you arrived. (fact)

30. SEQUENCE OF TENSES

In addition to information already given, keep in mind the following regarding sequence of tenses:

If the main verb is in the present or future, the subjunctive, if required, will be in the present if its time is present or future:

Duvido que ele venha.	I doubt that he will come.
Duvido que elas estejam em casa.	I doubt that they are home.

The subjunctive will be in the imperfect if its time is past:

Duvido que ele viesse.	I doubt that he came.

If the main verb is in the past, the subjunctive, if required, will be in the imperfect if it reflects action at the same time or later; it will be in the pluperfect (past perfect subjunctive) if it indicates previous action:

Eu duvidava que ele viesse.	I doubted that he would come.
Eu duvidava que ele tivesse vindo.	I doubted that he had come.

31. THE INFINITIVE

Portuguese has two types of infinitives: the impersonal and the personal.

The impersonal infinitive is used in most cases calling for an infinitive. Practically all infinitives end in *-ar* (first conjugation): *falar* (to speak); *-er* (second conjugation): *comer* (to eat) and *-ir* (third conjugation): *partir* (to leave). There is just one verb that ends in *-or: pôr* (to put), and it is not considered as one conjugation by itself.[16]

Os alunos não querem estudar.
The students don't want to study.

---

[16] Its compounds: *compôr, supôr, impôr, opôr* (to compose, to suppose, to impose, to oppose), etc., are conjugated like *pôr* plus the prefix: *componho, suponho, imponho,* etc.

Eles preferem ficar aqui.
They prefer to stay here.

Ele deve pagar a conta.
He must pay the bill.

Vou pôr o dinheiro aqui.
I'm going to put the money here.

The personal infinitive is a distinct feature of the Portuguese language. It is the infinitive which has a logical subject and endings as follows:

eu falar	*nós falarmos*
(tu falares)	*(vós falardes)*
você falar	*vocês falarem*
ele/ela falar	*eles/elas falarem*

The personal infinitive is usually used to avoid ambiguity and/or just for clarity. In the statement *Vão jantar depois de chegar,* it's not clear whose arrival we are talking about. If we use a subject for the verb to arrive—*Vão jantar depois de eu chegar (de nós chegarmos,* etc.)—the central idea becomes more precise.

Eles partiram sem nós sabermos.
They left without our knowing.

Mostly in the plural, the subject pronoun can be deleted since the verbal ending itself indicates the subject:

É preciso trabalhar para ganharmos dinheiro.
It's necessary for us to work to earn money.

Depois de estudarmos este livro, vamos saber falar português.
After studying this book, we will know how to speak Portuguese.

Note: The personal infinitive in Portuguese is used quite frequently in conversation. In several instances, it can replace some uses of the subjunctive. For example, as we have seen previously, the following conjunctions require the present (or imperfect) subjunctive:

CONJUNCTION	PREPOSITION
sem que	*sem*
para que + (present) subjunctive	• *para* + personal infinitive
até que	*para*

Ela pede para que nós fiquemos mais um pouco.
She is asking us to stay a little longer.

Não vamos sair até que vocês digam a verdade.
We don't want to leave until you tell the truth.

However, if we use a preposition instead, the personal infinitive can be used:

Ela pede para nós ficarmos mais um pouco.
She's asking us to stay a little longer.

Não vamos sair até vocês dizerem a verdade.
We're not going to leave until you tell (us) the truth.

Remember the impersonal expressions that will require the present (or imperfect) subjunctive:

É necessário que nós digamos e façamos isto.
It's necessary that we say and do this.

Era preciso que vocês fossem lá e comprassem isto.
It was necessary that you go and do this.

But, in most cases, the conjunction "que" can be deleted and the subjunctive is no longer required:

É necessário nós dizermos e fazermos isto.
It's necessary for us to say and do that.

Era preciso vocês irem lá e comprarem isto.
She needs you to go there and buy this.

In some instances, the personal infinitive can also replace the future subjunctive:

CONJUNCTION	PREPOSITION
depois que + future subjunctive	*depois de +* personal infinitive

Fut. subj. *Depois que nós fizermos isto, vamos sair.*
Pers. inf. *Depois de nós fazermos isto, vamos sair.*
            After we do this, we are going to leave.

Note that with regular verbs, the future subjunctive and personal infinitive have the same forms, for example:

Fut. subj. *Depois que nós falarmos com ele, vamos sair.*
Pers. inf. *Depois de nós falarmos com ele, vamos sair.*
            After we talk to him, we will leave.

Other examples:

(conjunction)   *É preciso que nós estudemos.*
(preposition)   *É preciso nós estudarmos.*
                It's necessary for us to study.

(conjunction)   *Eu fui lá sem que ela soubesse.*
(preposition)   *Eu fui lá sem ela saber.*
                I went there without her knowing it.

(conjunction)	*Vou ficar aqui até que eles cheguem.*
(preposition)	*Vou ficar aqui até eles chegarem.*
	I'm going to stay here until they arrive.

(conjunction)	*Nós iremos ao parque depois que você fizer isto.*
(preposition)	*Nós iremos ao parque depois de você fazer isto.*
	We will go to the park after you do this.

32. The Conditional

1. The present conditional is formed by adding the endings *-ia, -ias, -ia, -íamos, -íeis, -iam* to the infinitives of all three conjugations:

I	II	III
falar (to speak)	*aprender* (to learn)	*partir* (to leave)
falaria	*aprenderia*	*partiria*
(falarias)	*(aprenderias)*	*(partirias)*
falaria	*aprenderia*	*partiria*
falaríamos	*apredenríamos*	*partiríamos*
(falaríeis)	*(aprenderíeis)*	*(partiríeis)*
falariam	*aprenderiam*	*partiriam*

Note: The verbs *dizer, fazer,* and *trazer* add these endings to a shortened stem: *diria, faria, traria,* etc.

2. The conditional is used to express:

a. A future from a past point, being usually translated "would" and the meaning of the verb:

| *Ele me disse que chegaria às sete.* | He told me that he would arrive at seven. |

b. Probability or conjecture in the past:

Seriam oito horas, quando ele chegou.	It was probably eight o'clock when he arrived.
Que horas seriam quando ele chegou?	What time could it have been (I wonder what time it was) when he arrived?

c. A softened statement:

Eu gostaria de vê-lo.	I would like to see him.

d. The conclusion of certain conditional sentences (see Section 33, following).

3. The perfect conditional is formed with the conditional of *ter* (*haver* is used sometimes) and the past participle of the main verb:

Ele me teria falado . . .	He would have spoken to me . . .
Elas não teriam ido . . .	They would not have gone . . .

33. CONDITIONAL SENTENCES

Conditional sentences have two parts, the conditional or "if" clause and the conclusion. The following are the most common combinations.

1. A simple condition can be expressed with both verbs in the indicative. Sometimes the "if" factor is the equivalent of "when" or "whenever":

Se chove (está chovendo), não vamos.	If it is raining, we won't go.
Se ele entrou eu não o vi.	If he came in, I didn't see him.

Se ele chegava cedo vinha me ver.	If (whenever) he arrived early, he came to see me.

2. When the "if" clause expresses a simple condition (not a doubtful one) in the future, the future subjunctive is used in the "if" clause and the future indicative (or the present indicative) is used in the conclusion:

Se chover não iremos (vamos).	If it rains we won't go.

3. When the "if" clause expresses a doubtful condition in the future the imperfect subjunctive is used in the "if" clause and the conditional (or the imperfect indicative)[17] in the conclusion:

Se chovesse não iríamos (íamos).	If it should rain we would not go.

The same sequence is used to indicate a doubtful or contrary-to-fact situation in the present:

Se eu fosse rico viajaria (viajava) todos os verãos.	If I were rich I would travel every summer.

4. When the "if" clause expresses a condition contrary to fact in the past, the pluperfect (past perfect) subjunctive is used in the "if" clause and the conditional perfect (or the pluperfect indicative)[18] in the conclusion:

Se tivesse chovido não teríamos (tínhamos) ido.	If it had rained we would not have gone.

---

[17] The imperfect indicative is usually preferred in conversation.
[18] Preferred in conversation.

34. Commands and Requests

English uses the imperative (command) form more often and in more instances than Portuguese. Remember that commands imply "you," in either singular or plural sense. There are two types of commands in Portuguese: formal and informal.

FORMAL COMMANDS

Practically all Portuguese commands, affirmative or negative, will be given with the third person singular and plural forms of the present subjunctive.

As with the subjunctive, the stem is formed by removing the final *-o* of the first person singular of the present indicative *(eu)* form, and, for *-ar* verbs, adding *-e, -em* to form the singular and plural commands, respectively. For *-er* and *-ir* verbs, add *-a, -am:*

INFINITIVE	PRESENT INDICATIVE	IMPERATIVE		ENGLISH
		Singular:	Plural:	
falar	*eu falo*	*Fale!*	*Falem!*	Speak!
fazer	*eu faço*	*Faça!*	*Façam!*	Do!
vir	*eu venho*	*Venha!*	*Venham!*	Come!
pôr[19]	*eu ponho*	*Ponha!*	*Ponham!*	Put!

The following verbs have irregular command forms:

ser: seja, sejam	*Seja feliz!*	Be happy!
estar: esteja, estejam	*Estejam à vontade!*	Be at home!
ir: vá, vão	*Não vá lá.*	Don't go there.
dar: dê, dêem	*Dê-me mais um.*	Give me one more.

---

[19] Like *-er* verbs.

saber: saiba,   *Saiba o endereço*   Know his address.
  saibam   *dele.*
querer:[20] *queira,*   *Queiram sentar-se.*   Please sit down.
  queiram

There are a few spelling changes in some verbs in order
to maintain the original sound:

  1. Verbs ending in *-car* change the "c" to "qu" before the
      ending *-e:*

Explicar: Explique./Expliquem.   Explain.

  2. Verbs ending in *-çar* change the "ç" to "c" before the
      ending *-e:*

Dançar: Dance./Dancem. Dance.

  3. Verbs ending in *-gar* change the "g" to "gu" before the
      ending *-e:*

Pagar: Pague./Paguem.   Pay.

  4. Verbs ending in *-cer* change the "c" to "ç" before the
      ending *-a:*

Esquecer: Esqueça./Esqueçam.   Forget.

Commands with reflexive verbs:

The reflexive pronoun is usually *se.* Remember that when a
pronoun follows a verb it must be connected by a hyphen:

---

[20] The verb *querer* (to want) is mostly used to soften the imperative meaning "please." *Queira entrar* = Please come in.

	PRESENT		
INFINITIVE	INDICATIVE	IMPERATIVE	ENGLISH

		Singular:	Plural:	
Sentar-se	*(eu me sento)*	*Sente-se!*	*Sentem-se!*	Sit down!
Vestir-se	*(eu me visto)*	*Vista-se!*	*Vistam-se!*	Dress!

But, in the negative:

Não se corte.	Don't cut yourself.
Não se sente aqui.	Don't sit down here.

Commands with object pronouns:

As has just been said, in affirmative commands the object pronoun must follow the verb. However, whenever a vowel pronoun (*o, a, os,* or *as*) occurs after the plural command, a letter "n" is added to it. But remember that with the negative command the pronoun is placed without the "n" before the verb (because the verb is no longer the first element).[21]

Trago-o.	Bring it.
Mostre-lhes o quarto.	Show them the room.
Diga-me a verdade.	Tell me the truth.
Tragam-no.[22]	Bring it.
Levem-nas.	Take them.

But:

Não o traga.	Don't bring it.
Não o tragam.	Don't bring it.
Não lhes mostre.	Don't show them.

---

[21] See Lesson 14.

[22] In Brazil, avoid using these forms in speech. It's better to use the expressed object instead: *Tragam o livro. Levem as crianças.* (Bring the book. Take the children.)

Other examples:

Escreva-o.	Write it.
Escute!	Listen!
Não gastem tudo!	Don't spend everything!
Não me escreva mais!	Don't write me any more!
Termine tudo.	Finish everything.
Não venha antes das cinco.	Don't come before five.
Não lhe diga isto.	Don't tell him/her this.
Dê-lhe o troco.	Give her/him the change.
Traga-nos um café.	Bring us a (cup of) coffee.
Peça-lhe para ficar.	Ask him to stay.
Deite-se cedo.	Go to bed early.

INFORMAL COMMANDS

In informal, conversational style, the third person singular of the present indicative is used as the imperative. In this way, the "formal" command is more a grammatically correct command, whereas the indicative used as an imperative is preferred in Brazil as a kind of "soft" command. One will hear this form among Brazilians in almost all informal situations:

Fala com ele. (for *Fale . . .*)	Talk to him.
Vai lá. (for *Vá . . .*)	Go there.
Dá um café, por favor. (for *Dê . . .*)	Give (us, me) a coffee, please.
Fica quieto. (for *Fique . . .*)	Be quiet.
Não diz nada para ele (for *Não lhe diga . . .*)	Don't tell him anything.
Faz o favor . . . (for *Faça . . .*)	Do a favor . . .

Also in Brazil, the verb *querer* (or *poder*) followed by an infinitive is often used as an alternative to soften a request:

Você pode virar à esquerda, por favor?	Turn to the left, please?
Quer me dar um café, por favor?	Give me a (cup of) coffee, please?
Você podem esperar lá fora, por favor?	Wait outside, please?
Você quer repetir mais uma vez, por favor?	Repeat (it) once more, please?

It may be helpful to understand another common expression: *Vê se você . . .* In informal conversation, for stronger emphasis, these words denote more the sense of a command than that of a request. The tone of voice in which the words are said will reveal them as a command without sounding like an order:

Vê se você chega cedo. (for *Chegue . . .*).	(See that you) Arrive early.
Vê se vocês não fazem barulho. (for *Não façam . . .*)	Don't make noise.
Vê se não gasta muito. (for *Não gaste . . .*)	Don't spend much.
Vê se me deixa em paz (for *Deixe-me . . .*)	Leave me alone.

35. The Participle

1. The present participle is formed by adding *-ando, -endo,* and *-indo* to the stems of verbs of the three conjugations:

I		II	
falar	to speak	*aprender*	to learn
falando	speaking	*aprendendo*	learning

III	
partir	to leave
partindo	leaving

If an object pronoun follows the present participle, the two are joined with a hyphen:

falando-nos	speaking to us
escrevendo-lhe	writing to him
vendo-o	seeing him

2. The present participle is used in the progressive tenses (see the next section) and often much as in English:

Vi-o na praia, dormindo.	I saw him on the beach, sleeping.
Partindo (Ao partir), ele me deu seu cartão.	On leaving he gave me his card.

3. The past participle is formed by adding *-ado, -ido, -ido* to the stems of verbs of the three conjugations:

I		II	
falar	to speak	*aprender*	to learn
falado	spoken	*aprendido*	learned

III	
partir	to leave
partido	left

4. Irregular participles:

Pôr has the irregular present participle *posto*.

The following are some of the verbs that have irregular past participles:

INFINITIVE		IRREGULAR PAST PARTICIPLE
abrir	to open	*aberto*
cobrir	to cover	*coberto*
dizer	to say	*dito*
escrever	to write	*escrito*
fazer	to do, make	*feito*
pôr	to put	*posto*
ver	to see	*visto*
vir	to come	*vindo*

Some verbs have a regular participle and also a shortened form:

INFINITIVE		REGULAR	IRREGULAR
aceitar	to accept	*aceitado*	*aceito, aceite*
entregar	to deliver, give	*entregado*	*entregue*
ganhar	to earn, gain	**ganhado*	*ganho*
gastar	to spend	**gastado*	*gasto*
pagar	to pay	**pagado*	*pago*
morrer	to die	*morrido*	*morto*

Although both forms are used, there is a tendency for the regular form to be favored as the past participle of the perfect tenses and for the shortened form to be favored as an adjective:

Tínhamos aceitado todo o dinheiro.	We had accepted all the money.
O dinheiro não foi aceito.	The money was not accepted.

---

* These forms are not used with *ter*.

36. PROGRESSIVE TENSES

The Portuguese progressive tenses are formed with the present participle and the tenses of *estar* (although other verbs, such as *ir,* may also be used as the auxiliary verb):

Estou estudando.	I am studying.
Quando eles entraram na sala nós estávamos lendo o jornal.	When they entered the room we were reading the newspaper.
Elas estão divertindo-se.	They are having a good time.
Eles iam cantando.	They were singing. ("They went on singing.")

Portugal also uses *estar a* and the infinitive: *Estou a estudar.* I am studying.

37. THE PASSIVE VOICE

The passive voice is made up of the forms of *ser* with the past participle:

O Brasil foi descoberto em 1500 (mil e quinhentos).	Brazil was discovered in 1500.

The passive voice is used as in English. Very often, however, Portuguese uses *se* to express the passive (see Lesson 15 F).

38. TO BE

Ser and *estar* both mean "to be" in Portuguese. In general, *ser* indicates a characteristic or permanent state and *estar* a temporary condition or state. However, one should note the different uses of these verbs.

SER	ESTAR	
eu sou	*eu estou*	I am
(tu és)	*(tu estás)*	you are *(familiar)*
o senhor é	*o senhor está*	you are *(masc.)*
a senhora é	*a senhora está*	you are *(fem.)*
você é	*você está*	you are
ele é	*ele está*	he is
ela é	*ela está*	she is
nós somos	*nós estamos*	we are
(vós sois)	*(vós estais)*	(you are)
os senhores são	*os senhores estão*	you are
as senhoras são	*as senhoras estão*	you are
vocês são	*vocês estão*	you are
eles são	*eles estão*	they are
elas são	*elas estão*	they are

S E R

1. Indicates a characteristic or inherent quality:

Meu irmão é alto.	My brother is tall.
O livro é vermelho.	The book is red.
Ela é jovem.	She is young.
O gelo é frio.	Ice is cold.
Ele é inteligente.	He is intelligent.

2. Indicates an established or permanent location:

A capital é no Distrito Federal.	The capital is in the Federal District.
A escola é longe daqui.	The school is far from here.

3. Is used with a predicate noun or pronoun:

Ele é professor.	He is a professor.
Ela é aluna.	She is a student.

Somos americanos.   We are Americans.
É ele.   It is he.
Sou eu.   It is I.

4. Indicates origin or source:

Ele é de Lisboa.   He's from Lisbon.
Esta madeira é do Brasil. This wood is from Brazil.

5. Indicates material:

A casa é de pedra.   The house is made of stone.

6. Indicates possession:

Os livros são dele.   The books are his.
De quem é?   Whose is it?
É meu.   It is mine.

7. Is used in indicating the time:

São duas horas.   It is two o'clock.
É meio-dia.   It is noon.

8. Is used in impersonal expressions:

É tarde.   It is late.
É cedo.   It is early.
É possível.   It is possible.
É pena.   It's a pity.
Não é verdade?   Isn't it so?

9. Is used in forming the passive voice (see Section 37 of
   the grammar summary).

ESTAR

1. Expresses position or location:

Ele não está aqui.	He is not here.
Maria está em casa.	Mary is home.
Onde estão os livros?	Where are the books?
O jornal está na caixa.	The newspaper is in the box.
(x = sh)	

2. Indicates a transient quality or characteristic:

Ela está contente.	She is happy (pleased).
Estamos cansados.	We are tired.
Estou pronto.	I'm ready.
O café está frio.	The coffee is cold.
A janela está aberta (fechada).	The window is open (closed).
Ela está bonita hoje.	She is pretty today.

3. Is used to form the progressive tenses (see Section 36 above):

Eles estão falando (a falar ℗) de nós.	They are talking about us.

4. Is used in expressions about the weather:

Está frio hoje.	It is cold today.
No verão estará quente.	It will be hot in the summer.

5. Is used in certain other expressions (especially in Brazil):

Estou com fome.	I am hungry.
Eles estão com sede.	They are thirsty.

Note: The verb *ficar* (to remain) is quite popular in Brazil and is often used for *ser* or *estar:*

Onde fica a estação?	Where is the station?
Fica longe daqui.	It is far from here.
Ela fica contente.	She is happy (pleased).
Ele ficou doente.	He became ill.

39. THE FORMS OF REGULAR VERBS

CONJUGATION I	CONJUGATION II	CONJUGATION III

INFINITIVE

PRESENT

falar (to speak)	*aprender* (to learn)	*partir* (to leave)

PERSONAL INFINITIVE

falar	*aprender*	*partir*
(falares)	*(aprenderes)*	*(partires)*
falar	*aprender*	*partir*
falarmos	*aprendermos*	*partirmos*
(falardes)	*(aprenderdes)*	*(partirdes)*
falarem	*aprenderem*	*partirem*

PAST

ter falado	*ter aprendido*	*ter partido*
to have spoken	to have learned	to have left

PARTICIPLES

PRESENT

falando	*aprendendo*	*partindo*
speaking	learning	leaving

PAST

falado spoken   *aprendido* learned   *partido* left

INDICATIVE AND CONDITIONAL

PRESENT

falo	*aprendo*	*parto*
(falas)	*(aprendes)*	*(partes)*
fala	*aprende*	*parte*
falamos	*aprendemos*	*partimos*
(falais)	*(aprendeis)*	*(partis)*
falam	*aprendem*	*partem*

IMPERFECT

falava	*aprendia*	*partia*
(falavas)	*(aprendias)*	*(partias)*
falava	*aprendia*	*partia*
falávamos	*aprendíamos*	*partíamos*
(faláveis)	*(aprendíeis)*	*(partíeis)*
falavam	*aprendiam*	*partiam*

PRETERIT

falei	*aprendi*	*parti*
(falaste)	*(aprendeste)*	*(partiste)*
falou	*aprendeu*	*partiu*
falamos[23]	*aprendemos*	*partimos*
(falastes)	*(aprendestes)*	*(partistes)*
falaram	*aprenderam*	*partiram*

FUTURE

falarei	*aprenderei*	*partirei*
(falarás)	*(aprenderás)*	*(partirás)*
falará	*aprenderá*	*partirá*
falaremos	*aprenderemos*	*partiremos*
(falareis)	*(aprendereis)*	*(partireis)*
falarão	*aprenderão*	*partirão*

[23] *falámos* Ⓟ.

CONDITIONAL

falaria	aprenderia	partiria
(falarias)	(aprenderias)	(partirias)
falaria	aprenderia	partiria
falaríamos	aprenderíamos	partiríamos
(falaríeis)	(aprenderíeis)	(partiríeis)
falariam	aprenderiam	partiriam

PRESENT PERFECT

tenho	+	falado	aprendido	partido
(tens)	+	falado	aprendido	partido
tem	+	falado	aprendido	partido
temos	+	falado	aprendido	partido
(tendes)	+	falado	aprendido	partido
têm	+	falado	aprendido	partido

PLUPERFECT (COMPOUND)

tinha	+	falado	aprendido	partido
(tinhas)	+	falado	aprendido	partido
tinha	+	falado	aprendido	partido
tínhamos	+	falado	aprendido	partido
(tínheis)	+	falado	aprendido	partido
tinham	+	falado	aprendido	partido

PLUPERFECT (SIMPLE)[24]

falara	aprendera	partira
(falaras)	(aprenderas)	(partiras)
falara	aprendera	partira
faláramos	aprendêramos	partíramos
(faláreis)	(aprendêreis)	(partíreis)
falara	aprendera	partira

[24] The simple pluperfect has the same meaning as the compound pluperfect, but it is more a literary tense and is never used in conversation.

FUTURE PERFECT

terei	+	*falado*	*aprendido*	*partido*
(terás)	+	*falado*	*aprendido*	*partido*
terá	+	*falado*	*aprendido*	*partido*
teremos	+	*falado*	*aprendido*	*partido*
(tereis)	+	*falado*	*aprendido*	*partido*
terão	+	*falado*	*aprendido*	*partido*

CONDITIONAL PERFECT

teria	+	*falado*	*aprendido*	*partido*
(terias)	+	*falado*	*aprendido*	*partido*
teria	+	*falado*	*aprendido*	*partido*
teríamos	+	*falado*	*aprendido*	*partido*
(teríeis)	+	*falado*	*aprendido*	*partido*
teriam	+	*falado*	*aprendido*	*partido*

SUBJUNCTIVE

PRESENT

fale	*aprenda*	*parta*
(fales)	*(aprendas)*	*(partas)*
fale	*aprenda*	*parta*
falemos	*aprendamos*	*partamos*
(faleis)	*(aprendais)*	*(partais)*
falem	*aprendam*	*partam*

IMPERFECT

falasse	*aprendesse*	*partisse*
(falasses)	*(aprendesses)*	*(partisses)*
falasse	*aprendesse*	*partisse*
falássemos	*aprendêssemos*	*partíssemos*
(falásseis)	*(aprendêsseis)*	*(partísseis)*
falassem	*aprendessem*	*partissem*

FUTURE

falar	aprender	partir
(falares)	(aprenderes)	(partires)
falar	aprender	partir
falarmos	aprendermos	partirmos
(falardes)	(aprenderdes)	(partirdes)
falarem	aprenderem	partirem

PRESENT PERFECT

tenha	+	falado	aprendido	partido
(tenhas)	+	falado	aprendido	partido
tenha	+	falado	aprendido	partido
tenhamos	+	falado	aprendido	partido
(tenhais)	+	falado	aprendido	partido
tenham	+	falado	aprendido	partido

PLUPERFECT

tivesse	+	falado	aprendido	partido
(tivesses)	+	falado	aprendido	partido
tivesse	+	falado	aprendido	partido
tivéssemos	+	falado	aprendido	partido
(tivésseis)	+	falado	aprendido	partido
tivessem	+	falado	aprendido	partido

RADICAL-CHANGING VERBS

As indicated before (see Lesson 1, Vowels) the sounds of vowels vary in Portuguese, with open and closed qualities for the same vowel, as well as other variations. To have good pronunciation it is necessary to distinguish between these sounds. Certain verbs in Portuguese have variations in the stem (or radical, as it is also called), and these should be kept in mind. *Only some of these changes, with a few sample verbs, are given here.* Unless otherwise indicated, the change given pertains to those forms of the verb in which the stress falls on the last vowel of the stem: the 1, 2, 3, and 6 forms (the three singular and the third plural forms) of the present indicative and of the present subjunctive.

CONJUGATION I

levar	to take away	
secar	to dry	(open *e*)
cortar	to cut	
escovar	to brush	
jogar	to play (game)	
morar	to dwell, live	(open *o*)
notar	to note	
voltar	to return	
cear	to eat supper	
estrear	to use, wear for the first time	(*e* changes to *ei*)
passear	to take a walk or ride	
recear	to fear	
odiar	to hate	
remediar	to remedy	(*i* changes to *ei*)

CONJUGATION II

dever	to owe, to have to	(*e* changes to open *e* in 2, 3, 6—not in 1st form)
escrever	to write	
meter	to put	
correr	to run	
mover	to move	(open *o* in 2, 3, 6)

CONJUGATION III

competir	to compete	
conferir	to confer	
conseguir	to obtain	(*e* becomes *i* in 1;
despir (-se)	to undress (oneself)	*e* becomes open *e*
divertir (-se)	to amuse (oneself)	in 2, 3, 6 of
ferir	to wound	pres. ind.;
preferir	to prefer	*e* becomes *i* in

referir	to refer	all six forms of
repetir	to repeat	pres. subj.)
seguir	to follow	
servir	to serve	
vestir (-se)	to dress (oneself)	
mentir	to lie	(*e* becomes *i* in 1
sentir	to feel, to be sorry	of pres. ind. and
		in all pres. subj.)
		(*o* becomes *u* in 1;
cobrir	to cover	*o* becomes open *o*
dormir	to sleep	in 2, 3, 6 of
engolir	to swallow	pres. ind.;
tossir	to cough	*o* becomes *u* in all
		six forms of pres.
		subj.)
consumir	to consume	(*u* becomes open *o*
fugir	to flee	in 2, 3, 6 of
sacudir	to shake	pres. ind.)
subir	to go up	

SPELLING CHANGES IN VERBS

Some verb forms, as is true of other parts of speech, undergo spelling changes before certain endings. These changes are in the final consonant of the stem. To understand these cases better, consult Section 2 of the grammar summary.

1. Verbs ending in *-car:*

   In verbs ending in *-car* in the infinitive, the "c" changes to "qu" before *e*. This occurs in:

   a. The first person singular of the preterit
   b. All forms of the present subjunctive

Example: *ficar* (to remain, to be):

PRETERIT INDICATIVE	PRESENT SUBJUNCTIVE
fiquei	*fique*
(ficaste)	*(fiques)*
ficou	*fique*
ficamos[25]	*fiquemos*
(ficastes)	*(fiqueis)*
ficaram	*fiquem*

Some of the other verbs in -*car*:

atacar	to attack	*secar*	to dry
educar	to educate	*significar*	to signify, mean
explicar	to explain	*tocar*	to touch, play (music)
indicar	to indicate	*verificar*	to verify

2. Verbs ending in -*çar*:

In these verbs the "ç" changes to "c" before *e* in the same forms indicated above.

Example: *começar* (to begin):

PRETERIT INDICATIVE	PRESENT SUBJUNCTIVE
comecei	*comece*
(começaste)	*(comeces)*
começou	*comece*
começamos[26]	*comecemos*
(começastes)	*(comeceis)*
começaram	*comecem*

---

[25] *ficámos* Ⓟ.
[26] *começámos* Ⓟ.

Some of the other verbs in -*çar:*

abraçar	to embrace	*forçar*	to force
alcançar	to reach	*recomeçar*	to begin again
caçar	to hunt	*traçar*	to trace, sketch

3. Verbs ending in -*gar:*

In these verbs "g" becomes "gu" before *e* in the same forms indicated above.

Example: *chegar* (to arrive):

PRETERIT INDICATIVE	PRESENT SUBJUNCTIVE
cheguei	*chegue*
(chegaste)	*(chegues)*
chegou	*chegue*
chegamos[27]	*cheguemos*
(chegastes)	*(chegueis)*
chegaram	*cheguem*

Some of the other verbs in -*gar:*

apagar	to put out, erase
carregar	to load, transport
entregar	to deliver
fatigar	to fatigue
jogar	to play (game)
pegar	to seize
pagar	to pay
rogar	to beg, ask

4. Verbs ending in -*cer:*

---

[27] *chegámos* Ⓟ.

In these verbs "c" changes to "ç" before *o* or *a*. This occurs in:

a. The first person singular of the present indicative
b. All forms of the present subjunctive

Example: *conhecer* (to know):

PRESENT INDICATIVE	PRESENT SUBJUNCTIVE
conheço	*conheça*
(conheces)	*(conheças)*
conhece	*conheça*
conhecemos	*conheçamos*
(conheceis)	*(conheçais)*
conhecem	*conheçam*

Some of the other verbs in *-cer:*

abastecer	to supply
acontecer	to happen
agradecer	to be grateful
aparecer	to appear
carecer	to lack
compadecer	to pity
desaparecer	to disappear
desobedecer	to disobey
envelhecer	to age
esquecer	to forget
falecer	to die
favorecer	to favor
fornecer	to supply
merecer	to deserve
nascer	to be born
obedecer	to obey
oferecer	to offer
padecer	to suffer

parecer	to seem
permanecer	to remain
pertencer	to belong
reconhecer	to recognize

5. Verbs ending in *-ger:*

   In these verbs "g" changes to "j" before *o* or *a* in the same forms indicated above.

   Example: *proteger* (to protect):

PRESENT INDICATIVE	PRESENT SUBJUNCTIVE
protejo	*proteja*
(proteges)	*(protejas)*
protege	*proteja*
protegemos	*protejamos*
(protegeis)	*(protejais)*
protegem	*protejam*

   Some of the other verbs in *-ger:*

| *eleger* | to elect | *reger* | to rule |

6. Verbs ending in *-gir:*

   These verbs have the same changes as verbs ending in *-ger.* Some of these verbs are:

dirigir	to direct, to drive
erigir	to erect
exigir (x = z)	to demand
fugir	to flee
surgir	to emerge

7. Verbs ending in *-guer* or *-guir:*

In these verbs "gu" changes to "g" before *o* or *a*. This occurs in the same forms as in Section 4 above.

Example: *distinguir* (to distinguish):

PRESENT INDICATIVE	PRESENT SUBJUNCTIVE
distingo	*distinga*
(distingues)	*(distingas)*
distingue	*distinga*
distinguimos	*distingamos*
(distinguis)	*(distingais)*
distinguem	*distingam*

Some verbs in *-guer* and *-guir:*

erguer	to raise
conseguir	to obtain
extinguir (x = sh)	to extinguish
perseguir	to pursue
seguir	to follow

Seguir is also radical-changing (see "Radical-Changing Verbs" above), and its derivatives (such as *conseguir* and *perseguir*) show these changes:

PRESENT INDICATIVE	PRESENT SUBJUNCTIVE
sigo	*siga*
(segues)	*(sigas)*
segue	*siga*
seguimos	*sigamos*
(seguis)	*(sigais)*
seguem	*sigam*

40. IRREGULAR VERBS

Some of the irregular verbs in Portuguese are shown below. Only tenses that have irregular forms are given. Verbs with only radical changes or orthographic changes are not given. Imperative forms are not listed. Irregular participles are indicated.

Abrir (to open)

PAST PART.: *aberto*

Caber (to fit in)

PRES. IND.: *caibo, cabes, cabe, cabemos, cabeis, cabem*

PRES. SUBJ.: *caiba, caibas, caiba, caibamos, caibais, caibam*

PRET. IND.: *coube, coubeste, coube, coubemos, coubestes, couberam*

PAST PERF. IND.: *coubera, couberas, coubera, coubéramos, coubéreis, couberam*

IMPF. SUBJ.: *coubesse, coubesses, coubesse, coubéssemos, coubésseis, coubessem*

FUT. SUBJ.: *couber, couberes, couber, coubermos, couberdes, couberem*

Cair (to fall)

Like *sair* (to leave). See below.

Cobrir (to cover)

PAST. PART.: *coberto*

Conduzir (to conduct, lead [to], drive Ⓟ)

PRES. IND.: *conduzo, conduzes, conduz, conduzimos, conduzis, conduzem*

Construir (to construct)

PRES. IND.: *construo, constróis, constrói, construímos, construís, constroem*

IMPF. IND.:   *construía, construías, construía,*
                 construíamos, construíeis, construíam
PRET. IND.:   *construí, construíste, construiu,*
                 construímos, construístes, construíram
PAST PERF. IND.: *construíra, construíras, construíra,*
                 construíramos, construíreis, construíram
IMPF. SUBJ.:   *construísse, construísses, construísse,*
                 construíssemos, construísseis, construíssem
FUT. SUBJ.:   *construir, construíres, construir,*
                 construirmos, construirdes, construírem
PAST PART.:   *construído*

Crer (to believe)
PRES. IND.:   *creio, crês, crê, cremos, credes, crêem*
PRES. SUBJ.:   *creia, creias, creia, creiamos, creies, creiam*
PRET. IND.:   *cri, creste, creu, cremos, crestes, creram*

Dar (to give)
PRES. IND.:   *dou, dás, dá, damos, dais, dão*
PRES. SUBJ.:   *dê, dês, dê, demos, deis, dêem*
PRET. IND.:   *dei, deste, deu, demos, destes, deram*
PAST PERF. IND.: *dera, deras, dera, déramos, déreis, deram*
IMPF. SUBJ.:   *desse, desses, desse, déssemos, désseis,*
                 dessem
FUT. SUBJ.:   *der, deres, der, dermos, derdes, derem*

Despedir (to send away)
PRES. IND.:   *despeço, despedes, despede, despedimos,*
                 despedis, despedem
PRES. SUBJ.:   *despeça, despeças, despeça, despeçamos,*
                 despeçais, despeçam

Dizer (to say)
PRES. IND.:   *digo, dizes, diz, dizemos, dizeis, dizem*
PRES. SUBJ.:   *diga, digas, diga, digamos, digais, digam*

PRET. IND.:   *disse, disseste, disse, dissemos, dissestes,*
                   disseram
PAST PERF. IND.:   *dissera, disseras, dissera, disséramos,*
                   disséreis, disseram
IMP. SUBJ.:   *dissesse, dissesses, dissesse, disséssemos,*
                   dissésseis, dissessem
FUT. SUBJ.:   *disser, disseres, disser, dissermos, disserdes,*
                   disserem
FUT. IND.:   *direi, dirás, dirá, diremos, direis, dirão*
COND.:   *diria, dirias, diria, diríamos, diríeis, diriam*
PAST. PART.:   *dito*

Eleger (to elect)
PAST. PART.:   *elegido* and *eleito*

Erigir (to erect)
PAST PART.:   *erigido* and *ereto*

Escrever (to write)
PAST PART.:   *escrito*

Estar (to be)
PRES. IND.:   *estou, estás, está, estamos, estais, estão*
PRES. SUBJ.:   *esteja, estejas, esteja, estejamos, estejais,*
                   estejam
PRET. IND.:   *estive, estiveste, esteve, estivemos, estivestes,*
                   estiveram
PAST PERF. IND.:   *estivera, estiveras, estivera, estivéramos,*
                   estivéreis, estiveram
IMP. SUBJ.:   *estivesse, estivesses, estivesse, estivéssemos,*
                   estivésseis, estivessem
FUT. SUBJ.:   *estiver, estiveres, estiver, estivermos,*
                   estiverdes, estiverem

Extinguir (to extinguish) (x = sh)
PAST PART.:   *extinguido* and *extinto*

Fazer (to do, make)

PRES. IND.: *faço, fazes, faz, fazemos, fazeis, fazem*
PRES. SUBJ.: *faça, faças, faça, façamos, façais, façam*
PRET. IND.: *fiz, fizeste, fez, fizemos, fizestes, fizeram*
PAST PERF. IND.: *fizera, fizeras, fizera, fizéramos, fizéreis, fizeram*
IMPF. SUBJ.: *fizesse, fizesses, fizesse, fizéssemos, fizésseis, fizessem*
FUT. SUBJ.: *fizer, fizeres, fizer, fizermos, fizerdes, fizerem*
FUT. IND.: *farei, farás, fará, faremos, fareis, farão*
COND.: *faria, farias, faria, faríamos, faríeis, fariam*
PAST PART.: *feito*

Haver (to have)

PRES. IND.: *hei, hás, há, havemos, haveis, hão*
PRES. SUBJ.: *haja, hajas, haja, hajamos, hajais, hajam*
PRET. IND.: *houve, houveste, houve, houvemos, houvestes, houveram*
PAST PERF. IND.: *houvera, houveras, houvera, houvéramos, houvéreis, houveram*
IMPF. SUBJ.: *houvesse, houvesses, houvesse, houvéssemos, houvésseis, houvessem*
FUT. SUBJ.: *houver, houveres, houver, houvermos, houverdes, houverem*

Ir (to go)

PRES. IND.: *vou, vais, vai, vamos, ides, vão*
PRES. SUBJ.: *vá, vás, vá, vamos, vades, vão*
IMPF. IND.: *ia, ias, ia, íamos, íeis, iam*
PRET. IND.: *fui, foste, foi, fomos, fostes, foram*
PAST PERF. IND.: *fora, foras, fora, fôramos, fôreis, foram*
IMPF. SUBJ.: *fosse, fosses, fosse, fôssemos, fôsseis, fossem*
FUT. SUBJ.: *for, fores, for, formos, fordes, forem*

Ler (to read)

PRES. IND.:	*leio, lês, lê, lemos, ledes, lêem*
PRES. SUBJ.:	*leia, leias, leia, leiamos, leiais, leiam*
PRET. IND.:	*li, leste, leu, lemos, lestes, leram*

Medir (to measure)

PRES. IND.:	*meço, medes, mede, medimos, medis, medem*
PRES. SUBJ.:	*meça, meças, meça, meçamos, meçais, meçam*

Ouvir (to hear)

PRES. IND.:	*ouço, ouves, ouve, ouvimos, ouvis, ouvem*
PRES. SUBJ.:	*ouça, ouças, ouça, ouçamos, ouçais, ouçam*

Pedir (to ask)

PRES. IND.:	*peço, pedes, pede, pedimos, pedis, pedem*
PRES. SUBJ.:	*peça, peças, peça, peçamos, peçais, peçam*

Perder (to lose)

PRES. IND.:	*perco, perdes, perde, perdemos, perdeis, perdem*
PRES. SUBJ.:	*perca, percas, perca, percamos, percais, percam*

Poder (to be able)

PRES. IND.:	*posso, podes, pode, podemos, podeis, podem*
PRES. SUBJ.:	*possa, possas, possa, possamos, possais, possam*
PRET. IND.:	*pude, pudeste, pôde, pudemos, pudestes, puderam*
PAST PERF. IND.:	*pudera, puderas, pudera, pudéramos, pudéreis, puderam*
IMPF. SUBJ.:	*pudesse, pudesses, pudesse, pudéssemos, pudésseis, pudessem*
FUT. SUBJ.:	*puder, puderes, puder, pudermos, puderdes, puderem*

Pôr (to put)

PRES. IND.:	*ponho, pões, põe, pomos, pondes, põem*
PRES. SUBJ.:	*ponha, ponhas, ponha, ponhamos, ponhais, ponham*
IMPF. IND.:	*punha, punhas, punha, púnhamos, púnheis, punham*
PRET. IND.:	*pus, puseste, pôs, pusemos, pusestes, puseram*
PAST PERF. IND.:	*pusera, puseras, pusera, puséramos, puséreis, puseram*
IMPF. SUBJ.:	*pusesse, pusesses, pusesse, puséssemos, pusésseis, pusessem*
FUT. SUBJ.:	*puser, puseres, puser, pusermos, puserdes, puserem*
PAST. PART.:	*posto*
PRES. PART.:	*pondo*

Note: *Compor* and other verbs formed from *pôr* have the same irregularities as *pôr*.

Querer (to want)

PRES. IND.:	*quero, queres, quer, queremos, quereis, querem*
PRES. SUBJ.:	*queira, queiras, queira, queiramos, queirais, queiram*
PRET. IND.:	*quis, quiseste, quis, quisemos, quisestes, quiseram*
PAST PERF. IND.:	*quisera, quiseras, quisera, quiséramos, quiséreis, quiseram*
IMP. SUBJ.:	*quisesse, quisesses, quisesse, quiséssemos, quisésseis, quisessem*
FUT. SUBJ.:	*quiser, quiseres, quiser, quisermos, quiserdes, quiserem*

Rir (to laugh)

PRES. IND.:	*rio, ris, ri, rimos, rides, riem*
PRES. SUBJ.:	*ria, rias, ria, riamos, riais, riam*

Saber (to know)

PRES. IND.:	*sei, sabes, sabe, sabemos, sabeis, sabem*
PRES. SUBJ.:	*saiba, saibas, saiba, saibamos, saibais, saibam*
PRET. IND.:	*soube, soubeste, soube, soubemos, soubestes, souberam*
PAST PERF. IND.:	*soubera, souberas, soubera, soubéramos, soubéreis, souberam*
IMPF. SUBJ.:	*soubesse, soubesses, soubesse, soubéssemos, soubésseis, soubessem*
FUT. SUBJ.:	*souber, souberes, souber, soubermos, souberdes, souberem*

Sair (to go out, leave)

PRES. IND.:	*saio, sais, sai, saímos, saís, saem*
PRES. SUBJ.:	*saia, saias, saia, saiamos, saias, saiam*
IMPF. IND.:	*saía, saías, saía, saíamos, saíeis, saíam*
PRET. IND.:	*saí, saíste, saiu, saímos, saístes, saíram*
PAST PERF. IND.:	*saíra, saíras, saíra, saíramos, saíreis, saíram*
IMPF. SUBJ.:	*saísse, saísses, saísse, saíssemos, saísseis, saíssem*
FUT. SUBJ.:	*sair, saíres, sair, sairmos, saírdes, saírem*
PAST PART.:	*saído*

Ser (to be)

PRES. IND.:	*sou, és, é, somos, sois, são*
PRES. SUBJ.:	*seja, sejas, seja, sejamos, sejais, sejam*
IMPF. IND.:	*era, eras, era, éramos, éreis, eram*
PRET. IND.:	*fui, foste, foi, fomos, fostes, foram*
PAST PERF. IND.:	*fora, foras, fora, fôramos, fôreis, foram*
IMPF. SUBJ.:	*fosse, fosses, fosse, fôssemos, fôsseis, fossem*
FUT. SUBJ.:	*for, fores, for, formos, fordes, forem*

Ter (to have)

PRES. IND.:	*tenho, tens, tem, temos, tendes, têm*
PRES. SUBJ.:	*tenha, tenhas, tenha, tenhamos, tenhais, tenham*
IMPF. IND.:	*tinha, tinhas, tinha, tínhamos, tínheis, tinham*
PRET. IND.:	*tive, tiveste, teve, tivemos, tivestes, tiveram*
PAST PERF. IND.:	*tivera, tiveras, tivera, tivéramos, tivéreis, tiveram*
IMPF. SUBJ.:	*tivesse, tivesses, tivesse, tivéssemos, tivésseis, tivessem*
FUT. SUBJ.:	*tiver, tiveres, tiver, tivermos, tiverdes, tiverem*

Note: *Conter* and other verbs formed from *ter* have the same irregularities as *ter*.

Trazer (to bring)

PRES. IND.:	*trago, trazes, traz, trazemos, trazeis, trazem*
PRES. SUBJ.:	*traga, tragas, traga, tragamos, tragais, tragam*
PRET. IND.:	*trouxe,[28] trouxeste, trouxe, trouxemos, trouxestes, trouxeram*
PAST PERF. IND.:	*trouxera, trouxeras, trouxera, trouxéramos, trouxéreis, trouxeram*
IMPF. SUBJ.:	*trouxesse, trouxesses, trouxesse, trouxéssemos, trouxésseis, trouxessem*
FUT. SUBJ.:	*trouxer, trouxeres, trouxer, trouxermos, trouxerdes, trouxerem*
FUT. IND.:	*trarei, trarás, trará, traremos, trareis, trarão*
COND.:	*traria, trarias, traria, traríamos, traríeis, trariam*

---

[28] In these verb forms *x* is pronounced like *s* in *see*.

Valer (to be worth)

PRES. IND.:	*valho, vales, vale, valemos, valeis, valem*
PRES. SUBJ.:	*valha, valhas, valha, valhamos, valhais, valham*

Ver (to see)

PRES. IND.:	*vejo, vês, vê, vemos, vedes, vêem*
PRES. SUBJ.:	*veja, vejas, veja, vejamos, vejais, vejam*
PRET. IND.:	*vi, viste, viu, vimos, vistes, viram*
PAST PERF. IND.:	*vira, viras, vira, víramos, víreis, viram*
IMPF. SUBJ.:	*visse, visses, visse, víssemos, vísseis, vissem*
FUT. SUBJ.:	*vir, vires, vir, virmos, virdes, virem*
PAST PART.:	*visto*

Vir (to come)

PRES. IND.:	*venho, vens, vem, vimos, vindes, vêm*
PRES. SUBJ.:	*venha, venhas, venha, venhamos, venhais, venham*
IMPF. IND.:	*vinha, vinhas, vinha, vínhamos, vínheis, vinham*
PRET. IND.:	*vim, vieste, veio, viemos, viestes, vieram*
PAST PERF. IND.:	*viera, vieras, viera, viéramos, viéreis, vieram*
IMPF. SUBJ.:	*viesse, viesses, viesse, viéssemos, viésseis, viessem*
FUT. SUBJ.:	*vier, vieres, vier, viermos, vierdes, vierem*
PAST PART.:	*vindo*

Note: The present participle is also *vindo*.

Note: *Convir* (to suit, to agree) and other verbs formed from *vir* will have the same irregularities as *vir*.

LETTER WRITING

A. FORMAL INVITATIONS AND REPLIES

Pedro Pereira Sousa e Maria Sousa têm o prazer de convidar V. Excia. e Exma. Família para assistirem ao enlace matrimonial de (da) sua filha Glória com o Sr. Paulo Gomes, que se realizará na igreja de Santo Antônio[1] no dia 20 do corrente, às 18 horas. Depois da cerimônia,[2] haverá uma recepção na casa dos pais da noiva, à avenida Anchieta, 1529.

Peter Pereira Sousa and Mary Sousa take pleasure in inviting you and your family to the wedding of their daughter Gloria to Mr. Paulo Gomes, which will take place at St. Anthony's Church on the 20th of this month at 6 P.M. After the ceremony there will be a reception at the residence of the bride's parents, 1529 Anchieta Avenue.

José e Cecília Silva cumprimentam o senhor e a senhora Carlos Guimarães, e pedem que os honrem jantando na sua companhia, na próxima segunda-feira, às oito horas.

Joseph and Cecilia Silva extend their greetings to Mr. and Mrs. Charles Guimarães, and would be honored to have their company at dinner next Monday at eight o'clock.

O senhor e a senhora Guimarães, muito agradecidos, aceitam com grande prazer o convite do senhor e da senhora Silva para jantarem juntos na próxima segunda-feira, às oito horas, e aproveitam o ensejo para cumprimentá-los cordialmente.

[1] *António* Ⓟ.
[2] *Cerimónia* Ⓟ.

Mr. and Mrs. Guimarães will be delighted to dine with Mr. and Mrs. Silva next Monday at eight o'clock and take this opportunity to indicate their appreciation and to extend their kindest regards.

O senhor e a senhora Guimarães cumprimentam o senhor e a senhora Silva, agradecem muitíssimo o seu amável convite para jantar na próxima segunda-feira, mas lamentam não poderem aceitá-lo em virtude de já terem estabelecido um compromisso anteriormente, para a mesma data.

Mr. and Mrs. Guimarães extend their greetings to Mr. and Mrs. Silva and thank them for the kind invitation to dine with them on Monday, but regret that they will not be able to come due to a previous engagement.

Tomás e Margarida Freitas cumprimentam afetuosamente o senhor e a senhora Moreira da Silva e pedem que lhes dêem o grande prazer de participarem da festa com que comemorarão o aniversário de (da) sua filha Ana, festa essa que terá lugar no próximo domingo, 19 de março,[3] às nove horas da noite.

Thomas and Margaret Freitas extend their warmest greetings to Mr. and Mrs. Moreira da Silva and request the honor of their presence at a party celebrating the birthday of their daughter Ana, to be given on Sunday evening, March 19, at nine o'clock.

O senhor e a senhora Moreira da Silva agradecem muito o amável convite do senhor e da senhora Freitas, e expres-

[3] *Março* ℗.

sam o seu grande contentamento por terem a oportunidade de participar da festa do próximo domingo.

Mr. and Mrs. Moreira da Silva gratefully acknowledge the kind invitation of Mr. and Mrs. Freitas and will be most happy to attend the reception next Sunday.

B. THANK-YOU NOTES

2 de abril[4] de 2002

Minha cara Ana,

Escrevo-lhe não só para cumprimentá-la, como também para agradecer-lhe o formoso vaso que me mandou de presente. Coloquei-o em cima do piano, e você não pode imaginar o lindo efeito que faz.

Espero vê-la, amanhã, na festa que dá Carlota. Parece que essa reunião vai ser muito animada.

Meu desejo é que você e toda a família estejam bem. Aqui, tudo sem novidade.

Abraça-a (a) sua amiga dedicada.

Maria

_____

April 2, 2002

Dear Anna,

I'm writing you not only to say hello, but also to let you know how much I appreciate the beautiful vase you sent me as a gift. I put it on the piano, and you can't imagine the beautiful effect.

[4] *Abril* Ⓟ.

I hope to see you at Carlota's party tomorrow. I think it's going to be a very lively affair.

I hope you and your family are well. Here, everything is fine.

Your friend,

                                                                Mary

C. BUSINESS LETTERS

Rua Tobias Barreto, 1326
São Paulo, S. P.

5 de julho[5] de 2002

Sr. Júlio Matos
Avenida Rio Branco, 213
Rio de Janeiro, R. J.

Ilmo. Sr:

   Junto remeto-lhe um cheque de Cr$6.000,00 para obtenção de uma assinatura anual da revista Branco e Negro, que é dirigida por V. S.[6]

                                       Atenciosamente,
                                       João Carlos Martins

[5] *Julho* Ⓟ.
[6] *V. S.* stands for *Vossa Senhoria,* a correspondence term for "you."

Rua Tobias Barreto, 1326
São Paulo. S. P.

July 5, 2002

Mr. Júlio Matos
Avenida Rio Branco, 213
Rio de Janeiro, R. J.

Dear Sir:

Enclosed please find a check for 6,000 cruzeiros for a year's subscription of your magazine *Branco e Negro*.

Very truly yours,
João Carlos Martins

Lopes, Nunes & Cia.
Rua de Madalena, 154
Lisboa, Portugal

2 de maio[7] de 2002

Aos Srs.
Gomes, Lima & Cia.
Rua Nova d' Alfândega, 110
Porto

Prezados Senhores:

Temos a satisfação de apresentar-lhes o portador desta, o
Sr. Alberto Rocha, nosso gerente de vendas, que visitará as
principais cidades dessa região.

Não é preciso dizer-lhes que ficaremos imensamente
gratos pelas atenções que lhe dispensarem.

Aproveitamos a oportunidade para agradecer-lhes ante-
cipadamente o que fizerem pelo Sr. Rocha, e subscrevemo-
nos muito atenciosamente.

De VV.SS.
Atos. e Obos.

Lopes, Nunes & Cia.

João Lopes
Presidente

---

[7] maio Ⓑ.

Lopes, Nunes & Co.
Rua de Madalena, 154
Lisbon, Portugal

May 2, 2002

Gomes, Lima & Co.
Rua Nova d'Alfândega, 110
Oporto

Gentlemen:

We have the pleasure of introducing to you the bearer of this letter, Mr. Alberto Rocha, our sales manager, who will be visiting the principal cities of your region.

Needless to say, we will greatly appreciate any courtesy you may extend to him.

Thanking you in advance, we remain

Very truly yours,
Lopes, Nunes & Cia.

João Lopes
President

D. INFORMAL LETTERS

2 de fevereiro[8]

Meu caro José,

Foi com grande prazer que recebi a sua última carta. Para ir direto ao assunto, vou contar-lhe a grande notícia. Finalmente decidimos fazer a projetada (projectada Ⓟ) viagem a Lisboa, onde pretendemos ficar todo o mês de julho (Julho Ⓟ).

Naturalmente Maria está encantada, muito ansiosa de visitar o país dos seus avós e de conhecer você e sua amável esposa. Temos muitas coisas que comentar e espero que você possa livrar-se de outros compromissos durante esses dias.

Os negócios vão bem por agora e espero que continuem assim, de vento em popa. Na semana passada estive com o Alberto, e ele perguntou por você.

Ficarei muito agradecido se você puder reservar-nos um quarto num hotel, pertinho do prédio em que mora.

Escreva-me contando o que tem acontecido ultimamente, e o que lhe parece esta notícia.

Mando lembranças a Helena, e você, receba um abraço de (do) seu amigo

João

[8] *Fevereiro* Ⓟ.

February 2

Dear Joseph,

I was very happy to get your last letter. Without further delay I'm going to spring the big news. We have finally decided to take the trip to Lisbon, where we expect to spend all of July.

Naturally, Mary is delighted, being most anxious to visit the country of her grandparents and to meet you and your charming wife. We have much to talk about, and I hope you will be able to free yourself of other obligations during that period.

Business is good now, and I hope we'll continue to have smooth sailing. I saw Al last week, and he asked about you.

I'd appreciate it very much if you could reserve a room for us in a hotel near the building in which you are staying.

Write and let me know what has been going on lately and what you think of the news.

Give my regards to Helen.

Yours,
John

E. FORMS OF SALUTATIONS AND COMPLIMENTARY CLOSINGS

FORMAL

1. Salutations:

Excelentíssimo Senhor:	Dear Sir: (Your Excellency:)
Amigo e Senhor:	Dear Sir:
Illustríssimo Senhor:	Dear Sir:
Prezado Senhor:	Dear Sir:
Senhor:	Sir:
Senhora:	Madam:
Senhorita:	Miss:
Senhor Diretor:[9]	Dear Director:

Note: The above phrases can be used in the plural
(*Excelentíssimos Senhores, Amigos e Senhores*, etc.)
and in the feminine (*Excelentíssima Senhora, Amiga e
Senhora*, etc.). They can also be used with names:
Prezado Senhor Pereira: (Dear Mr. Pereira:).

2. Initial or opening statements:

Acusamos o recebimento de (da) sua carta de 12 deste e aproveitamo-nos para . . .	We hereby acknowledge receipt of your letter of the 12th of this month and take this opportunity to . . .
Agradecemos a sua atenciosa carta, datada a de 7 do mês corrente . . .	We greatly appreciate your kind letter of the 7th of this month . . .

[9] *Director* Ⓟ.

Cumpre-nos anunciar-lhes que . . .	Please be advised that . . .
É com grande prazer que respondo à sua estimada carta . . .	I take pleasure in answering your letter . . .
Em reposta à carta de VV. SS.[10] de 28 do mês passado, cumpre-nos informar-lhes que . . .	In answer to your letter of the 28th of last month, please be advised that . . .
Estou em posse de (da) sua carta de 22 de junho[11] e cumpre-me avisá-lo que . . .	I am in receipt of your letter of June 22 and am pleased to inform you that . . .
Muito grato ficaria a V.S. se me mandasse . . .	I would appreciate it very much if you would send me . . .
Recebi (a) sua atenciosa carta de 15 do corrente e apresso-me a . . .	I have received your letter of the 15th of this month and I hasten to . . .
Temos a satisfação de comunicar-lhe que . . .	We are pleased to announce that . . .

3. Closing statements:

---

[10] *VV. SS.* stands for *Vossas Senhorios,* "you" plural; *de VV. SS.* "your."
[11] *Junho* Ⓟ.

The following statements are roughly the equivalent of "Sincerely yours."

Apresento-lhes os meus sinceros cumprimentos

Aproveitamos o ensejo para lhes renovarmos os nossos protestos de consideração e estima

Com os nossos protestos de sincera estima e elevado apreço, subscrevemos-nos

Subscrevemo-nos com estima e consideração

Com estima e consideração	Very truly yours . . .
Desde já, muito gratos, somos atenciosamente	
Com os nossos atenciosos cumprimentos . . .	With our best regards . . .
Na expectativa de uma breve resposta . . .	Hoping to hear from you soon . . .
Na esperança de recebermos seus comentários favoráveis . . .	Hoping to receive a favorable response . . .
Respeitosamente . . .	Respectfully . . .

The above may be followed by phrases such as the following, which correspond to our "Very truly yours" or "Sincerely yours":

De Vossa Senhoria   *De V. S.*
Atento e Obrigado

De Vossas Senhorias   *De VV. SS.*
Amigos e Muito Gratos
Muito Atentos e Gratos, etc.

Note: These are usually written in the abbreviated forms given to the right.

INFORMAL

1. Salutations:

Amigo Carlos	My friend Charles
Meu caro Alberto	My dear Albert
Meu prezado Amigo	My dear Friend
Minha filha Querida	My dearest Daughter
Minha querida Cecília	My dear Cecilia
Prezado Amigo	Dear Friend
Prezado Alfredo	Dear Alfred
Prezado Maria	Dear Mary
Querida Mamãe	Dearest Mother
Querida Sobrinha	Dear Niece

2. Complimentary closings:

Abraça-o o amigo
Aceite um grande abraço do amigo
Aceite os cumprimentos
Envia-lhe um abraço de sua grande amiga
Recebam um abraço do seu
Seu amigo muito grato
Um abraço do seu

Note: The phrases above amount to "Yours," "Affectionately yours," or corresponding expressions.

Até à vista	Until I see you again
Cordialmente	Cordially
Seu filho carinhoso	Your loving son

F. FORM OF THE ENVELOPE

Lopes, Nunes & Cia.
Rua de Madalena, 154
Lisboa

                Aos Srs.
                Gomes, Lima & Cia.
                Rua Nova D'Alfândega, 110
                PORTO

João Carlos Martins
Rua Tobias Barreto, 1326
São Paulo, S. P.

                Ilmo. Sr.
                Júlio Matos
                Avenida Rio Branco, 213
                RIO DE JANEIRO, R. J.

Ilmo. Sr.
José Pereira Martins
Rua Castilho, 73
LISBOA, PORTUGAL

                João Santos
                Praia do Flamengo, 376
                RIO DE JANEIRO, R. J.

OTHER EXAMPLES

Exmo. Sr. Dr. Carlos de Silveria
Praça da Sé, 379
SÃO PAULO, S.P.

Sra. Carmen Pereira
Avenida Rui Barbosa, 322
RIO DE JANEIRO, R.J.

Srta. Maria da Silva
Av. P.A. Cabral, 92
LISBOA, PORTUGAL